CHICKASAW BY BLOOD
ENROLLMENT CARDS
1898-1914

VOLUME II

TRANSCRIBED BY
JEFF BOWEN
NATIVE STUDY
Gallipolis, Ohio
USA

Originally published:
Baltimore, Maryland
2010

Reprinted by:

Native Study LLC
Gallipolis, OH
www.nativestudy.com

Library of Congress Control Number: 2020915583

ISBN: 978-1-64968-040-2

Made in the United States of America.

Other Books and Series by Jeff Bowen

1901-1907 Native American Census Seneca, Eastern Shawnee, Miami, Modoc, Ottawa, Peoria, Quapaw, and Wyandotte Indians (Under Seneca School, Indian Territory)

1932 Census of The Standing Rock Sioux Reservation with Births And Deaths 1924-1932

Census of The Blackfeet, Montana, 1897- 1901 Expanded Edition

Eastern Cherokee by Blood, 1906-1910, Volumes I thru XIII

Choctaw of Mississippi Indian Census 1929-1932 with Births and Deaths 1924-1931 Volume I

Choctaw of Mississippi Indian Census 1933, 1934 & 1937, Supplemental Rolls to 1934 & 1935 with Births and Deaths 1932-1938, and Marriages 1936-1938 Volume II

Eastern Cherokee Census Cherokee, North Carolina 1930-1939 Census 1930-1931 with Births And Deaths 1924-1931 Taken By Agent L. W. Page Volume I

Eastern Cherokee Census Cherokee, North Carolina 1930-1939 Census 1932-1933 with Births And Deaths 1930-1932 Taken By Agent R. L. Spalsbury Volume II

Eastern Cherokee Census Cherokee, North Carolina 1930-1939 Census 1934-1937 with Births and Deaths 1925-1938 and Marriages 1936 & 1938 Taken by Agents R. L. Spalsbury And Harold W. Foght Volume III

Seminole of Florida Indian Census, 1930-1940 with Birth and Death Records, 1930-1938

Texas Cherokees 1820-1839 A Document For Litigation 1921

Choctaw By Blood Enrollment Cards 1898-1914 Volumes I thru XVII

Starr Roll 1894 (Cherokee Payment Rolls) Districts: Canadian, Cooweescoowee, and Delaware Volume One

Starr Roll 1894 (Cherokee Payment Rolls) Districts: Flint, Going Snake, and Illinois Volume Two

Starr Roll 1894 (Cherokee Payment Rolls) Districts: Saline, Sequoyah, and Tahlequah; Including Orphan Roll Volume Three

Other Books and Series by Jeff Bowen

Cherokee Intruder Cases Dockets of Hearings 1901-1909 Volumes I & II

Indian Wills, 1911-1921 Records of the Bureau of Indian Affairs
Books One thru Seven;

Native American Wills & Probate Records 1911-1921

Turtle Mountain Reservation Chippewa Indians 1932 Census with Births & Deaths, 1924-1932

Chickasaw By Blood Enrollment Cards 1898-1914 Volume I

Visit our website at **www.nativestudy.com** to learn more about these
and other books and series by Jeff Bowen

This whole series is dedicated to my wife and best friend, Kathy.

ENROLLMENT CARDS FOR THE
FIVE CIVILIZED TRIBES
1898-1914

On 93 rolls of this microfilm publication are reproduced the enrollment cards that were prepared by the staff of the Commission to the Five Civilized Tribes between 1898 and 1914. These records are part of Records of the Bureau of Indian Affairs, Record Group (RG) 75, and are housed in the Archives Branch of the Federal Archives and Records Center, Fort Worth, Tex. An act of Congress approved March 3, 1893 (27 Stat. 645), authorized the establishment of the Commission to negotiate agreements with the Cherokee, Choctaw, Chickasaw, Creek, and Seminole tribes providing for the dissolution of the tribal governments and the allotment of land to each tribal member. Senator Henry L. Dawes of Massachusetts was appointed Chairman of this Commission on November 1, 1893, after which it has commonly been referred to as the Dawes Commission. The Commission was authorized by an act of Congress approved June 28, 1898 (30 Stat. 495), to prepare citizenship (tribal membership) rolls for each tribe. These final rolls were the basis for allotment. Under this act, subsequent acts, and resulting agreements negotiated with each tribe, the Commission received applications for membership covering more than 250,000 people and enrolled more than 101,000. The tribal membership rolls were closed on March 4, 1907, by an act of Congress approved on April 26, 1906 (34 Stat. 370), although an additional 312 persons were enrolled under an act approved August 1, 1914. The Commission enrolled individuals as "citizens" of a tribe under the following categories: Citizens By Blood, Citizens by Marriage, New Born Citizens By Blood (enrolled under an act of Congress approved March 3, 1905), Minor Citizens By Blood (enrolled under an act of Congress approved April 26, 1906), Freedmen (former black slaves of Indians, later freed and admitted to tribal citizenship), New Born Freedmen, and Minor Freedmen. Delaware Indians adopted by the Cherokee tribe were enrolled as a separate group within the Cherokee. Within each enrollment category, the Commission generally maintained three types of cards: "Straight" cards for persons whose applications were approved, "D" cards for persons whose applications were considered doubtful and subject to question, and "R" cards for persons whose applications were rejected. Persons listed on "D" cards were subsequently transferred to either "Straight" or "R" cards depending on the Commission's decisions. All decisions of the Commission were sent to the Secretary of the Interior for final approval.

An enrollment card, sometimes referred to by the Commission as a "census card," records the information provided by individual applications submitted by members of the same family group or household and includes notation of the actions taken. The information given for each applicant includes name, roll number (individual's number if enrolled), age, sex, degree of Indian blood, relationship to the head of the family group, parents' names, and references to enrollment on earlier rolls used by the Commission for verification of eligibility. The card often includes references to kin-related enrollment cards and notations about births, deaths, changes in marital status, and actions taken by the Commission and the Secretary of the Interior. Within each enrollment category, the cards are arranged numerically by a "field" or "census card" number, which is separate from the roll number. The index to the final rolls, which is reproduced on roll 1 of this publication, provides the roll number for each person while the final rolls themselves provide the census card numbers for each enrollee. No indexes have been located for the majority of the "D" and "R" cards. There are a few Mississippi Choctaw "Identified" and "Field Cards" as well as some Chickasaw "Cancelled" that refer to person never finally enrolled.

National Archives and Records Administration
American Indians Catalogue, p. 41

INTRODUCTION

The following Introduction describes the considerations employed in transcribing the Chickasaw enrollment cards that comprise the basis for this series. The Chickasaw by Blood enrollment cards, sometimes called "census cards" by the Dawes Commission, were pre-printed cards or loose sheets of paper labeled **Chickasaw Nation. Chickasaw Roll (Not Including Freedmen) with Residence County**. The heading **Post Office** appeared on the left side of each card, and **Card No., Field No.** on the right. The cards were further broken down into the categories *Dawes No., Name, Relationship to Person First Named, Age, Sex, Blood, Tribal Enrollment (Year, Town, Page), Name of Father, Year, Town, Name of Mother, Year, Town*, as well as *Tribal Enrollments of Parents*. For whatever reason, no card numbers were recorded in the corresponding field on any of the cards.

This and subsequent volumes have been transcribed from National Archives microfilm series M-1186: Roll 67, 1-662 and Roll 68, 663-1424. The page format of this transcription does not follow the microfilm exactly, owing to the space restrictions of the book format, but I have endeavored to include all categories of information supplied in the original. Also, the Dawes Roll No. has been relegated to the Notes area of each transcribed page. The notes section also contains information such as, Other name listings, Transfers to different cards, Birth dates, Death dates, listings on various payrolls with years, even sometimes a mention of a spouse in the doubtful category with card number, spouse possibly from another tribe, or a marriage license and certificate that was on file along with location. Sometimes the notes contain revealing information such as the following, "5/31/99. It is reported that Wm. Washington has this woman on his place and had parties to marry and they have never lived together—Investigate." Interestingly, this tidbit was found not under the representation of Wm. Washington but under that of Head of Household "Frank Osavior." Finally, the category "County" indicates the status of Non-Citizen, ethnicity, or Creek Roll, Cherokee Roll, Chocktaw Roll, etc.

Jeff Bowen
Gallipolis, OH
NativeStudy.com

Chickasaw Enrollment Cards 1898-1914
Chickasaw by Blood   Volume II

RESIDENCE: Choctaw Nation   **COUNTY**   **CARD NO.**

POST OFFICE: Stewart, Ind. Ter.   **FIELD NO.**

NAME	RELATION-SHIP TO PERSON	AGE	SEX	BLOOD	TRIBAL ENROLLMENT		
					YEAR	COUNTY	PAGE
1 Brown, Susan	FIRST NAMED	40	F	Full	1897	Chick residing in Choctaw N. 1st Dist.	69
2 Sealy, Henry	Son	10	M	"	1897	" " " "	69
3 McLish, Lee	"	3	"	"	1897	" " " "	69
4 Sealy, Permelia	Dau	11	F	"	1897	" " " "	72

TRIBAL ENROLLMENT OF PARENTS

	NAME OF FATHER	YEAR	COUNTY	NAME OF MOTHER	YEAR	COUNTY
1	Wesley Brown	Dead	Chickasaw Roll	Is-ka-ha-ga	Dead	Chickasaw Roll
2	Isum Sealy	1897	Chick residing in Choctaw N. 1st Dist.	No. 1		
3	(Illegible) McLish	1897	" " " "	No. 1		
4	Isum Sealy	1897	" " " "	No. 1		

(NOTES)

No. 3 On Chickasaw Roll as Lon C. Brown.
No. 4 Originally listed on Chickasaw card No. 1440, Dec. 24, 1902, and
transferred to this card Jan. 25, 1905. See testimony taken Jan. 10, 12, 14 and 16, 1905.

Sept. 7/98.

RESIDENCE: Choctaw Nation   **COUNTY**   **CARD NO.**

POST OFFICE: Stewart, Ind. Ter.   **FIELD NO.**

NAME	RELATION-SHIP TO PERSON	AGE	SEX	BLOOD	TRIBAL ENROLLMENT		
					YEAR	COUNTY	PAGE
1 Laflore, Bensey	FIRST NAMED	26	F	1/2	1897	Chick residing in Choctaw N. 3rd Dist.	69
2 Watson, Ida	Dau	8	F	1/4			

TRIBAL ENROLLMENT OF PARENTS

	NAME OF FATHER	YEAR	COUNTY	NAME OF MOTHER	YEAR	COUNTY
1	Adam Laflore	Dead	Choctaw Roll	Micey Sealy		
2	Elias Watson	"	Atoka Co. Choctaw Nation	No. 1		

(NOTES)

No. 1 Also on 1896 Choctaw Census Roll Page 342 #13039 as Bensy L. Wade
     Micey Sealy aiknowledged[sic] to be a Chickasaw (full blood *(remainder illegible)*
No. 2 On Choctaw Roll 1896 Atoka County No. 14000.
No. 2 On Choctaw Census Record No. 2 Page 485. Transferred to Chickasaw Roll by Dawes Com   Sept. 7/98.

Chickasaw Enrollment Cards 1898-1914
Chickasaw by Blood   Volume II

RESIDENCE: Pontotoc COUNTY					CARD NO.		
POST OFFICE: Jeff, Ind. Ter.					FIELD NO.		

NAME	RELATION-SHIP TO PERSON FIRST NAMED	AGE	SEX	BLOOD	TRIBAL ENROLLMENT		
					YEAR	COUNTY	PAGE
1 Immotichey, Sam	NAMED	28	M	Full	1897	Pontotoc	57
2 " Melvina	Dau	3	F	"			

TRIBAL ENROLLMENT OF PARENTS						
NAME OF FATHER	YEAR	COUNTY	NAME OF MOTHER	YEAR	COUNTY	
1 Davis Immotichey	Dead	Pontotoc	Martha Immotichey	Dead	Pontotoc	
2 No. 1			Elsie Immotichey	1897	"	

(NOTES)

No. 1 now husband of Lizzie Brown, Chick 125
No. 2 Proof of birth Feby. 5, 1902.

P.O. Hogan, I.T. 10/15/1902   Sept. 7/98.

RESIDENCE: Pontotoc COUNTY					CARD NO.		
POST OFFICE: Jeff, Ind. Ter.					FIELD NO.		

NAME	RELATION-SHIP TO PERSON FIRST NAMED	AGE	SEX	BLOOD	TRIBAL ENROLLMENT		
					YEAR	COUNTY	PAGE
1 Ayakatubby, Cyrus	NAMED	25	M	Full	1897	Pontotoc	54

TRIBAL ENROLLMENT OF PARENTS						
NAME OF FATHER	YEAR	COUNTY	NAME OF MOTHER	YEAR	COUNTY	
1 Thompson Ayakatubby	1897	Pontotoc	Sallie	Dead	Pontotoc	

(NOTES)

No. 1 Died Jan. 15th 1899. Proof of Death filed July 16th 1901.

Sept. 7/98.

RESIDENCE: Pontotoc COUNTY					CARD NO.		
POST OFFICE: Jeff, Ind. Ter.					FIELD NO.		

NAME	RELATION-SHIP TO PERSON FIRST NAMED	AGE	SEX	BLOOD	TRIBAL ENROLLMENT		
					YEAR	COUNTY	PAGE
1 Brown, Henderson	NAMED	22	M	Fi"	1897	Pickens	18

TRIBAL ENROLLMENT OF PARENTS						
NAME OF FATHER	YEAR	COUNTY	NAME OF MOTHER	YEAR	COUNTY	
1 John Brown	Dead	Pontotoc	Caroline Brown	Dead	Pontotoc	

(NOTES)

No. 1 is now the husband of Kate Wilson, on Chick *(remainder illegible)*   Sept. 7 1898.

2

RESIDENCE: Pontotoc   **COUNTY**   **CARD NO.**
POST OFFICE: Conway, Ind. Ter.   **FIELD NO.**

	NAME	RELATION-SHIP TO PERSON FIRST NAMED	AGE	SEX	BLOOD	TRIBAL ENROLLMENT		
						YEAR	COUNTY	PAGE
1	Perry, Jeff	NAMED	23	M	Full	1897	Pontotoc	42
2	" Lula	Wife	20	F	"	1897	"	42
3	" Benny	Son	2	M	"	1897	"	42
4	" Bettie	Dau	6mo	F	"			

	NAME OF FATHER	YEAR	COUNTY	NAME OF MOTHER	YEAR	COUNTY
1	Filmore Perry	Dead	Chickasaw Roll	Sha-ne-cha	Dead	Chickasaw Roll
2	Culberson Harris	"	Tishomingo	Louviney	"	Tishomingo
3	No. 1			No. 2		
4	No. 1			No. 2		

(NOTES)

No. 2 On Chickasaw Roll as Eula Perry
No. 2 Died Feb. 12th 1902; Evidence of Death filed July 2nd 1902
No. 4 Proof of Birth received and filed Nov. 13th 1902   *(No. 4 Dawes' Roll No. 1851)*

Sept. 7/98.

RESIDENCE: Choctaw Nation   **COUNTY**   **CARD NO.**
POST OFFICE: Waupunuka, Ind. Ter.   **FIELD NO.**

	NAME	RELATION-SHIP TO PERSON FIRST NAMED	AGE	SEX	BLOOD	TRIBAL ENROLLMENT		
						YEAR	COUNTY	PAGE
1	Pound, William T.	NAMED	50	M	I.W.	1897	Chickasaw living in Choctaw N. 3rd Dist.	81
2	" Cornelia Eldora	Wife	28	F	1/16	1897	" " " "	60
3	" Lillie	Dau	9	F	1/32	1897	" " " "	60
4	" Lela S	"	7	"	1/32	1897	" " " "	60
5	" Helena	"	3	"	1/32	1897	" " " "	60
6	" Mabel A.	"	8mo	"	1/32			

TRIBAL ENROLLMENT OF PARENTS

	NAME OF FATHER	YEAR	COUNTY	NAME OF MOTHER	YEAR	COUNTY
1	David W. Pound	Dead	Non-Citizen	Mary A. Pound	Dead	Non-Citizen
2	Jackson Wright		Choctaw Roll	Delilah Wright	1897	Pontotoc
3	No. 1			No. 2		
4	No. 1			No. 2		
5	No. 1			No. 2		
6	No. 1			No. 2		

Chickasaw Enrollment Cards 1898-1914
Chickasaw by Blood   Volume II

(NOTES)

No. 1 On Chickasaw Roll as W.F. Pound   *(No. 1 Dawes' Roll No. 6)*
No. 2 "   "   " " E.C. "
No. 4 "   "   " " Lula S. "
No. 6 Enrolled Nov. 3/99.
(Remainder illegible)

P.O. of #2 Hamden I.T. 3/23/03   Sept. 7/98.

RESIDENCE: Pontotoc **COUNTY**   **CARD NO.**
POST OFFICE: Waupunuka, Ind. Ter.   **FIELD NO.**

	NAME	RELATIONSHIP TO PERSON FIRST NAMED	AGE	SEX	BLOOD	TRIBAL ENROLLMENT YEAR	COUNTY	PAGE
1	Wright, Delila	NAMED	62	F	1/2	1897	Pontotoc	
2	Hassell, Willie	Niece	18	"	1/2			
3	~~Smith, Ona Edward~~	~~G. Dau~~	~~7mo~~	~~M~~	~~1/4~~			
4	Hassell, Bernice	" "	6mo	F	1/4			

TRIBAL ENROLLMENT OF PARENTS

	NAME OF FATHER	YEAR	COUNTY	NAME OF MOTHER	YEAR	COUNTY
1	*(Name Illegible)*	Dead	Non-Citizen	Catherine Moore	Dead	Chickasaw Roll
2	*(Name Illegible)*	"	Chickasaw Roll	*(Name Illegible)*	"	Non-citizen
3	*(Name Illegible)*	"	Non-Citizen	No. 2		
4	W.T. Hassell		" "	No. 2		

(NOTES)

(All notations illegible)

P.O. Berwyn, I.T.   Sept. 7/98.

RESIDENCE: Pontotoc **COUNTY**   **CARD NO.**
POST OFFICE: Pontotoc, Ind. Ter.   **FIELD NO.**

	NAME	RELATIONSHIP TO PERSON FIRST NAMED	AGE	SEX	BLOOD	TRIBAL ENROLLMENT YEAR	COUNTY	PAGE
1	Cravatt, Raorders H.	NAMED	28	M	3/4	1897	Pontotoc	54
2	" Mary	Wife	27	F	Full	1897	"	54
3	" Irvin	Son	4	M	7/8	1897	"	54
4	" Cora	Dau	5mo	F	7/8			
5	" Elvina	"	5mo	"	7/8			

Chickasaw Enrollment Cards 1898-1914
Chickasaw by Blood   Volume II

	TRIBAL ENROLLMENT OF PARENTS					
NAME OF FATHER	YEAR	COUNTY	NAME OF MOTHER	YEAR	COUNTY
1 Henderson Cravatt	Dead	Chickasaw Roll	Melvina Cravatt	Dead	Chickasaw Roll
2 A-cha-ca-ton-ly	"	" "	Katsey McCarty	1897	Pontotoc
3 No. 1			No. 2		
4 No. 1			No. 2		
5 No. 1			No. 2		

(NOTES)

No. 1 On Chickasaw Roll as Henderson H. Cravatt
No. 2 "   "   "   " Mary McCarty
No. 5 Enrolled July 11, 1901
No. 4 Died Sept. 10, 1900 - proof of death filed Dec. 23, 190?

P.O. address, Jesse, I.T.   Sept. 7/98.

RESIDENCE: Pontotoc COUNTY   CARD NO.
POST OFFICE: Center, Ind. Ter.   FIELD NO.

	NAME	RELATION-SHIP TO PERSON FIRST NAMED	AGE	SEX	BLOOD	TRIBAL ENROLLMENT		
						YEAR	COUNTY	PAGE
1	Duffy, Patrick		37	M	I.W.			
2	" Edith Ethel	Wife	19	F	3/4	1897	Pontotoc	48
3	" Ethel Cecelai	Dau	7mo	"	3/8			
4	" Esther Clementine	"	1mo	"	3/8			

	TRIBAL ENROLLMENT OF PARENTS					
NAME OF FATHER	YEAR	COUNTY	NAME OF MOTHER	YEAR	COUNTY
1 Joseph Duffy	Dead	Non-Citizen	Maria Duffy	Dead	Non-Citizen
2 Isaac Burris	1897	Pontotoc	Celia F. Burris	1897	Pontotoc
3 No. 1			No. 2		
4 No. 1			No. 2		

(NOTES)

No. 2 On Chickasaw Roll as E.E. Burris
No. 3 Enrolled June 7th 1900
No. 4 Born Nov. 5th 1901. Enrolled Dec. 18th 1901.

Sept. 7 1898.

5

Chickasaw Enrollment Cards 1898-1914
Chickasaw by Blood Volume II

RESIDENCE: Pontotoc COUNTY CARD NO.
POST OFFICE: Minco, I.T. FIELD NO.

	NAME	RELATION-SHIP TO PERSON FIRST NAMED	AGE	SEX	BLOOD	TRIBAL ENROLLMENT		
						YEAR	COUNTY	PAGE
1	Johnson, Adelaide B.	NAMED	33	F	1/16	1897	Pontotoc	66
2	" Gertruce	Dau	14	"	1/8	1897	"	66
3	" Ira Montford	Son	12	M	1/8	1897	"	66
4	" James Wolf	"	10	"	1/8	1897	"	66
5	" Charles Boggy	"	7	"	1/8	1897	"	66
6	" Vivian	Dau	3	F	1/8	1897	"	66

TRIBAL ENROLLMENT OF PARENTS

	NAME OF FATHER	YEAR	COUNTY	NAME OF MOTHER	YEAR	COUNTY
1	C.L. Campbell	Dead	Non-Citizen	Sally L. Campbell	1897	Pickens
2	Montford J. Johnson	"	Pontotoc	No. 1		
3	" " "	"	"	No. 1		
4	" " "	"	"	No. 1		
5	" " "	"	"	No. 1		
6	" " "	"	"	No. 1		

(NOTES)

No. 1 On Chickasaw Roll as A.B. Johnson
No. 2 "   "   " " Gettie "
No. 3 "   "   " " Ira "
No. 4 "   "   " " J.W. "
No. 5 "   "   " " Charles "

Sept. 7 1898.

RESIDENCE: Pontotoc COUNTY CARD NO.
POST OFFICE: Newcastle, Ind. Ter. FIELD NO.

	NAME	RELATION-SHIP TO PERSON FIRST NAMED	AGE	SEX	BLOOD	TRIBAL ENROLLMENT		
						YEAR	COUNTY	PAGE
1	Johnson, E.B.	NAMED	35	M	1/8	1897	Pontotoc	64
2	" Mollie E.	Wife	32	F	I.W.	1897	"	81
3	" Veta	Dau	10	"	1/16	1897	"	64
4	" Ina	"	8	"	1/16	1897	"	64
5	" Neal R.	Son	6	M	1/16	1897	"	64
6	" Montford T	"	4	"	1/16	1897	"	64
7	" Graham Belten	"	2	"	1/16	1897	"	89
8	" Froma Adelaide	Dau	3mos	F	1/16			

6

| 9 | " | Benj. F. | Bro | 18 | M | 1/8 | 1897 | | " | | 65 |
| 10 | " | Arline | Dau | 1mo | F | 1/16 | | | | | |

TRIBAL ENROLLMENT OF PARENTS

	NAME OF FATHER	YEAR	COUNTY	NAME OF MOTHER	YEAR	COUNTY
1	Montford T. Johnson	Dead	Pontotoc	Mary E. Johnson	Dead	Non-Citizen
2	R.M. Graham	"	Non-Citizen	Marillias Graham		" "
3	No. 1			No. 2		
4	No. 1			No. 2		
5	No. 1			No. 2		
6	No. 1			No. 2		
7	No. 1			No. 2		
8	No. 1			No. 2		
9	Montford T. Johnson	Dead	Pontotoc	Mary E. Johnson	Dead	Non-Citizen
10	No. 1			No. 2		

(NOTES)

No. 3 On Chickasaw Roll as Vita Johnson
No. 6 " " " " Mont E. "
No. 7 " " " " Benton G. "   *(No. 7 Dawes' Roll No. 4650)*
No. 9 " " " " Berry F. "
No. 10 Enrolled Aug. 18 1900
No. 7 Proof of Birth received and filed Sep. 15 1902
No. 8 Evidence of Birth received and filed Feb. 13 1902.

P.O. Norman, OK 12/17/02.   Sept. 7/98.

RESIDENCE:	Pontotoc	COUNTY				CARD NO.			
POST OFFICE:	Johnson, Ind. Ter.					FIELD NO.			

	NAME		RELATION-SHIP TO PERSON	AGE	SEX	BLOOD	TRIBAL ENROLLMENT		
							YEAR	COUNTY	PAGE
1	Johnston,	Joseph E.	FIRST NAMED	39	M	1/8	1897	Pontotoc	61
2	"	Mary Catherine	Wife	36	F	I.W.	1897	"	80
3	"	Emely	Dau	15	"	1/16	1897	"	61
4	"	Viola	"	13	"	1/16	1897	"	61
5	"	Neoma	"	10	"	1/16	1897	"	61
6	"	Henry	Son	8	M	1/16	1897	"	61
7	"	Sydney	"	6	"	1/16	1897	"	61
8	"	Jesse	"	4	"	1/16	1897	"	61
9	"	Carrie	Dau	1	F	1/16	1897	"	89

10	"	Robert E.		Son	4mo	M	1/16			
11	"	Edwin Bates		"	3 1/2 mo	"	1/16			

TRIBAL ENROLLMENT OF PARENTS

	NAME OF FATHER	YEAR	COUNTY	NAME OF MOTHER	YEAR	COUNTY
1	Thos. Johnston	Dead	Non-Citizen	Elizabeth Johnston	Dead	Pontotoc
2	Henry White		" "	Lou White		Non Citizen
3	No. 1			No. 2		
4	No. 1			No. 2		
5	No. 1			No. 2		
6	No. 1			No. 2		
7	No. 1			No. 2		
8	No. 1			No. 2		
9	No. 1			No. 2		
10	No. 1			No. 2		
11	No. 1			No. 2		

(NOTES)

No. 1 On Chickasaw Roll as J.E. Johnson
No. 2 "   "   " " M.C. Johnston   *(No. 2 Dawes' Roll No. I.W. 302)*
No. 5 "   "   " " Meoma
No. 8 "   "   " " Jessie Johnson
No. 9 Evidence of Birth received and filed Nov. 1st 1902   *(No. 9 Dawes' Roll No. 4049)*
No. 10 Enrolled Nov. 3rd 1899
No. 11 Enrolled Oct. 3rd 1901
No. 3 Married to Chas L. Williams and *(remainding illegible)* 3/20/99
    See testimony of No. 1 reference to enrollment of No. 2 taken Oct. 20 1902.

P.O. Seems now to be Roff, I.T.   Sept. 7/98.

RESIDENCE:	Pontotoc	COUNTY				CARD NO.			
POST OFFICE:	Johnson, Ind. Ter.					FIELD NO.			

	NAME	RELATION-SHIP TO PERSON FIRST NAMED	AGE	SEX	BLOOD	TRIBAL ENROLLMENT		
						YEAR	COUNTY	PAGE
1	Bouie, Eva		18	F	1/16	1897	Pontotoc	61
2	" Henry	Son	14mo	M	1/32	1897		88
3	" Nathan B.	Husband	27	"	I.W.			
4	" William N.	Son	2mo	"	1/32			
5	" Lois	Dau	1wk	F	1/32			

8

	TRIBAL ENROLLMENT OF PARENTS					
NAME OF FATHER	YEAR	COUNTY	NAME OF MOTHER	YEAR	COUNTY
1	Josh Davis (I.W.)	Dead	Chickasaw Roll	Puss Davis	Dead	Pontotoc
2	N.C. Bouie		Non Citizen	No. 1		
3	Thomas Bouie		" "	Nancy Bouie	Dead	Non-Citizen
4	No. 3			No. 1		
5	No. 3			No. 1		

(NOTES)

No. 1 On Chickasaw Roll as Eva Buil - wife of N.C. Bouie a non citizen

No. 2 Proof of Birth filed Oct. 27th 1902   *(No. 2 Dawes' Roll No. 4048)*

No. 3 Enrolled Mar 20th 1899   *(No. 3 Dawes' Roll No. 251)*

No. 4 Enrolled Nov. 3rd 1899

No. 5 Born June 7th 1902. Enrolled June 14th 1902

P.O. McGee, I.T.   Sept. 7/98.

RESIDENCE: Pontotoc *COUNTY*   *CARD NO.*

POST OFFICE: Stonewall, Ind. Ter.   *FIELD NO.*

	NAME	RELATION-SHIP TO PERSON FIRST NAMED	AGE	SEX	BLOOD	TRIBAL ENROLLMENT		
						YEAR	COUNTY	PAGE
1	Illetewahke, Charles		45	M	Full			
2	" Betsey	Wife	25	F	"	1897	Pontotoc	58
3	" Caroline	Dau	7	"	"	1897	Pontotoc	58
4	" Malvina	"	5	"	"	1897	Pontotoc	58
5	" Peggy	"	3	"	"	1897	Pontotoc	58
6	" Joseph	Son	4m	M	"			
7	" Noah	"	18	"	"	1897	Pontotoc	58
8	" Sam	"	13	"	"	1897	Pontotoc	58
9	" Cathy	Dau	10	F	"	1897	Pontotoc	58

	TRIBAL ENROLLMENT OF PARENTS					
NAME OF FATHER	YEAR	COUNTY	NAME OF MOTHER	YEAR	COUNTY
1	Eletewaleky	Dead	Chickasaw Roll	Sikey Hawkins	1897	Pontotoc
2	Henderson Porter	"	Pontotoc	Mollie Porter	1897	"
3	No. 1			No. 2		
4	No. 1			No. 2		
5	No. 1			No. 2		
6	No. 1			No. 2		
7	No. 1			Kissie *(Illegible)*	Dead	Pontotoc
8	No. 1			" "	"	"

9

9	No. 1			"	"		"		"

(NOTES)

No. 1 Admitted by Act of Legislature, Oct. 28th 1895. See Exhibit "A" Card No 285

No. 1 Is a Son of Sike Hawkins, Chickasaw Field Card No. D.384.

No. 6 Died March 3rd 1900. Proof of Death filed Sept. 4th 1901.

See letter of E.J. Ball, relative to present surname of this family Sept. 4th 1901.

(No. 7 Dawes' Roll No. 4045)

(No. 8 Dawes' Roll No. 4046)

(No. 9 Dawes' Roll No. 4047)

Sept. 7/98.

RESIDENCE: Pontotoc   **COUNTY**   **CARD NO.**

POST OFFICE: Ada, Ind. Ter.   **FIELD NO.**

	NAME	RELATION-SHIP TO PERSON FIRST NAMED	AGE	SEX	BLOOD	TRIBAL ENROLLMENT		
						YEAR	COUNTY	PAGE
1	Colbert, George	NAMED	45	M	Full	1897	Pontotoc	41
2	" Sukey	Wife	30	F	"	1897	Pontotoc	41
3	" Nora	Dau	11	"	"	1897	Pontotoc	41
4	" Dougherty	Son	7	M	"	1897	Pontotoc	41
5	" Richard Floyd	"	3	"	"	1897	Pontotoc	41
6	" Abijah	"	4mos	"	"			
7	" Laura D.	Dau	3wks	F	"			

TRIBAL ENROLLMENT OF PARENTS

	NAME OF FATHER	YEAR	COUNTY	NAME OF MOTHER	YEAR	COUNTY
1	Dougherty Colbert	Dead	Pontotoc	Jincy	Dead	Pontotoc
2	Ben Courtney	1897	Tishomingo	*(Name Illegible)*	"	Tishomingo
3	No. 1			No. 2		
4	No. 1			No. 2		
5	No. 1			No. 2		
6	No. 1			No. 2		
7	No. 1			No. 2		

(NOTES)

No. 5 On Chickasaw Card as Floyd Colbert

No. 6 Evidence of Birth received and filed Feb. 14 1902

No. 7 Born Aug ? 1902 *(remainder illegible)*

Sept. 7/98

10

Chickasaw Enrollment Cards 1898-1914
Chickasaw by Blood   Volume II

RESIDENCE: Pontotoc *COUNTY*					*CARD NO.*			
POST OFFICE: Jeff, Ind. Ter.					*FIELD NO.*			

NAME	RELATION-SHIP TO PERSON FIRST NAMED	AGE	SEX	BLOOD	TRIBAL ENROLLMENT		
					YEAR	COUNTY	PAGE
1 Anderson, Minnie	FIRST NAMED	24	F	Full	1897	Chick residing in Choctaw N. 3rd Dist.	73

TRIBAL ENROLLMENT OF PARENTS

NAME OF FATHER	YEAR	COUNTY	NAME OF MOTHER	YEAR	COUNTY
1 Frank Anderson	Dead	Tishomingo	*(Name Illegible)*	Dead	Tishomingo

(NOTES)

No. 1 is now wife of Johnson Willis, Chick # *(remainder illegible)*

Sept. 7/98.

RESIDENCE: Pontotoc *COUNTY*					*CARD NO.*			
POST OFFICE: Franks, Ind. Ter.					*FIELD NO.*			

NAME	RELATION-SHIP TO PERSON FIRST NAMED	AGE	SEX	BLOOD	TRIBAL ENROLLMENT		
					YEAR	COUNTY	PAGE
1 Parnacher, Roberson	NAMED	38	M	Full			
2 " Lizzie	Wife	27	F	"	1897	Pontotoc	?

TRIBAL ENROLLMENT OF PARENTS

NAME OF FATHER	YEAR	COUNTY	NAME OF MOTHER	YEAR	COUNTY
1 Parnacher	Dead	Pontotoc	Fannie	Dead	Pontotoc
2 Dave Burris	"	"	Cassie Burris	"	Chickasaw Roll

(NOTES)

(Remainder illegible)

Sept. 7/98.

RESIDENCE: Pontotoc *COUNTY*					*CARD NO.*			
POST OFFICE: Stonewall, Ind. Ter.					*FIELD NO.*			

NAME	RELATION-SHIP TO PERSON FIRST NAMED	AGE	SEX	BLOOD	TRIBAL ENROLLMENT		
					YEAR	COUNTY	PAGE
1 Parnacher, Calvin	NAMED	34	M	Full			
2 " Nannie	Dau	10	F	"	1897	Pontotoc	?

TRIBAL ENROLLMENT OF PARENTS

NAME OF FATHER	YEAR	COUNTY	NAME OF MOTHER	YEAR	COUNTY
1 Parnacher	Dead	Pontotoc	Fannie	Dead	Pontotoc
2 No. 1			Lousanna	1897	"

Chickasaw Enrollment Cards 1898-1914
Chickasaw by Blood Volume II

(NOTES)

No. 1 Admitted by Act of Legislature, Oct. 28 1895. See Exhibit "A" Card No. 285.

Sept. 7/98.

RESIDENCE: Pontotoc COUNTY   CARD NO.

POST OFFICE: Pontotoc, Ind. Ter.   FIELD NO.

NAME	RELATION-SHIP TO PERSON FIRST NAMED	AGE	SEX	BLOOD	TRIBAL ENROLLMENT		
					YEAR	COUNTY	PAGE
1 McGee, Lucy	NAMED	23	F	Full	1897	Pontotoc	53
2 Greenwood, Gincy	Dau	8	F	"	1897	"	53
3 " Bert	Son	7	M	"	1897	"	53
4 " Lee	"	6	M	"	1897	"	53
5 " Catherine	Dau	4	F	"	1897	"	53
6 " Joseph	Son	4mo	M	"			
7 McGee, Harriet	Dau	13mos	F	"			

TRIBAL ENROLLMENT OF PARENTS

	NAME OF FATHER	YEAR	COUNTY	NAME OF MOTHER	YEAR	COUNTY
1	Batish Williams	Dead	Pontotoc	Selena	Dead	Pontotoc
2	Sam Greenwood	"	"	No. 1		
3	" "	"	"	No. 1		
4	" "	"	"	No. 1		
5	" "	"	"	No. 1		
6	" "	"	"	No. 1		
7	Reubin McGee	1897	"	No. 1		

(NOTES)

No. 1 is now the wife of Reubin McGee, on Chickasaw Care #907

See letter of Reubin McGee filed *(remainder illegible)*

No. 6 Died in March 1899. Proof of Death filed June 30th 1900

No. 7 Enrolled April 27th 1901

Sept. 7/98.

RESIDENCE: Pontotoc COUNTY   CARD NO.

POST OFFICE: Conner, Ind. Ter.   FIELD NO.

NAME	RELATION-SHIP TO PERSON FIRST NAMED	AGE	SEX	BLOOD	TRIBAL ENROLLMENT		
					YEAR	COUNTY	PAGE
1 Sealy, Malinda	NAMED	21	F	Full	1897	Pontotoc	55
2 Greenwood, Nolis	Son	1	M	"			
3 " Alpheus	"	1mo	"	"			

4	Owens, Abe		"	2	M	7/8				

TRIBAL ENROLLMENT OF PARENTS

	NAME OF FATHER	YEAR	COUNTY	NAME OF MOTHER	YEAR	COUNTY
1	Gipson Ishtonubby	Dead	Pontotoc	Julia Hotubby	1897	Pontotoc
2	Isaac Greenwood	1897	"	No. 1		
3	" "	1897	"	No. 1		
4	Solomon Owens	1897	"	No. 1		

(NOTES)

No. 2 Died February 11 1899. Proof of Death filed July 15th 1901
No. 3 Born July 12, 1898. Proof of birth filed Oct. 20, 1903.   *(No. 3 Dawes' Roll No. 4767)*
No. 4 Born Jany 1901, proof of birth filed Oct. 20, 1903.   *(No. 4 Dawes' Roll No. 4768)*
No. 4 is illegitimate
Orig. application for No. 4, was made Dec. 1, 1902

P.O. Viola, I.T. 11/29/02   Sept. 7/98.

RESIDENCE: Pontotoc *COUNTY*   CARD NO.
POST OFFICE: Conner, Ind. Ter.   FIELD NO.

	NAME	RELATIONSHIP TO PERSON FIRST NAMED	AGE	SEX	BLOOD	TRIBAL ENROLLMENT		
						YEAR	COUNTY	PAGE
1	Hotubby, Julia		50	F	Full	1897	Pontotoc	55
2	" Somie	Son	14	M	"	1897	"	55
3	" Robert	"	8	"	"	1897	"	55
4	" Annie	Dau	12	F	"	1897	"	55

TRIBAL ENROLLMENT OF PARENTS

	NAME OF FATHER	YEAR	COUNTY	NAME OF MOTHER	YEAR	COUNTY
1	Ligua	Dead	Pontotoc	Sow-we-sha	Dead	Pontotoc
2	John Hotubby	"	"	No. 1		
3	" "	"	"	No. 1		
4	" "	"	"	No. 1		

(NOTES)

No. 3 Also on Chickasaw Roll as Harry Hotuby
No. 4   "   "   "   "   " Susan Hotubby
No. 4 died in May 1899; proof of death filed December 1899.

P.O. Viola, I.T. Apr. 4/04   Sept. 7/98.

13

Chickasaw Enrollment Cards 1898-1914
Chickasaw by Blood   Volume II

RESIDENCE: Pontotoc COUNTY					CARD NO.			
POST OFFICE: Stonewall, Ind. Ter.					FIELD NO.			

	NAME	RELATION-SHIP TO PERSON FIRST NAMED	AGE	SEX	BLOOD	TRIBAL ENROLLMENT		
						YEAR	COUNTY	PAGE
1	Collins, J.D.	NAMED	64	M	Full	1897	Pontotoc	54
2	" Salina E.	Wife	52	F	"	1897	"	54
3	" Alphus	Son	19	M	"	1897	"	54
4	" Lee	G Son	10	M	1/2	1897	"	90
5	Perry, Clifton	" "	15	"	Full	1897	"	54
6	Vance, Jefferson	Nephew	40	"	"	1897	"	54
7	Killcrease, Stanwaity	G Son	19mo	"	"			
8	Leader, Jesse	G Dau	15	F	"	1897	"	49

TRIBAL ENROLLMENT OF PARENTS

	NAME OF FATHER	YEAR	COUNTY	NAME OF MOTHER	YEAR	COUNTY
1	Tish-oh-to-????-tubby	Dead	Chickasaw Roll	Ish-te-mah-le-cha	Dead	Chickasaw Roll
2	Ah-mol-sho-tubby	"	" "	She-mul-li-ke	"	" "
3	No. 1			No. 2		
4	Jack Allman		Non-citizen	Mary Collins	Dead	Pontotoc
5	Jimmie Perry	1897	Pontotoc	" "	"	"
6	Ker-nun-che-tubby	Dead	Chickasaw Roll	Isht-te-mun-ne-te	"	"
7	Eastman Killcrease	1897	Pontotoc	Mary Collins	"	"
8	Simon Leader	Dead	"	" "	"	"

(NOTES)

No. 1 Died April 24th 1902. Proof of Death filed May 10th 1902

No. 2 Died Feby 3rd 1901. Evidence of Death filed May 16th 1901

No. 4 Registered under Act of Legislature approved July 31/97. Page *(illegible)*

No. 4 On 1897 and 1893 Pay Roll, Pontotoc County as Pikey Allmon; On 1896 Chickasaw Roll Page 49 as Pikey Allmon

No. 6 On Chickasaw Roll as Jeff Vance

No. 7 Affidavit as to Birth received and filed Nov. 6th 1902   *(No. 7 Dawes' Roll No. 4043)*

No. 8 On Chickasaw Roll as Jessie Leader   *(No. 8 Dawes' Roll No. 4044)*

No. 8 is a full blood Chickasaw Indian. See affidavit of Serena Collins filed Sept 13th 1902.

Sept. 7/98.

RESIDENCE: Pontotoc	***COUNTY***	***CARD NO.***	
POST OFFICE: Palmer, Ind. Ter,		***FIELD NO.***	

	NAME	RELATION-SHIP TO PERSON FIRST NAMED	AGE	SEX	BLOOD	TRIBAL ENROLLMENT		
						YEAR	COUNTY	PAGE
1	Aldrich, Susan N.		28	F	Full	1897	Pontotoc	49
2	" Ada E.	Dau	5	"	"	1897	"	49
3	" Eula L.	"	3	"	"	1897	"	49
4	" Cyntha C	"	6mo	"	"			
5	" Annie L.	"	3mo	"	"			
6	" Allie Latitia	"	2mo	"	"			
7	" Albert Alonzo	Husband	33	M	I.W.			

TRIBAL ENROLLMENT OF PARENTS

	NAME OF FATHER	YEAR	COUNTY	NAME OF MOTHER	YEAR	COUNTY
1	Ellis McGee	1897	Chick residing in Choctaw N. 2nd Dist.	Lucinda Ned	Dead	Tishomingo
2	A.A. Aldrich		Non-Citizen	No. 1		
3	" " "		" "	No. 1		
4	" " "		" "	No. 1		
5	" " "		" "	No. 1		
6	" " "		" "	No. 1		
7	W.D. Aldrich	1897	non-citz	Cynthia Aldrich	Dead	non-citz

(NOTES)

No. 1 is wife of Albert Alonzo Aldrich *(remainder illegible)*
No. 3 On Chickasaw Card as W.L. Aldrich
No. 4 Evidence of Birth received and filed April 8th 1902.
No. 5 Enrolled Nov. 3/99.
No. 6 Born Feb. 6, 1902. Enrolled April 8th 1902.
No. 7 Transferred from Chickasaw card #D.108, April 1, 1903. See decision of March 16, 1903.

P.O. Sulphur, I.T, Sept. 7/98.

RESIDENCE: Choctaw Nation	***COUNTY***	***CARD NO.***	
POST OFFICE: Calvin, Ind. Ter.		***FIELD NO.***	

	NAME	RELATION-SHIP TO PERSON FIRST NAMED	AGE	SEX	BLOOD	TRIBAL ENROLLMENT		
						YEAR	COUNTY	PAGE
1	Stick, Kinney		28	M	Full	1897	Pontotoc	68
2	" Malissa	Wife	45	F	1/2	1897	"	68
3	" Fannie	Dau	8	"	3/4	1897	"	68
4	" Silsey	"	5	"	3/4	1897	"	68

5	Leader, Elmina	Step Dau	19	"	3/4	1897		"		68
6	" Wilson	" Son	17	M	3/4	1897		"		68
7	" Johnson	" "	13	M	3/4	1897		"		68
8	" Nettie	G. St Son[sic]	3mo	"	3/4					

TRIBAL ENROLLMENT OF PARENTS

	NAME OF FATHER	YEAR	COUNTY	NAME OF MOTHER	YEAR	COUNTY
1	Martin Stick	Dead	Chickasaw Roll	Magy Stick	Dead	Pontotoc
2	E-fi-chey Benton	"	Choctaw "	Nellie Benton	"	"
3	No. 1			(Illegible)		
4	No. 1			(Illegible)		
5	Tom Leader	Dead	(Illegible)	(Illegible)		
6	" "	"	(Illegible)	(Illegible)		
7	Johnie "	"	(Illegible)	(Illegible)		
8	Ben Perry			(Illegible)		

(NOTES)

No. 2 On Chickasaw roll as Malissa Leader
No. 3 "   "   " " Fannie   "
No. 4 "   "   " " Silsey   "
No. 7 "   "   " " John   "
No. 8 is the illegitimate child of No. 5. Enrolled Aug 6th 1900.

Sept. 7/98.

RESIDENCE:	Pontotoc	COUNTY				CARD NO.			
POST OFFICE:	Franks, Ind. Ter.					FIELD NO.			

	NAME	RELATION-SHIP TO PERSON FIRST NAMED	AGE	SEX	BLOOD	TRIBAL ENROLLMENT		
						YEAR	COUNTY	PAGE
1	Tohm, Wilson	NAMED	35	M	Full	1897	Pontotoc	40
2	Underwood, Silena	Wife	37	F	"			
3	Tohm, Nedo	Dau	7	"	"	1897	Pontotoc	40
4	" Maggie	"	4	"	"	1897	"	40
5	" Mamie	"	10mo	"	"			
6	" Acey	Wife	30	"	"	1897	"	40
7	Underwood, Martha Hoey	Dau of No. 2	8mo	F	1/2			

TRIBAL ENROLLMENT OF PARENTS

	NAME OF FATHER	YEAR	COUNTY	NAME OF MOTHER	YEAR	COUNTY
1	Ah-na-kan-tubby	Dead	Chickasaw Roll	Margaret	Dead	Pontotoc
2	Te-ho-tubby	"	" "	Sike	1897	"
3	No. 1			No. 2		

16

Chickasaw Enrollment Cards 1898-1914
Chickasaw by Blood   Volume II

4	No. 1			No. 2		
5	No. 1			No. 6		
6	Te-ho-tubby			Sike	1897	Pontotoc
7	Jim Underwood			No. 2		

(NOTES)

No. 1 On Chickasaw Roll as Wilson Tom

No. 2 Admitted by Act of Council Oct 28 1895. See exhibit "A" Card No. 285' No. 2 is known as Silena Underwood
Nov. 13 1902   *(No. 2 Dawes' Roll No. 4041)*

No. 3 On Chickasaw Roll as Nita Tom

No. 4   "   "   "   " Maggie Tom

No. 5 Evidence of Birth filed May 2nd 1902

No. 6 Admitted by Act of *(as written)* Oct 28 1895; above referred to *(remainder illegible)*

No. 6 On Chickasaw Roll 1897 ad Casey Hawkins

No. 7 Born March 17th 1902; Enrolled Nov. 14 1902   *(No. 7 Dawes' Roll No. 4042)*

See testimony of May 2nd 1902 as to separation of Nos. 1 & 2 and also as to Nos 1 & 6 living together and
marriages and divorce.   See affidavit of No. 2 as to having been the wife of No. 1 filed Sept. 18th 1902.

Sept. 7/99.

RESIDENCE: Pontotoc   COUNTY   CARD NO.

POST OFFICE: Conner, Ind. Ter.   FIELD NO.

NAME	RELATION-SHIP TO PERSON FIRST	AGE	SEX	BLOOD	TRIBAL ENROLLMENT		
					YEAR	COUNTY	PAGE
1 Grayson, John	NAMED	28	M	Full	1897	Pontotoc	55
2 " Louisa	Wife	38	F	"	1897	"	55
3 Collins, Lema	Step Dau	15	"	"	1897	"	55
4 " Oscie	" Son	13	M	"	1897	"	55
5 Grayson, Tennie	Dau	1mo	F	"			
6 Underwood, Willie Bond	Son of No. 3	3mo	M	"			

TRIBAL ENROLLMENT OF PARENTS

	NAME OF FATHER	YEAR	COUNTY	NAME OF MOTHER	YEAR	COUNTY
1	Toney Grayson	Dead	Pontotoc	Sally Grayson	Dead	Pontotoc
2	Pos-ka-tubby	"	"	Ah-ho-we-cha	"	"
3	John Collins	"	"	No. 2		
4	" "	"	"	No. 2		
5	No. 1			No. 2		
6	*(Name Illegible)*		Pontotoc	No. 3		

(NOTES)

No. 5 Enrolled 8/4/99

(Remainder illegible)   *(No. 6 Dawes' Roll No. 4749)*   Sept. 7 1898.

17

Chickasaw Enrollment Cards 1898-1914
Chickasaw by Blood   Volume II

RESIDENCE: Tishomingo   COUNTY   CARD NO.

POST OFFICE: Conner, Ind. Ter.   FIELD NO.

NAME	RELATION- SHIP TO PERSON FIRST NAMED	AGE	SEX	BLOOD	TRIBAL ENROLLMENT		
					YEAR	COUNTY	PAGE
1 Ned, John	NAMED	38	M	Full	1897	Tishomingo	36
2 " Susanna **DEAD**	Wife	35	F	"	1897	"	36
3 Jones. Ellen	Dau	14	"	"	1897	"	36
4 Ned, Osborne	Son	8	M	"	1897	"	36
5 " Ida	Dau	3	F	"	1897	"	36
6 " Abe	Son	8mo	M	"			
7 Jones, James	Gr Son	1	"	3/4			
8 " Moses	"	2mo	"	3/4			

TRIBAL ENROLLMENT OF PARENTS

	NAME OF FATHER	YEAR	COUNTY	NAME OF MOTHER	YEAR	COUNTY
1	Duncan Ned	Dead	Chickasaw Roll	A-na-ya-ho-ha	Dead	Chickasaw Roll
2	Wilson Alexander	"	" "	Ro-ye-ho-ke	1897	Tichomingo
3	No. 1			(Illegible)		
4	No. 1			(Illegible)		
5	No. 1			(Illegible)		
6	No. 1			(Illegible)		
7	Wesley Jones	1897	Pontotoc	(Illegible)		
8	" "	"	"	(Illegible)		

(NOTES)

No. 2 On Chickasaw Roll as Susan

No. 2 Died March 30th 1901. Proof of Death filed July 2nd 1901

No. 3 is now the wife of Wesley Jones on Chickasaw Card #1202. See affidavit as to marriage filed herein May 19th 1902

No. 6 Evidence of Birth received and filed March 19th 1902

No. 7 Born May 6th 1901. Enrolled May 19th 1902

No. 8 Born Sept 15th 1902; Enrolled Nov. 21st 1902.   (No. 8 Dawes' Roll No. 4040)

No. 3 P.O. Albanny, I.T. 11/21/1902

P.O. Connerville, I.T. 5/25/04   Sept. 7 1898.

18

RESIDENCE: Pontotoc   *COUNTY*   *CARD NO.*

POST OFFICE: Jesse, Ind. Ter.   *FIELD NO.*

	NAME	RELATION-SHIP TO PERSON FIRST NAMED	AGE	SEX	BLOOD	TRIBAL ENROLLMENT		
						YEAR	COUNTY	PAGE
1	Johnson, Landers **DEAD**	NAMED	29	M	Full	1897	Pontotoc	50
2	" Eliza	Wife	27	F	"	1897	"	50
3	" Ema	Dau	9	"	"	1897	"	50
4	" Rena	"	3	"	"	1897	"	50
5	" Mulford	Son	6mo	M	"			

TRIBAL ENROLLMENT OF PARENTS

	NAME OF FATHER	YEAR	COUNTY	NAME OF MOTHER	YEAR	COUNTY
1	Ah-cah-nah-te	Dead	Chickasaw Roll	Sko-nah-he	Dead	Chickasaw Roll
2	Henry Davis	"	" "	Rhoda	"	" "
3	No. I			No. 2		
4	No. I			No. 2		
5	No. I			No. 2		

(NOTES)

No. I Died May 15, 1902; Proof of Death filed July 8ᵗʰ 1902

No. 2 *(remainder illegible)*   *(No. 2 Dawes' Roll No. 4039)*

(Notation illegible)   *(No. 5 Dawes' Roll No. 4748)*

P.O. Hogan, I.T.   Sept. 7/98.

RESIDENCE: Choctaw Nation   *COUNTY*   *CARD NO.*

POST OFFICE: Guertie, Ind. Ter.   *FIELD NO.*

	NAME	RELATION-SHIP TO PERSON FIRST NAMED	AGE	SEX	BLOOD	TRIBAL ENROLLMENT		
						YEAR	COUNTY	PAGE
1	Colbert, Edmon	NAMED	25	M	Full	1897	Chick residing in Choctaw N. ? Dist.	68
2	" Martha	Wife	25	F	1/2	1897	" " " "	68
3	" Joshua	Son	3	M	3/4	1897	" " " "	68
4	" Ben	"	Imo	"	3/4			

TRIBAL ENROLLMENT OF PARENTS

	NAME OF FATHER	YEAR	COUNTY	NAME OF MOTHER	YEAR	COUNTY
1	Ben Colbert	Dead	Chickasaw Roll	Nellie Colbert		Chickasaw Roll
2	John Lewis		Choctaw Roll	Ah-litch-ta		Chick residing in Choctaw N Iˢᵗ Dist.
3	No. I			No. 2		

19

4	No. 1			No. 2		

(NOTES)

No. 3 On Chickasaw Roll as *(illegible)*
No. 2 is daughter of John Lewis on Choctaw Card #4941 and Hullechen Lewis on Chickasaw Card *(illegible)*
No. 4 Born Aug. 30th 1898. Proof of Birth filed Feby 17th 1903.

Sept. 7th 1898.

RESIDENCE: Choctaw Nation	COUNTY				CARD NO.		
POST OFFICE: Guertie, Ind. Ter.					FIELD NO.		
NAME	RELATIONSHIP TO PERSON FIRST NAMED	AGE	SEX	BLOOD	TRIBAL ENROLLMENT		
					YEAR	COUNTY	PAGE
1 Lawrence, Sinie		20	F	Full	1893	Pontotoc	P.R.#2 46
2 " Anna Isabelle	Dau	15mo	"	"	1897	"	91
3 " Niola D.	"	2mo	"	"			

TRIBAL ENROLLMENT OF PARENTS

NAME OF FATHER	YEAR	COUNTY	NAME OF MOTHER	YEAR	COUNTY
1 Co-ah-che-che Brown	Dead	Chickasaw Roll	Annie Brown	1897	Pontotoc
2 S.S. Lawrence	"	Atoka Co. Choctaw Roll	No. 1		
3 " " "	"	" "	No. 1		

(NOTES)

No. 1 Wife of S.S. Lawrence *(remainder illegible)*
No. 1 On Chickasaw Roll *(illegible)* "Dead" as Sinie Brown
No. 2 " " " as Anna Isabelle Lawrence
No. 2 Died Nov. 30th 1900. Proof of Death filed Nov. 12th 1902.

P.O. Ada, I.T. 11/10/02.

No. 1 Enrolled Oct. 14/98.
" 2 " Sept. 7/98.
" 3 " Nov. 3/99.

RESIDENCE: Pontotoc	COUNTY				CARD NO.		
POST OFFICE: Ada, Ind. Ter.					FIELD NO.		
NAME	RELATIONSHIP TO PERSON FIRST NAMED	AGE	SEX	BLOOD	TRIBAL ENROLLMENT		
					YEAR	COUNTY	PAGE
1 Ishtincheyou, Fomister		46	M	1/2			
2 " Annie	Wife	46	F	Full	1897	Pontotoc	43

TRIBAL ENROLLMENT OF PARENTS

NAME OF FATHER	YEAR	COUNTY	NAME OF MOTHER	YEAR	COUNTY
1 Ishtincheyou	Dead	Chickasaw Roll	Sippey		

2	Cha-ta-ha			Sim-a-ho-ke		1897	Pontotoc

(NOTES)

No. I was admitted by Act of Council Oct. 28, 1895 as Famister Ishtincheyon
   See Certified Copy hereto attached and marked Exhibit "A"
No. 2 On Chickasaw Roll as Annie Ishtinchea

Sept. 7/98.

RESIDENCE: Choctaw Nation   **COUNTY**   **CARD NO.**
POST OFFICE: Kiowa, Ind. Ter.   **FIELD NO.**

NAME	RELATION-SHIP TO PERSON FIRST NAMED	AGE	SEX	BLOOD	TRIBAL ENROLLMENT		
					YEAR	COUNTY	PAGE
1 Pound, Tom	FIRST NAMED	23	M	1/4	1897	Chick residing in Choctaw N. 1st Dist.	70
2 " Mattie	Wife	29	F	I.W.			
3 " ~~Ruby~~	~~Dau~~	~~4mo~~	"	~~1/8~~	DIED		
4 " ~~Marie~~	"	~~4mo~~	"	~~1/8~~	DIED		

TRIBAL ENROLLMENT OF PARENTS

	NAME OF FATHER	YEAR	COUNTY	NAME OF MOTHER	YEAR	COUNTY
1	George Pound I.W.	1897	Chick residing in Choctaw N. 1st Dist.	Carrie Pound	1897	Chick residing in Choctaw N. 1st Dist
2	Rufus Shepard	Dead	Non-Citizen	Sarah Shephard[sic]	Dead	Non-Citizen
3	No. I			No. 2		
4	No. I			No. 2		

(NOTES)

No. 2 Enrolled Oct. 13/98.
No. 2 Married as a Choctaw
No. 3 Enrolled March 6, 1899
No. 3 Died Sept 27th 1900. Proof of Death filed Oct. 20th 1902.
No. 4 Enrolled Sept. 7th 1900
No. 4 Died Oct. 27th 1901. Proof of Death filed Oct. 20th 1902.

P.O. Rush Springs, I.T. Oct. 16, 1902.   Sept. 7/98.

RESIDENCE: Choctaw Nation   **COUNTY**   **CARD NO.**
POST OFFICE: Kiowa, Ind. Ter.   **FIELD NO.**

NAME	RELATION-SHIP TO PERSON FIRST NAMED	AGE	SEX	BLOOD	TRIBAL ENROLLMENT		
					YEAR	COUNTY	PAGE
1 Colbert, Theodore	FIRST NAMED	29	M	1/2	1897	Chick residing in Choctaw N. 1st Dist.	70

	TRIBAL ENROLLMENT OF PARENTS					
	NAME OF FATHER	YEAR	COUNTY	NAME OF MOTHER	YEAR	COUNTY
1	James Colbert	1897	Chick residing in Choctaw N. 1st Dist.	Mary Colbert	Dead	Chick residing in Choctaw N. 1st Dist.

(NOTES)

(All Notations Illegible)

Sept. 7/1898.

RESIDENCE: Choctaw Nation **COUNTY** **CARD NO.**

POST OFFICE: Kiowa, Ind. Ter. **FIELD NO.**

	NAME	RELATIONSHIP TO PERSON FIRST NAMED	AGE	SEX	BLOOD	TRIBAL ENROLLMENT		
						YEAR	COUNTY	PAGE
1	Colbert, Katinka		53	F	I.W.	1897	Chick residing in Choctaw N. 1st Dist.	82
2	" Emil Frank	Son	20	M	1/4	1897	" " " "	70
3	" Oscar	"	17	M	1/4	1897	" " " "	70
4	" Eula	Gr. Dau	2wks	F	1/8			
5	" Annie E.	Wife of No. 2	23	F	I.W.			

	TRIBAL ENROLLMENT OF PARENTS					
	NAME OF FATHER	YEAR	COUNTY	NAME OF MOTHER	YEAR	COUNTY
1	Rodinska	Dead	Non-citizen	*(Name Illegible)*	Dead	Non-citizen
2	James Colbert	"	Chick residing in Choctaw N 1st Dist.	No. 1		
3	" "	"	" " " "	No. 1		
4	No. 3			Anna Colbert		white woman
5	J.H. Reynolds		non citizen	M.A. Reynolds		non citizen

(NOTES)

No. 1 Admitted as a Choctaw by Intermarriage Card No. *(remainder illegible)*
in 1896 Choctaw Case #985 under Act of Congress of June 10, 1896. No appeal.
No. 2 is the husband of Annie E. Colbert on Chickasaw Card #D.354.
No. 3 is the husband of *(Illegible)* Colbert on Chickasaw Card #D.353. Feb. 11th 1902.
No. 4 Born Feb. 22nd 1902; Enrolled March 8th 1902
(Notation illegible)
(Notation illegible)
No. 5 transferred from Chickasaw Card D.354 April 7, 1904.
See decision of March 15, 1904.

Sept. 7th 1898.

RESIDENCE: Choctaw Nation   *COUNTY*   CARD NO.

POST OFFICE: Kiowa, Ind. Ter.   FIELD NO.

	NAME	RELATION-SHIP TO PERSON FIRST NAMED	AGE	SEX	BLOOD	TRIBAL ENROLLMENT		
						YEAR	COUNTY	PAGE
1	Colbert, James E.	FIRST NAMED	39	M	1/2	1897	Chick residing in Choctaw N 1st Dist.	69
2	" Nina	Wife	30	F	I.W.	1897	" " " "	82
3	" James	Son	13	M	1/4	1897	" " " "	69
4	" Leila	Dau	10	F	1/4	1897	" " " "	70
5	" Holmes	Son	8	M	1/4	1897	" " " "	70
6	" Zona	Dau	1 1/2	F	1/4	1897	" " " "	91
7	" Ben	Son	6wks	M	1/4			

TRIBAL ENROLLMENT OF PARENTS

	NAME OF FATHER	YEAR	COUNTY	NAME OF MOTHER		YEAR	COUNTY
1	James Colbert	Dead	Chick residing in Choctaw N 1st Dist.	Mary Colbert		Dead	Chick residing in Choctaw N 1st Dist.
2	O'neil		non citizen	Katinka Colbert	(I.W.)	1897	" " " "
3	No. 1			No. 2			
4	No. 1			No. 2			
5	No. 1			No. 2			
6	No. 1			No. 2			
7	No. 1			No. 2			

(NOTES)

No. 2 was admitted as Intermarried Choctaw by Dawes Commission   *(No. 2 Dawes' Roll No. 202)*
    Under Act of Congress June 10th 1896 Choctaw Card #966   No Appeal
No. 4 On Chickasaw Roll as Lula Colbert
No. 6 "   "   "   " Zana   "   *(No. 6 Dawes' Roll No. 4038)*
No. 6 Proof of Birth received and file Sept. 11 1902
No. 7 Enrolled March 22, 1901.

Sept. 7 1898.

RESIDENCE: Pontotoc   *COUNTY*   CARD NO.

POST OFFICE: Stonewall, Ind. Ter.   FIELD NO.

	NAME	RELATION-SHIP TO PERSON FIRST NAMED	AGE	SEX	BLOOD	TRIBAL ENROLLMENT		
						YEAR	COUNTY	PAGE
1	Johnson, Stone	FIRST NAMED	23	M	Full	1897	Pontotoc	??

TRIBAL ENROLLMENT OF PARENTS

	NAME OF FATHER	YEAR	COUNTY	NAME OF MOTHER	YEAR	COUNTY
1	John Wesley	Dead	Pontotoc	Sena Carney	1897	Pontotoc

(NOTES)

(All Notations illegible)   Sept. 7/98.

RESIDENCE: Pontotoc COUNTY					CARD NO.			
POST OFFICE: Stonewall, Ind. Ter.					FIELD NO.			
NAME	RELATION-SHIP TO PERSON FIRST NAMED	AGE	SEX	BLOOD	TRIBAL ENROLLMENT			
					YEAR	COUNTY	PAGE	
1 Carney, Reubin	NAMED	47	M	Full	1897	Pontotoc	40	
2 " Sena	Wife	48	F	"	1897	"	40	
3 Killcrease, Emaline	Dau	18	F	"	1897	"	40	
4 Carney, Andrew	Son	16	M	"	1897	"	40	
5 " Annie	Dau	9	F	"	1897	"	40	
6 Johnson, Malissie	Step Dau	21	"	"	1897	"	59	
7 Killcrease, Eddie	Gr. Dau	5mo	"	"				

	TRIBAL ENROLLMENT OF PARENTS						
NAME OF FATHER	YEAR	COUNTY	NAME OF MOTHER	YEAR	COUNTY		
1 Char-ta-ha	Dead	Chickasaw Roll	Se-ma-ho-ke	1897	Pontotoc		
2 Sta-non-tubby	"	" "	Sippey	1897	"		
3	No. 1		Laney	Dead	"		
4	No. 1		No. 2				
5	No. 1		No. 2				
6 John Wesley	Dead	Pontotoc	No. 2				
7 Thompson Killcrease	1897	"	No. 3				

(NOTES)

No. 2 Died May 17th 1900; Proof of Death filed June 20th 1901
No. 3 is now the wife of Thompson Killcrease, Chickasaw Card #142.
    Evidence of marriage requested, received and filed April 20 1902
No. 6 Died about March 10th 1900. Proof of Death filed June ? 1901
No. 7 Born Jany 24th 1902. Enrolled March ? 1902

P.O. Russell, I.T.   Sept. 7/98.

RESIDENCE: Pontotoc COUNTY					CARD NO.			
POST OFFICE: Stonewall, Ind. Ter.					FIELD NO.			
NAME	RELATION-SHIP TO PERSON FIRST NAMED	AGE	SEX	BLOOD	TRIBAL ENROLLMENT			
					YEAR	COUNTY	PAGE	
1 Carney, Burney	NAMED	20	M	Full	1897	Pontotoc	49	
2 " Joseph	Wife	18	F	"	1897	"	49	

24

Chickasaw Enrollment Cards 1898-1914
Chickasaw by Blood   Volume II

3	" Martha	Dau	Iwk	"	"				
4	" Mary	"	Imo	"	"				

TRIBAL ENROLLMENT OF PARENTS

	NAME OF FATHER	YEAR	COUNTY	NAME OF MOTHER	YEAR	COUNTY
1	Reuben Carney	1897	Pontotoc	Laney	Dead	Pontotoc
2	Edward Davis	1897	"	Easter	1897	"
3	No. 1			No. 2		
4	No. 1			No. 2		

(NOTES)

No. 3 Evidence of Birth reeived and filed March ? 1902
No. 4 Enrolled Sept. 16th 1901.

Sept. 7/98.

RESIDENCE:	Choctaw Nation	COUNTY				CARD NO.			
POST OFFICE:	Conway, Ind. Ter.					FIELD NO.			

NAME	RELATION-SHIP TO PERSON FIRST NAMED	AGE	SEX	BLOOD	TRIBAL ENROLLMENT		
					YEAR	COUNTY	PAGE
1 Harris, Caroline	NAMED	17	F	Full			
2 Rushing, Chas. William	Son	2wk	M	1/2			

TRIBAL ENROLLMENT OF PARENTS

	NAME OF FATHER	YEAR	COUNTY	NAME OF MOTHER	YEAR	COUNTY
1	Culberon Harris	Dead	Chickasaw Roll	Viney Harris	Dead	Chickasaw Roll
2	Joe Rushing	"	Non-Citizen	No. 1		

(NOTES)

(All Notations Illegible)

Sept. 7/98.

RESIDENCE:	Choctaw Nation	COUNTY				CARD NO.			
POST OFFICE:	Conway, Ind. Ter.					FIELD NO.			

	NAME	RELATION-SHIP TO PERSON FIRST NAMED	AGE	SEX	BLOOD	TRIBAL ENROLLMENT		
						YEAR	COUNTY	PAGE
1	Goer, Mary	NAMED	29	F	Full			
2	" Simon	Son	13	M	1/2			
3	" Angeline	Dau	10	F	1/2			
4	" Doney	"	6	"	1/2			
5	" Henderson	Son	3	M	1/2			
6	" Elmarina	Dau	3mo	F	1/2			

25

	TRIBAL ENROLLMENT OF PARENTS						
	NAME OF FATHER	YEAR	COUNTY	NAME OF MOTHER	YEAR	COUNTY
1	Martin Stick	Dead	Chickasaw Roll	Viney Harris	Dead	Chickasaw Roll
2	William Goer		Atoka County Choctaw Nation	No. I		
3	" "		" "	No. I		
4	" "		" "	No. I		
5	" "		" "	No. I		
6	" "		" "	No. I		

(NOTES)

All except No. 6 are on Choctaw Census Record No. 2 Page 212. Transferred to Chickasaw Roll by Dawes Commission.

No. I wife of William Goer Chickasaw Roll Card No. 52.

No. I On Choctaw Roll 1896, Atoka County No. 4969.

No. 2 "   "   " 1896 "   "   " 4970 as Simeon Goer

No. 3 "   "   " 1896 "   "   " 4972

No. 4 "   "   " 1896 "   "   " 4973 as Daney Goer

No. 5 "   "   " 1896 "   "   " 4971

No. 6 Evidence of Birth Received and filed Feb. 28th 1902.

Sept. 7/98

RESIDENCE: Choctaw Nation COUNTY					CARD NO.		
POST OFFICE: Calvin, Ind. Ter.					FIELD NO.		

NAME	RELATION-SHIP TO PERSON	AGE	SEX	BLOOD	TRIBAL ENROLLMENT		
					YEAR	COUNTY	PAGE
1 Perriman, Lizzie	FIRST NAMED	7	F	1/2	1897	Chick residing in Choctaw N. 1st Dist.	70
2 " George	Bri	5	M	1/2	1897	" " " "	70

	TRIBAL ENROLLMENT OF PARENTS						
	NAME OF FATHER	YEAR	COUNTY	NAME OF MOTHER	YEAR	COUNTY
1	Alesi Perriman		Creek Roll	Agnes Perriman	Dead	Chick residing in Choctaw N. 1st Dist.
2	" "		" "	" "	"	" " " " "

(NOTES)

Sept. 7/98.

Chickasaw Enrollment Cards 1898-1914
Chickasaw by Blood   Volume II

RESIDENCE: Pontotoc   COUNTY   CARD NO.

POST OFFICE: Conway, Ind. Ter.   FIELD NO.

	NAME	RELATION-SHIP TO PERSON FIRST NAMED	AGE	SEX	BLOOD	TRIBAL ENROLLMENT		
						YEAR	COUNTY	PAGE
1	Stick, Billie		38	M	Full	1897	Pontotoc	41
2	" Nellie	Wife	40	F	"	1897	"	41
3	" Katie	Dau	10	"	"	1897	"	41
4	" Mattie	"	9	"	"	1897	"	41
5	" Lillie	"	7	"	"	1897	"	41
6	" Eddie	Son	5	M	"	1897	"	42
7	" Ida	Dau	4mo	F	"			
8	Kuctchubby, Josephine	Step Dau	14	"	"	1897	"	41
9	Stick, Emily	Dau	5mo	"	"			

TRIBAL ENROLLMENT OF PARENTS

	NAME OF FATHER	YEAR	COUNTY	NAME OF MOTHER	YEAR	COUNTY
1	Martin Stick	Dead	Pontotoc	Biney Stick	Dead	Pontotoc
2	Ed Leader	1897	"	Zahley	"	"
3	No. 1			No. 2		
4	No. 1			No. 2		
5	No. 1			No. 2		
6	No. 1			No. 2		
7	No. 1			No. 2		
8	Bob Kuctchubby			No. 2		
9	No. 1			No. 2		

(NOTES)

No. 1 On Chickasaw Roll as Bill Stick
No. 2 "   "   " " Nellie "
No. 7 Died Dec' 13th 1898. Evidence of Death filed June 30th 1902
No. 9 Enrolled May 24th 1900

Sept. 6/98.

RESIDENCE: Pontotoc   COUNTY   CARD NO.

POST OFFICE: McGee, Ind. Ter.   FIELD NO.

	NAME	RELATION-SHIP TO PERSON FIRST NAMED	AGE	SEX	BLOOD	TRIBAL ENROLLMENT		
						YEAR	COUNTY	PAGE
1	Keel, Billie		40	M	Full	1897	Pontotoc	39
2	" Lizzie	Wife	32	F	"	1897	"	39
3	" Ella	Dau	12	"	"	1897	"	39

Chickasaw Enrollment Cards 1898-1914
Chickasaw by Blood   Volume II

#	Name	Relationship	Age	Sex	Blood	Year	County	Page
4	" Ida	"	11	"	"	1897	"	39
5	" Ada	"	9	"	"	1897	"	39
6	" William	Son	7	M	"	1897	"	39
7	" Lewellen	"	4	"	"	1897	"	39
8	" Jonas	"	1	"	"	1897	"	39
9	" Leo	"	5mo	"	"	1897	"	39

TRIBAL ENROLLMENT OF PARENTS

	NAME OF FATHER	YEAR	COUNTY	NAME OF MOTHER	YEAR	COUNTY
1	Isam Keel	Dead	Pontotoc	Siney	Dead	Chickasaw Roll
2	Newton	"	"	Salina Walton	1897	Pontotoc
3	No. 1			No. 2		
4	No. 1			No. 2		
5	No. 1			No. 2		
6	No. 1			No. 2		
7	No. 1			No. 2		
8	No. 1			No. 2		
9	No. 1			No. 2		

(NOTES)

No. 2 On Chickasaw Roll as Mre Billie Keel
Nos. 3, 4, 5, 6, and 7 On Chickasaw Roll as "Five Children"
No. 8 Died Aug. 30, 1899. Proof of Death filed Nov. 12, 1902
No. 9 Enrolled Aug. 17th 1901.

Sept. 6/98

RESIDENCE: Pontotoc COUNTY						CARD NO.		
POST OFFICE: Conner, Ind. Ter.						FIELD NO.		

NAME	RELATION-SHIP TO PERSON FIRST NAMED	AGE	SEX	BLOOD	TRIBAL ENROLLMENT		
					YEAR	COUNTY	PAGE
1 Ko-you-hokey		75	F	Full	1897	Pontotoc	55

TRIBAL ENROLLMENT OF PARENTS

	NAME OF FATHER	YEAR	COUNTY	NAME OF MOTHER	YEAR	COUNTY
1	O-no-ho-chubby	Dead	Chickasaw Roll	La-ga	Dead	Chickasaw Roll

(NOTES)

Sept. 6, 1898.

Chickasaw Enrollment Cards 1898-1914
Chickasaw by Blood   Volume II

RESIDENCE: Pontotoc   **COUNTY**   **CARD NO.**

POST OFFICE: Purcell, Ind. Ter.   **FIELD NO.**

	NAME	RELATION-SHIP TO PERSON FIRST NAMED	AGE	SEX	BLOOD	TRIBAL ENROLLMENT		
						YEAR	COUNTY	PAGE
1	White, Leona	NAMED	13	F	1/2	1897	Pontotoc	63
2	" Alice	Sister	10	"	12	1908	"	63

TRIBAL ENROLLMENT OF PARENTS

	NAME OF FATHER	YEAR	COUNTY	NAME OF MOTHER	YEAR	COUNTY
1	John White		Non citizen	Annie Billie	1897	Pontotoc
2	" "		" "	" "	"	"

(NOTES)

Sept. 6/98.

RESIDENCE: Pontotoc   **COUNTY**   **CARD NO.**

POST OFFICE: Conner, Ind. Ter.   **FIELD NO.**

	NAME	RELATION-SHIP TO PERSON FIRST NAMED	AGE	SEX	BLOOD	TRIBAL ENROLLMENT		
						YEAR	COUNTY	PAGE
1	James. Dinson	NAMED	22	M	Full	1897	Tishomingo	35
2	" June	Wife	36	F	"	1897	"	36
3	" Culberson	Son	1	M	"			
4	Alexander, Myatt	Step Son	8	"	"	1897	Tishomingo	36
5	" Joseph	" "	5	"	"	1908	"	35

TRIBAL ENROLLMENT OF PARENTS

	NAME OF FATHER	YEAR	COUNTY	NAME OF MOTHER	YEAR	COUNTY
1	??-??-na-tubby	Dead	Pontotoc	Elizabeth	Dead	Pontotoc
2	Duncan Ned	"	"	Ah-no-le-ho-la	"	"
3	No. 1			No. 2		
4	Gilman Alexander	Dead	Tishomingo	No. 2		
5	" "	"	"	No. 2		

(NOTES)

No. 2 On Chickasaw Roll as Jane Alexander
No. 3 Eviodence of Birth received and filed March 20. 1902

Sept. 6, 1898.

29

Chickasaw Enrollment Cards 1898-1914
Chickasaw by Blood   Volume II

RESIDENCE: Pontotoc   COUNTY

CARD NO.

POST OFFICE: Oakman, Ind. Ter.

FIELD NO.

NAME	RELATION-SHIP TO PERSON FIRST NAMED	AGE	SEX	BLOOD	TRIBAL ENROLLMENT		
					YEAR	COUNTY	PAGE
1 Porter, Harrison	NAMED	24	M	Full	1897	Pontotoc	60
2 " Icey	Wife	30	F	"	1897	"	39

TRIBAL ENROLLMENT OF PARENTS

NAME OF FATHER	YEAR	COUNTY	NAME OF MOTHER	YEAR	COUNTY
1 Oshway Porter	1897	Pontotoc	Salina	1897	Pontotoc
2 Ho-pah-kin-tubby	Dead	Chickasaw Roll	Lousanna	Dead	Chickasaw Roll

(NOTES)

(All notations illegible)

Sept. 6, 1898.

RESIDENCE: Choctaw Nation   COUNTY

CARD NO.

POST OFFICE: Guertie, Ind, Ter.

FIELD NO.

NAME	RELATION-SHIP TO PERSON FIRST NAMED	AGE	SEX	BLOOD	TRIBAL ENROLLMENT		
					YEAR	COUNTY	PAGE
1 Leader, Isabinda	NAMED	32	F	Full			
2 " Odis	Son	17	M	1/2			
3 " Aaron	"	13	"	1/2			
4 " Jim	"	3	"	1/2			
5 " Alice	Dau	20	F	1/2			
6 " Melinda	"	2	"	1/2			
7 " Mary	"	1wk	"	1/2			

TRIBAL ENROLLMENT OF PARENTS

NAME OF FATHER	YEAR	COUNTY	NAME OF MOTHER	YEAR	COUNTY
1 Aaron Frazier	Dead	Chickasaw Roll	Malinda James	Dead	Chickasaw Roll
2 John Leader		" "	No. 1		
3 " "		" "	No. 1		
4 " "		" "	No. 1		
5 " "		" "	No. 1		
6 " "		" "	No. 1		
7 " "		" "	No. 1		

(NOTES)

All on Choctaw Census Record No. 2, Page 342.
No. 1 Wife of John Leader, Choctaw Card 212, *(remainder illegible)*
No. 1 On Choctaw Roll 1896 Atoka County No. 8296 as Isabinda Leader
No. 2 "   "   " 1896   "   "   " 8298

30

No. 3 "   "   " 1896   "   "   " 8299
No. 4 "   "   " 1896   "   "   " 8300
No. 5 "   "   " 1896   "   "   " 8301
No. 6 "   "   " 1896   "   "   " 8302
No. 7 Born March 21st 1902; Enrolled April 1st 1902

Sept. 6/98.

RESIDENCE: Pontotoc COUNTY					CARD NO.			
POST OFFICE: Stonewall, Ind. Ter.					FIELD NO.			
NAME	RELATION-SHIP TO PERSON FIRST NAMED	AGE	SEX	BLOOD	TRIBAL ENROLLMENT			
					YEAR	COUNTY	PAGE	
1 James, Jennie	NAMED	51	F	1/4	1897	Pontotoc	41	
2 " Osceola W.	Son	21	M	1/2	1897	"	41	
3 Statler, Dacie	Dau	18	F	1/2	1897	"	41	
4 " Lelia	Grand Dau	4mo	"	1/4				
5 " Gale	husband of No. 3	30	M	I.W.				

TRIBAL ENROLLMENT OF PARENTS

	NAME OF FATHER	YEAR	COUNTY	NAME OF MOTHER	YEAR	COUNTY
1	John Byrd	Dead	Non citizen	Mary Byrd	Dead	Chickasaw Roll
2	Simon D. James	"	Chickasaw Roll	No. 1		
3	" " "	"	" "	No. 1		
4	Gale Statler		white man	No. 3		
5	(Illegible) Statler		non citizen	Martha Statler		non-citizen

(NOTES)

No. 2 On Chickasaw Roll as O.W. James
No. 3 "   "   "   " Daisy "
No. 3 is now the wife of Gale Statler, on Chickasaw Card D.262, Feby. 19th 1900
No. 4 Enrolled May 24th 1900
No. 5 transferred from Chickasaw card #D.262 March 29, 1903. See
     decision of March 13, 1903.

Sept. 6/98.

RESIDENCE: Choctaw Nation COUNTY					CARD NO.			
POST OFFICE: Oconce, Ind. Ter.					FIELD NO.			
NAME	RELATION-SHIP TO PERSON FIRST NAMED	AGE	SEX	BLOOD	TRIBAL ENROLLMENT			
					YEAR	COUNTY	PAGE	
1 Jemison, Eula	NAMED	25	F	1/2		(Illegible information)		

2	"	Joe	Son	6	M	1/4		*(Illegible information)*	
3	"	Gertrude	Dau	2	F	1/4		*(Illegible information)*	
4	"	Jennie	"	2wks	"	1/4			
5	"	Vera	"	6wk	"	1/4			
6	"	William P.	Husband	33	M	I.W.			

TRIBAL ENROLLMENT OF PARENTS

	NAME OF FATHER	YEAR	COUNTY	NAME OF MOTHER	YEAR	COUNTY
1	*(Name Illegible)*	Dead	Chickasaw Roll	Jennie James	1897	Pontotoc
2	*(Name Illegible)*		Non-Citizen	*(Name Illegible)*		*(Illegible)*
3	*(Name Illegible)*		" "	No. 1		*(Illegible)*
4	*(Name Illegible)*		" "	No. 1		*(Illegible)*
5	*(Name Illegible)*		" "	No. 1		*(Illegible)*
6	*(Name Illegible)*		" "	*(Name Illegible)*		Non citizen

(NOTES)

(All Notations illegible)

Sept. 6/98.

RESIDENCE:	Choctaw Nation	COUNTY		CARD NO.	
POST OFFICE:	Jeff, Ind. Ter.			FIELD NO.	

	NAME	RELATION-SHIP TO PERSON FIRST NAMED	AGE	SEX	BLOOD	TRIBAL ENROLLMENT		
						YEAR	COUNTY	PAGE
1	Scott, John P.	NAMED	38	M	I.W.			
2	" Phoebe	Wife	26	F	1/4			
3	" Andrew J.	Son	6	M	1/8			
4	" John	"	3	"	1/8			
5	" Laura	Dau	1	F	1/8			
6	" Lula Elizabeth	"	2mo	"	1/8			

TRIBAL ENROLLMENT OF PARENTS

	NAME OF FATHER	YEAR	COUNTY	NAME OF MOTHER	YEAR	COUNTY
1	Andrew J. Scott	Dead	Non-citizen	Margaret Scott	Dead	Non-Citizen
2	Ben *(Illegible)*	"	Choctaw	Salina Walton	?	Pontotoc
3	No. 1			No. 2		
4	No. 1			No. 2		
5	No. 1			No. 2		
6	No. 1			No. 2		

(NOTES)

See decision of June 13 '04.

No. 1 Admitted as intermarried Chickasaw by Dawes Com. in 1896. *(No. 1 Dawes' Roll No. 383)*

No. 1 Admitted by Dawes Com. Case No. 157, on Choctaw Intermarried Roll Page 101

(Remainder illegible)

Sept. 6th 1898

Chickasaw Enrollment Cards 1898-1914
Chickasaw by Blood   Volume II

RESIDENCE: Pontotoc   COUNTY   CARD NO.
POST OFFICE: Stonewall, Ind. Ter,   FIELD NO.

NAME	RELATION-SHIP TO PERSON FIRST NAMED	AGE	SEX	BLOOD	TRIBAL ENROLLMENT		
					YEAR	COUNTY	PAGE
1 Henderson, Tom	NAMED	50	M	Full	1897	Pontotoc	39
2 " Nancy	Wife	42	F	"	1897	"	39
3 " Frances	Step-Dau	16	"	"	1897	"	39
4 Gipson, Wilburn	Step-Son	18	M	"	1897	"	39
5 Perkins, Lena	Ward	8	F	"	1897	"	39
6 Dyer, Cisen	Step-Dau	23	"	"	1897	"	39
7 Factor, McCurtain	Ward	5	M	"	1897	"	P.R. #1 137

TRIBAL ENROLLMENT OF PARENTS

NAME OF FATHER	YEAR	COUNTY	NAME OF MOTHER	YEAR	COUNTY
1 (Name Illegible)	Dead	Chickasaw Roll	Te-mo-lak-ke	Dead	Chickasaw Roll
2 (Name Illegible)	"	" "	Fo-lo-he	"	" "
3 John (Illegible)		Pontotoc	No. 2		
4 Gipson, James	1897	"	No. 2		
5 (Illegible) Greenwood	Dead	"	Sarah Greenwood	Dead	Pontotoc
6 (Illegible) Dyer	"	"	No. 2		
7 Willie Factor	"	"	(Illegible) Factor	Dead	Pontotoc

(NOTES)

No. 4 is now married to Liza Benton (remainder illegible)
No. 6 On Chickasaw Roll as Decero Dyer, (remainder illegible)
(Notation illegible)
No. 5 died, July 14, 1900; -proof of death filed Dec. 12, 1902
No. 6 died Nov. 4, 1901; proof of death filed Dec. 12, 1902.

P.O. Jesse, I.T. 12/1/02.   Sept. 6. 1898.

RESIDENCE: Pontotoc   COUNTY   CARD NO.
POST OFFICE: Conway, Ind. Ter.   FIELD NO.

NAME	RELATION-SHIP TO PERSON FIRST NAMED	AGE	SEX	BLOOD	TRIBAL ENROLLMENT		
					YEAR	COUNTY	PAGE
1 McLane, Ainusiah	NAMED	21	M	Full	1897	Pontotoc	95

TRIBAL ENROLLMENT OF PARENTS

NAME OF FATHER	YEAR	COUNTY	NAME OF MOTHER	YEAR	COUNTY
1 John McLane	1897	Pontotoc	Kilsey	Dead	Chickasaw Roll

Chickasaw Enrollment Cards 1898-1914
Chickasaw by Blood   Volume II

(NOTES)

No. 1 On 1893 Chickasaw Pay Roll No. 2, Page 157 as *(Illegible)* McLane

Sept. 6/98.

	NAME	RELATION- SHIP TO PERSON FIRST NAMED	AGE	SEX	BLOOD	TRIBAL ENROLLMENT		
						YEAR	COUNTY	PAGE

RESIDENCE: Pontotoc COUNTY   CARD NO.
POST OFFICE: Allen, Ind. Ter.   FIELD NO.

	NAME	RELATION-SHIP TO PERSON FIRST NAMED	AGE	SEX	BLOOD	YEAR	COUNTY	PAGE
1	McLane, John	NAMED	50	M	Full	1897	Pontotoc	?
2	" *(Illegible)*	Wife	40	F	"	1897	"	?
3	" *(Illegible)*	Son	19	M	"	1897	"	?
4	" *(Illegible)*	Dau	13	F	"	1897	"	95
5	" Odus	Son	12	M	"	1897	"	95

TRIBAL ENROLLMENT OF PARENTS

	NAME OF FATHER	YEAR	COUNTY	NAME OF MOTHER	YEAR	COUNTY
1	*(Name Illegible)*	Dead	Chickasaw Roll	*(Name Illegible)*	Dead	Chickasaw Roll
2	*(Name Illegible)*	"	" "	*(Illegible)* James		Pontotoc
3	No. 1			Kilsey	Dead	Chickasaw Roll
4	No. 1			"	"	" "
5	No. 1			"	"	" "

(NOTES)

(All Notations illegible)

Sept. 6/98.

RESIDENCE: Pontotoc COUNTY   CARD NO.
POST OFFICE: Jeff, Ind. Ter.   FIELD NO.

	NAME	RELATION-SHIP TO PERSON FIRST NAMED	AGE	SEX	BLOOD	YEAR	COUNTY	PAGE
1	Gipson, Albert	NAMED	30	M	Full	1897	Pontotoc	51
2	" Malina	Wife	30	F	"	1897	"	51
3	" Abner	Son	9	M	"	1897	"	51
4	" Eddie	"	5	"	"	1897	"	51
5	" Elizie	S.Dau	15	F	"	1897	"	51
6	Shico, Elonzo	Ward	7	M	"	1897	Tishomingo	35

TRIBAL ENROLLMENT OF PARENTS

	NAME OF FATHER	YEAR	COUNTY	NAME OF MOTHER	YEAR	COUNTY
1	Gipson	Dead	Chickasaw Roll	Sallie	Dead	Chickasaw Roll
2	*(Name Illegible)*	"	" "	Ha-we-ok-tey	"	" "

34

3	No. 1			No. 2		
4	No. 1			No. 2		
5	David Ayakatubby	Dead	Chickasaw Roll	No. 2		
6	Frank Shico	1897	Pontotoc	Susanna Alowatubbie	1897	Tishomingo

(NOTES)

No. 2 Died March 6th 1902; Proof of Death filed March 17th 1902.

Sept. 6/98.

RESIDENCE:	Pontotoc	COUNTY				CARD NO.		
POST OFFICE:	Conway, Ind. Ter.					FIELD NO.		

NAME	RELATION-SHIP TO PERSON FIRST NAMED	AGE	SEX	BLOOD	TRIBAL ENROLLMENT		
					YEAR	COUNTY	PAGE
1 Alexander, Annie		15	F	1/2	1897	Pontotoc	60

TRIBAL ENROLLMENT OF PARENTS						
NAME OF FATHER	YEAR	COUNTY	NAME OF MOTHER		YEAR	COUNTY
1 Stephen Alexander		Chick Freedman	Louiney		Dead	Pontotoc

(NOTES)

No. 1 Died April, 1902. Proof of Death filed *(Illegible)* 1902.

Sept. 6/98.

RESIDENCE:	Choctaw Nation	COUNTY				CARD NO.		
POST OFFICE:	Tandy, Ind. Ter.					FIELD NO.		

NAME	RELATION-SHIP TO PERSON FIRST NAMED	AGE	SEX	BLOOD	TRIBAL ENROLLMENT		
					YEAR	COUNTY	PAGE
1 Johnston, William		45	M	1/8	1897	Chick residing in Choctaw N. 1st Dist.	70

TRIBAL ENROLLMENT OF PARENTS						
NAME OF FATHER	YEAR	COUNTY	NAME OF MOTHER		YEAR	COUNTY
1 Jack Johnston	Dead	Non-Citz	Mary Johnston		Dead	Chickasaw Roll

(NOTES)

No. 1 On 1897 Chickasaw Roll as William Johnson.

Husband of Lu?etia Johnston, Choctaw Card No. *(illegible)*

Sept. 6/98.

Chickasaw Enrollment Cards 1898-1914
Chickasaw by Blood   Volume II

RESIDENCE: Pontotoc COUNTY					CARD NO.			
POST OFFICE: Stonewall, Ind. Ter.					FIELD NO.			

NAME	RELATION-SHIP TO PERSON FIRST NAMED	AGE	SEX	BLOOD	TRIBAL ENROLLMENT			
					YEAR	COUNTY		PAGE
1 Harrison, Lucy		42	F	Full	1897	Pontotoc		?

TRIBAL ENROLLMENT OF PARENTS

NAME OF FATHER	YEAR	COUNTY	NAME OF MOTHER	YEAR	COUNTY
1 *(Name Illegible)*	Dead	Chickasaw Roll	*(Name Illegible)*	Dead	Chickaaw Roll

(NOTES)

(Illegible notation)   *(No. 1 Dawes' Roll No. 826)*

No. 1 Died Sept. 1901; Proof of Death filed *(Illegible)*1902.

Sept. 6/98.

RESIDENCE: Pontotoc COUNTY					CARD NO.			
POST OFFICE: Stonewall, Ind. Ter.					FIELD NO.			

	NAME	RELATION-SHIP TO PERSON FIRST NAMED	AGE	SEX	BLOOD	TRIBAL ENROLLMENT		
						YEAR	COUNTY	PAGE
1	Harrison, Daniel P.	NAMED	36	M	1/2	1897	Pontotoc	40
2	" Mary	Wife	28	F	I.W.	1897	"	80
3	" William	Son	19	M	3/4	1897	"	40
4	" Laura	Dau	15	F	3/4	1897	"	40
5	" Tina	"	12	"	3/4	1897	"	40
6	" Cecelia	"	8	"	3/4	1897	"	40
7	" Mamie	"	6	"	1/4	1897	"	40
8	" Pearl	"	4	"	1/4	1897	"	40
9	" Mary	"	2	"	1/4			
10	" Ella	"	8mo	"	1/4			
11	" Frances V.	"	1mo	"	1/4			
12	" Arthur D.	Son	2wks	M	1/4			

TRIBAL ENROLLMENT OF PARENTS

	NAME OF FATHER	YEAR	COUNTY	NAME OF MOTHER	YEAR	COUNTY
1	Wm F. Harrison	Dead	Non Citizen	Mary Harrison	Dead	Pontotoc
2				Berthena Bradshaw		Non-Citizen
3	No. 1			Lucy Harrison	1897	Pontotoc
4	No. 1			" "	"	"
5	No. 1			" "	"	"
6	No. 1			" "	"	"
7	No. 1			No. 2		

Chickasaw Enrollment Cards 1898-1914
Chickasaw by Blood   Volume II

8	No. 1			No. 2		
9	No. 1			No. 2		
10	No. 1			No. 2		
11	No. 1			No. 2		
12	No. 1			No. 2		

(NOTES)

No. 1 On Chickasaw Roll as D.P. Harrison
No. 3 "   "   "   " William H "
No. 9 Evidence of Birth received and filed Feb. 27 1902
No. 10 "   "   "   "   "   " Feb. 27 1902
No. 11 Enrolled June 8/99
No. 12 Born July 27th 1902. Enrolled Aug. 7th 1902
  (Some notations illegible)

No. 2 Enrolled Sept. 5/98.
All others   "   Sept. 6/98.

RESIDENCE: Pontotoc COUNTY   CARD NO.
POST OFFICE: Pontotoc, Ind. Ter.   FIELD NO.

NAME	RELATION-SHIP TO PERSON FIRST NAMED	AGE	SEX	BLOOD	TRIBAL ENROLLMENT		
					YEAR	COUNTY	PAGE
1 Levi, Edmon	NAMED	26	M	Full	1897	Pontotoc	55
2 " Milsey	Wife	30	F	"	1897	"	55
3 " Jackson	Son	5	M	"	1897	"	55
4 " Mattie	Dau	1	F	"			

TRIBAL ENROLLMENT OF PARENTS

	NAME OF FATHER	YEAR	COUNTY	NAME OF MOTHER	YEAR	COUNTY
1	Levi	Dead	Tishomingo	Kamimey	Dead	Tishomingo
2	Jno. McLean	1897	Pontotoc	Elizabeth McLean	"	Pontotoc
3	No. 1			No. 2		
4	No. 1			No. 2		

(NOTES)
Evidence of Birth for No. 4 received and filed *(Illegible)* 28, 1902.

Sept. 6/98.

RESIDENCE: Pontotoc COUNTY   CARD NO.
POST OFFICE: Wynnewood, Ind. Ter.   FIELD NO.

NAME	RELATION-SHIP TO PERSON FIRST NAMED	AGE	SEX	BLOOD	TRIBAL ENROLLMENT		
					YEAR	COUNTY	PAGE
1 Nelson, Columbus	NAMED	56	M	1/2	1897	Pontotoc	48

37

2	*(Blank on microfilm)*								
3	" John	Son	18	M	1/4	1897	Pontotoc		48
4	" Malissa	Dau	11	F	1/4	1897	"		48
5	" Fate	Son	9	M	1/4	1897	"		48
6	" Lula	Dau	7	F	1/4	1897	"		48
7	" Eliza	"	1	"	1/4				
8	" Sim	Son	4mo	M	1/4				

TRIBAL ENROLLMENT OF PARENTS

	NAME OF FATHER	YEAR	COUNTY	NAME OF MOTHER	YEAR	COUNTY
1	John Nelson	Dead	Non-Citizen	Catherine Nelson	Dead	Pontotoc
2						
3	No. 1			Anna Nelson	Dead	Non-Citizen
4	No. 1			" "	"	" "
5	No. 1			" "	"	" "
6	No. 1			" "	"	" "
7	No. 1			Susan Nelson		White Woman
8	No. 1			" "		" "

(NOTES)

No. 4 On Chickasaw Roll as Maulsy Nelson
No. 5 "   "   "   " Lute   "
No. 7 Affidavit of attending physician to be supplied
No. 7 Died March 2nd 1899. Proof of Death filed May 20th 1902.
No. 8 Enrolled Decr 13th 1899

Oct. 5/98.

RESIDENCE: Pontotoc COUNTY					CARD NO.			
POST OFFICE: Stonewall, Ind. Ter.					FIELD NO.			
NAME	RELATION-SHIP TO PERSON FIRST NAMED	AGE	SEX	BLOOD	TRIBAL ENROLLMENT			
					YEAR	COUNTY		PAGE
1 Brown, Tecumseh		25	M	Full	1897	Pontotoc		53

TRIBAL ENROLLMENT OF PARENTS

	NAME OF FATHER	YEAR	COUNTY	NAME OF MOTHER	YEAR	COUNTY
1	*(Name Illegible)*	1897	Pontotoc	Kilsey Brown	Dead	Pontotoc

(NOTES)

Sept. 6th 1898.

Chickasaw Enrollment Cards 1898-1914
Chickasaw by Blood   Volume II

RESIDENCE: Choctaw Nation   *COUNTY*   *CARD NO.*

POST OFFICE: Lehigh, Ind. Ter.   *FIELD NO.*

	NAME	RELATION-SHIP TO PERSON FIRST NAMED	AGE	SEX	BLOOD	TRIBAL ENROLLMENT		
						YEAR	COUNTY	PAGE
1	Sealy, Susan		40	F	Full	1897	Chick residing in Choctaw N. 3rd Dist.	74
2	" Culberson	Son	23	M	"	1897	" " " "	74
3	" Amelia	Dau	16	F	"	1897	" " " "	74
4	Monroe, Josephine	"	12	"	"	1897	" " " "	74
5	Dick, Martin	Son of No. 4	23mo	M	7/8			

TRIBAL ENROLLMENT OF PARENTS

	NAME OF FATHER	YEAR	COUNTY	NAME OF MOTHER	YEAR	COUNTY
1	Tecumseh Jefferson	Dead	Chickasaw Roll	Temayoke	Dead	Chickasaw Roll
2	Tom Sealy	"	Chick residing in Choctaw N 3rd Dist	No. 1		
3	" "	"	" " " "	No. 1		
4	Willis Monroe	1897	" " " "	No. 1		
5	Taylor Dick	1896	Atoka	No. 4		

(NOTES)

No. 4 is wife of Taylor Dick Choctaw Card #5506
No. 3 Died Sept. 20, 1902; Proof of Death filed *(illegible)*
No. 5 Born Aug. 8/02, appl. first received Oct. 17/02
(Remainder illegible)

Sept. 6/98.

RESIDENCE: Choctaw Nation 3rd Dist.   *COUNTY*   *CARD NO.*

POST OFFICE: Tuskahoma, Ind. Ter.   *FIELD NO.*

	NAME	RELATION-SHIP TO PERSON FIRST NAMED	AGE	SEX	BLOOD	TRIBAL ENROLLMENT		
						YEAR	COUNTY	PAGE
1	Anderson, Rogers		48	M	1/2			
2	" Kissie **DEAD**	Wife	40	F	Full	1897	Chick residing in Choctaw Nation	73
3	" Raynie	Son	6	M	3/4			
4	" Clifford **DEAD**	"	1	"	3/4			
5	" Bonnie	"	14	"	3/4			
6	" Osborne	"	16	"	3/4	1897	Chick residing in Choctaw Nation	73
7	" Freeman	;;	11	"	3/4			

39

Chickasaw Enrollment Cards 1898-1914
Chickasaw by Blood   Volume II

8	" Willie		"	9	"			

	TRIBAL ENROLLMENT OF PARENTS						
	NAME OF FATHER	YEAR	COUNTY	NAME OF MOTHER	YEAR	COUNTY
1	Reuben Anderson	Dead	Choctaw Roll	Hettie Anderson	Dead	Chickasaw Roll
2	(Name Illegible)		Chickasaw Roll	(Name Illegible)	"	" "
3	No. 1			No. 2		
4	No. 1			No. 2		
5	No. 1			Peggy		Chick residing in Choctaw N 3rd Dist
6	No. 1			No. 2		
7	No. 1			No. 2		
8	No. 1			No. 2		

(NOTES)

All but Nos 2 & 4 on Choctaw Census Record No. 1, Page 20 (remainder illegible)

No. 1 On Choctaw Roll 1896 Jacks Fork County #484.   (No. 1 Dawes' Roll No. Void)

No. 3 " " " 1896 " " " #489 as Rayney Anderson

No. 5 " " " 1896 " " " #486 as Bunnie Anderson   (No. 5 Dawes' Roll No. Void)

No. 6 " " " 1896 " " " #485   No. 6 Dawes' Roll No. Void)

No. 7 " " " 1896 " " " #487

No. 8 " " " 1896 " " " #488

No. 2 Died Dec' 15th 1898. Evidence of Death filed July 3rd 1902.

No. 4 Died May 5th 1899; Evidence of Death filed July 3rd 1902.

No. 5 Died June 27th 1901; Evidence of Death filed July 3rd 1902.

(Other notations illegible.)

CANCELLED Stamped across card

Sept. 6th 1898.

RESIDENCE: Pontotoc   COUNTY   CARD NO.

POST OFFICE: Stonewall, Ind. Ter.   FIELD NO.

NAME	RELATION-SHIP TO PERSON FIRST NAMED	AGE	SEX	BLOOD	TRIBAL ENROLLMENT		
					YEAR	COUNTY	PAGE
1 Immotichey, Elsey	NAMED	31	F	1/2	1897	Pontotoc	57

	TRIBAL ENROLLMENT OF PARENTS						
	NAME OF FATHER	YEAR	COUNTY	NAME OF MOTHER	YEAR	COUNTY
1	Harmon Patterson	Dead	Choctaw Roll	Su-lo-ko-che	Dead	Chickasaw Roll

(NOTES)

No. 1 Died May 11th 1901; Proof of Death filed July 20th 1901.

Sept. 6th 1899.

Chickasaw Enrollment Cards 1898-1914
Chickasaw by Blood   Volume II

RESIDENCE: Choctaw Nation 3rd D.   COUNTY _____   CARD NO. _____
POST OFFICE: Calvin, Ind. Ter. _____   FIELD NO. _____

NAME	RELATION-SHIP TO PERSON FIRST	AGE	SEX	BLOOD	TRIBAL ENROLLMENT		
					YEAR	COUNTY	PAGE
1 Davis, Mary E.	NAMED	4	F	1/8			

TRIBAL ENROLLMENT OF PARENTS

NAME OF FATHER	YEAR	COUNTY	NAME OF MOTHER	YEAR	COUNTY
1 John W. Davis		Non-Citizen	Mary J. Davis	Dead	Chickasaw Roll

(NOTES)
On Choctaw Census Record No. 2 Page 74 *(remainder illegible)*
Also   "   "   Roll 1896 Atoka County, No. *(illegible)*

Sept. 6/98.

RESIDENCE: Pontotoc   COUNTY _____   CARD NO. _____
POST OFFICE: Allen, Ind. Ter. _____   FIELD NO. _____

NAME	RELATION-SHIP TO PERSON FIRST	AGE	SEX	BLOOD	TRIBAL ENROLLMENT		
					YEAR	COUNTY	PAGE
1 Alexander, Tennessee	NAMED	20	F	Full	1897	Pontotoc	44
2 Harjo, Mary	Dau	3	"	1/2	1897	"	44
3 " Oscar	Son	1	M	1/2			
4 " Salina	Dau	?	F	1/2			

TRIBAL ENROLLMENT OF PARENTS

NAME OF FATHER	YEAR	COUNTY	NAME OF MOTHER	YEAR	COUNTY
1 John Alexander	1897	Pontotoc	Salina	Dead	Pontotoc
2 Narkoche	1897	*(Illegible)*	No. 1		
3 "	1897	"	No. 1		
4 "		"	No. 1		

(NOTES)
No. 3 Born Feb. 26, 1897; Proof of Birth filed Nov. 19/03
No. 4 was born May 8, 1901; application received March ?, 1905, under Act of Congress; approved March 8, 1905.

RESIDENCE: Pontotoc   COUNTY _____   CARD NO. _____
POST OFFICE: Hart, Ind. Ter. _____   FIELD NO. _____

NAME	RELATION-SHIP TO PERSON FIRST	AGE	SEX	BLOOD	TRIBAL ENROLLMENT		
					YEAR	COUNTY	PAGE
1 Burnett, Rufus	NAMED	52	M	I.W.	1897	Pontotoc	80
2 " Harriet J.	Wife	48	F	1/2	1897	"	49

| 3 | " | Charles M | Son | 11 | M | 1/4 | 1897 | " | 49 |
| 4 | " | Benjamin Franklin | " | 7 | " | 1/4 | 1897 | " | 49 |

TRIBAL ENROLLMENT OF PARENTS

	NAME OF FATHER	YEAR	COUNTY	NAME OF MOTHER	YEAR	COUNTY
1	*(Illegible)* Burnett	Dead	Non-Citizen	Nancy Burnett	Dead	Non-Citizen
2	Sampson Folsom	"	Chickasaw Roll	Kittie Colbert	"	Chickasaw Roll
3	No. 1			No. 2		
4	No. 1			No. 2		

(NOTES)

No. 1 On Chickasaw Roll as Ruff. Burnett   *(No. 1 Dawes' Roll No. 201)*
No. 4 "   "   "   " B.F. Burnett
No. 2 "   "   "   " H.J. Burnett
No. 3 "   "   "   " Chas. M. Burnett
　　See additional testimony of No. 1 taken Oct. 22, 1902.

Sept. 6/98.

RESIDENCE:	Choctaw Nation	COUNTY		CARD NO.	
POST OFFICE:	Lehigh, Ind. Ter.			FIELD NO.	

	NAME	RELATION-SHIP TO PERSON FIRST NAMED	AGE	SEX	BLOOD	TRIBAL ENROLLMENT		
						YEAR	COUNTY	PAGE
1	~~James, John Clay~~	NAMED	~~19~~	~~M~~	~~1/8~~			
2	" Willie C.	Bro	17	M	1/8			
3	" Lorinda	Sister	15	F	1/8			

TRIBAL ENROLLMENT OF PARENTS

	NAME OF FATHER	YEAR	COUNTY	NAME OF MOTHER	YEAR	COUNTY
1	Henry C. James		Choctaw Roll	Lorinda	Dead	Chickasaw Roll
2	" " "		" "	"	"	" "
3	" " "		" "	"	"	" "

(NOTES)

　　All these names are on Choctaw Census Record No. 2, Page 305; transferred by Dawes Com - their father is on Choctaw Card No. *(illegible)*
No. 1 on Choctaw Roll 1896, Atoka County No. 7301 as John C. James
No. 2 "   "   " 1896 "   "   " 7302 as W.C.   "
No. 3 "   "   " 1896 "   "   " 7303 as Lorindy   "
No. 1 Died February 13, 1899. Evidence of death filed March 26, 1900.
　　Transferred to Choc. Card No. 5376 Oct. 16, 1902 - written across card.

Sept. 6/98.

Chickasaw Enrollment Cards 1898-1914
Chickasaw by Blood   Volume II

RESIDENCE: Pontotoc COUNTY					CARD NO.			
POST OFFICE: Stonewall, Ind. Ter.					FIELD NO.			
NAME	RELATION-SHIP TO PERSON FIRST NAMED	AGE	SEX	BLOOD	TRIBAL ENROLLMENT			
					YEAR	COUNTY	PAGE	
1 McCarty, Tom	NAMED	23	M	Full	1897	Pontotoc	54	
2 " Nancy	Wife	46	F	1/2	1897	"	49	

	TRIBAL ENROLLMENT OF PARENTS						
NAME OF FATHER	YEAR	COUNTY	NAME OF MOTHER	YEAR	COUNTY		
1 A-chok-a-tam-ly	Dead	Pontotoc	Katsey McCarty	1897	Pontotoc		
2 Cobb	"	Non-Citizen	Liney	Dead	Chickasaw Roll		

(NOTES)

No. 2 On Chickasaw Roll as Nancy Underwood.

Sept. 6/98.

RESIDENCE: Pontotoc COUNTY					CARD NO.			
POST OFFICE: Jeff, Ind. Ter.					FIELD NO.			
NAME	RELATION-SHIP TO PERSON FIRST NAMED	AGE	SEX	BLOOD	TRIBAL ENROLLMENT			
					YEAR	COUNTY	PAGE	
1 Folsom, Sampson	NAMED	23	M	1/2	1897	Pontotoc	52	

	TRIBAL ENROLLMENT OF PARENTS						
NAME OF FATHER	YEAR	COUNTY	NAME OF MOTHER	YEAR	COUNTY		
1 Bartoneby Folsom	Dead	Pontotoc	Cassie Folsom	Dead	Pontotoc		

(NOTES)

No. 1 Also on 1897 Chickasaw Roll Page 94.

Sept. 6/98.

RESIDENCE: Pontotoc COUNTY					CARD NO.			
POST OFFICE: Stonewall, Ind. Ter.					FIELD NO.			
NAME	RELATION-SHIP TO PERSON FIRST NAMED	AGE	SEX	BLOOD	TRIBAL ENROLLMENT			
					YEAR	COUNTY	PAGE	
1 Frazier, James	NAMED	56	M	Full	1897	Pontotoc	52	
2 " Sylvia	Wife	46	F	"	1897	"	52	
3 " Agnes	Dau	25	F	"	1897	"	52	
4 " Mary	Ward	6	F	"	1897	"	53	
5 Burris, Ada	Ward	11	"	"	1897	"	54	

	TRIBAL ENROLLMENT OF PARENTS						
	NAME OF FATHER	YEAR	COUNTY	NAME OF MOTHER	YEAR	COUNTY	
1	Harry Frazier	Dead	Chickasaw Roll	Shu-*(Illegible)*	Dead	Chickasaw Roll	
2	Old Man Tilluk	"	Pontotoc	*(Name Illegible)*	"	"	"
3	No. 1			No. 2			
4	Charley Frazier	Dead	Pontotoc	Rachael Frazier	Dead	Pontotoc	
5	Sydney Burris	1897	Chick residing in Choctaw N. 1st D.	Julie McCurtin	"	"	

(NOTES)

No. 1 Died April 1st, 1901. Evidence of Death filed May *(illegible)*

RESIDENCE: Pontotoc   COUNTY   CARD NO.

POST OFFICE: Stonewall, Ind. Ter.   FIELD NO.

	NAME	RELATION-SHIP TO PERSON FIRST NAMED	AGE	SEX	BLOOD	TRIBAL ENROLLMENT		
						YEAR	COUNTY	PAGE
1	McCarty, Katsey	NAMED	50	F	Full	1897	Pontotoc	54
2	" Somie	Son	26	M	"	1897	"	54
3	" Raymond	G.Son	7mo	"	"			
4	" Rena	G.Dau	7mo	F	"			

	TRIBAL ENROLLMENT OF PARENTS						
	NAME OF FATHER	YEAR	COUNTY	NAME OF MOTHER	YEAR	COUNTY	
1	James She-was-he	Dead	Chickasaw Roll	E-ma-nok-te	Dead	Chickasaw Roll	
2	A-chak-a-tam-by	"	Pontotoc	No. 1			
3	No. 2			Rachael Frazier	Dead	Pontotoc	
4	No. 2			" "	"	"	

(NOTES)

No. 3 Died July 13, 1899. Proof of Death filed Aug. 11, 1902.

No. 4 Died Aug. 4, 1899. Proof of Death filed Aug. 11, 1902.

P.O. address is near Jesse.   Sept. 6/98.

RESIDENCE: Pontotoc   COUNTY   CARD NO.

POST OFFICE: Hart, Ind. Ter.   FIELD NO.

	NAME	RELATION-SHIP TO PERSON FIRST NAMED	AGE	SEX	BLOOD	TRIBAL ENROLLMENT		
						YEAR	COUNTY	PAGE
1	Filmore, Henny	NAMED	18	M	3/4	1897	Pontotoc	49
2	Thomas, Sallie	~~1/2 Sist.~~	~~16~~	~~F~~	~~1/2~~	~~1897~~	"	~~49~~

	TRIBAL ENROLLMENT OF PARENTS					
	NAME OF FATHER	YEAR	COUNTY	NAME OF MOTHER	YEAR	COUNTY
1	Sam Filmore	Dead	Pontotoc	Harriet Burnett	1897	Pontotoc
2	~~Isaac Thompson~~	"	~~Chickasaw Roll~~	" "	"	"

(NOTES)

No. 2 placed on Card 1552. *(Remainder illegible)* Sept. 12/1899.

P.O. Roff, I.T. 12/19/02.

Sept. 6/98.

RESIDENCE: Pontotoc COUNTY — CARD NO.
POST OFFICE: Ada, Ind. Ter. — FIELD NO.

	NAME	RELATIONSHIP TO PERSON FIRST NAMED	AGE	SEX	BLOOD	TRIBAL ENROLLMENT		
						YEAR	COUNTY	PAGE
1	Porter, Wisdom B.		21	M	Full	1897	Pontotoc	44
2	" Johnson	Bro	18	"	"	1897	"	60

	TRIBAL ENROLLMENT OF PARENTS					
	NAME OF FATHER	YEAR	COUNTY	NAME OF MOTHER	YEAR	COUNTY
1	Osheray Porter	1897	Pontotoc	Sabena	1897	Pontotoc
2	" "	1897	"	"	1897	"

(NOTES)

No. 2 in Ardmore jail awaiting trial
Jackson Porter Son of No. 1 and Annie Leader
illegitimate child enrolled on Chickasaw 232.
June 5, 1900.

No. 1 on Chickasaw Roll as W.B. Porter
No. 1 Died March 9, 1902, proof of death filed July 25, 1902.

RESIDENCE: Pontotoc COUNTY — CARD NO.
POST OFFICE: Conway, Ind. Ter. — FIELD NO.

	NAME	RELATIONSHIP TO PERSON FIRST NAMED	AGE	SEX	BLOOD	TRIBAL ENROLLMENT		
						YEAR	COUNTY	PAGE
1	Carney, Sampson		46	M	Full	1897	Pontotoc	43
2	" Fene	Wife	48	F	"	1897	"	43
3	" Thomas	Son	16	M	"	1897	"	43
4	" Harriet	Dau	13	F	"	1897	"	43

	TRIBAL ENROLLMENT OF PARENTS					
	NAME OF FATHER	YEAR	COUNTY	NAME OF MOTHER	YEAR	COUNTY
1	Billy Carney	Dead	Chickasaw Roll	Tu-wa-sha	Dead	Chickasaw Roll

2	*(Name Illegible)*	"	"	"	Ak-a-lo-he	"	"	"
3	No. 1				No. 2			
4	No. 1				No. 2			

(NOTES)

P.O. Ada, I.T. 2/2-04.   Sept. 6/98.

| RESIDENCE: | Pontotoc COUNTY | | | | | CARD NO. | | |
| POST OFFICE: | Stonewall, Ind. Ter. | | | | | FIELD NO. | | |

	NAME	RELATION-SHIP TO PERSON FIRST NAMED	AGE	SEX	BLOOD	TRIBAL ENROLLMENT		
						YEAR	COUNTY	PAGE
1	McLean, Liesing	NAMED	28	F	Full	1897	Pontotoc	45
2	~~Parnacher, Niayana~~	~~Dau~~	~~8~~	~~"~~	~~"~~	~~1897~~	~~"~~	~~45~~
3	" Devet	Son	8	M	"	1897	"	45
4	" Nonles	"	5	"	"	1897	"	45
5	Beans, Tienie	Dau	15mo	F	"			

TRIBAL ENROLLMENT OF PARENTS

	NAME OF FATHER	YEAR	COUNTY	NAME OF MOTHER	YEAR	COUNTY
1	John McLean	1897	Pontotoc	Salina McLean	Dead	Pontotoc
2	~~Calvin Parnacher~~	~~1897~~	"	~~No. 1~~		
3	" "	1897	"	No. 1		
4	" "	1897	"	No. 1		
5	Phelan Beans	1897	"	No. 1		

(NOTES)

No. 1 On Chickasaw Roll as Lizaann Parnacher
No. 2 "   "   " " Mary   "
No. 3 "   "   " " Dave   "
No. 4 "   "   " " Nolis   "
No. 2 is duplicate of Nannie Parnacher on Chickasaw card No. 298.
Her enrollment cancelled under departmental *(remainder illegible)*   *(No. 5 Dawes' Roll No. 4783)*
                                                                    Sept. 6/98.

| RESIDENCE: | Pontotoc COUNTY | | | | | CARD NO. | | |
| POST OFFICE: | Conner, Ind. Ter. | | | | | FIELD NO. | | |

	NAME	RELATION-SHIP TO PERSON FIRST NAMED	AGE	SEX	BLOOD	TRIBAL ENROLLMENT		
						YEAR	COUNTY	PAGE
1	Hillhouse, Louisa	NAMED	38	F	Full	1897	Pontotoc	55
2	" Jefferson	Son	20	M	"	1897	"	55

TRIBAL ENROLLMENT OF PARENTS						
NAME OF FATHER	YEAR	COUNTY	NAME OF MOTHER	YEAR	COUNTY
1 John Goodise	Dead	Panola	Kizia Kemp	Dead	Panola
2 Israel Hillhouse	"	"	No. 1		

(NOTES)

No. 2 On Chickasaw roll as Jeff.   *(No. 2 Dawes' Roll No. 4037)*

Sept. 6/98.

RESIDENCE: Pontotoc COUNTY								
POST OFFICE: Waupanuka, Ind. Ter.					FIELD NO.	CARD NO.		

NAME	RELATION-SHIP TO PERSON FIRST NAMED	AGE	SEX	BLOOD	TRIBAL ENROLLMENT		
					YEAR	COUNTY	PAGE
1 Skeen, Cicero A.		45	M	I.W.	1897	Pontotoc	81
2 " Matilda	Wife	42	F	1/2	1897	Pontotoc	59
3 " James Walter	Son	18	M	1/4	1897	"	59
4 " Emily Frances	Dau	16	F	1/4	1897	"	59
5 " Cora Tamsie	"	11	F	1/4	1897	"	59

TRIBAL ENROLLMENT OF PARENTS						
NAME OF FATHER	YEAR	COUNTY	NAME OF MOTHER	YEAR	COUNTY
1 James C. Skeen	Dead	Non Citizen	Emily Skeen	Dead	Non Citizen
2 Sampson Fulsom	"	Chickasaw Roll	Cahenne Fulsom	"	Chickasaw Roll
3	No. 1		No. 2		
4	No. 1		No. 2		
5	No. 1		No. 2		

(NOTES)

No. 1 On Chickasaw Roll as C.A. Skeen   *(No. 1 Dawes' Roll No. 789)*
No. 1 Admitted by Dawes Com. Case No. 165. No appeal taken.
No. 3 On Chickasaw Roll as Walter
No. 4 "   "   "   " Fannie
No. 5 "   "   "   " Cora.

Sept. 6/98.

RESIDENCE: Pontotoc COUNTY								
POST OFFICE: Conner, Ind. Ter.					FIELD NO.	CARD NO.		

NAME	RELATION-SHIP TO PERSON FIRST NAMED	AGE	SEX	BLOOD	TRIBAL ENROLLMENT		
					YEAR	COUNTY	PAGE
1 Hughes, A.B.		26	M	I.W.	1897	Pontotoc	81
2 " Mamie	Wife	19	F	Full	1897	"	55

3	"	Missouri V.	Dau	2	"	1/2	1897		"		90
4	"	Fannie C.	"	6mo	"	1/2					
5	"	Erila A.	"	2mo	"	1/2					
6	"	Ma,oe M/	"	2mo	"	1/2					

TRIBAL ENROLLMENT OF PARENTS

	NAME OF FATHER	YEAR	COUNTY	NAME OF MOTHER	YEAR	COUNTY
1	Wm Hughes	Dead	Non Citizen	Maggie Hughes	Dead	Non Citizen
2	Henderson Cravatt	"	Pontotoc	Melvina Alexander	"	Pontotoc
3	No. 1			No. 2		
4	No. 1			No. 2		
5	No. 1			No. 2		
6	No. 1			No. 2		

(NOTES)

No. 3 registered under Act of Legislature July 31/97, Chick Roll page 90.
No. 5 Enrolled Sept 12th 1900.
No. 3 On Chickasaw roll as Missouri Vivian Hughes.
" 6 Born April 8, 1902. Enrolled June 18, 1902.
No. 4 Born March 20, 1898 Evidence of Birth filed July 8, 1902
No. 3 Proof of birth received and filed Sept. 18, 1902.

(No. 1 Dawes' Roll No. 200)
(No. 2 Dawes' Roll No. 768)
(No. 3 Dawes' Roll No. 4036)
(No. 4 Dawes' Roll No. 769)
(No. 5 Dawes' Roll No. 770)
(No. 6 Dawes' Roll No. 771)

P.O. Durwood, 6/19/02.

Sept. 6/98.

RESIDENCE: Pontotoc COUNTY						CARD NO.			
POST OFFICE: Conner, Ind. Ter.						FIELD NO.			

	NAME	RELATIONSHIP TO PERSON FIRST NAMED	AGE	SEX	BLOOD	TRIBAL ENROLLMENT		
						YEAR	COUNTY	PAGE
1	Greenwood, Hogen	NAMED	57	M	1/2	1897	Pontotoc	55
2	" Mahali	Wife	35	F	Full	1897	"	55
3	" ~~Stephen~~	~~Son~~	~~17~~	~~M~~	~~3/4~~	~~1897~~	~~"~~	~~55~~
4	" Linsey	Dau	12	F	3/4	1897	"	55
5	" Jesse	Son	5	M	3/4	1897	"	55
6	" Lottie	Dau	1	F	3/4	1897	"	90
7	Welsey, Lizzie	Ward	4	F	Full	1897	Pontotoc	55
8	Greenwood, Bessie	Dau	10mo	F	3/4			

TRIBAL ENROLLMENT OF PARENTS

	NAME OF FATHER	YEAR	COUNTY	NAME OF MOTHER	YEAR	COUNTY
1	Toney Grayson	Dead	Creek adopted Chick	Martha	Dead	Chickasaw Roll
2	Calvin Alexander	"	Pontotoc	Betsey Alexander	1897	Pontotoc

3	~~No. 1~~			~~Mary~~		~~Dead~~	~~Pontotoc~~
4	No. 1			No. 2			
5	No. 1			No. 2			
6	No. 1			No. 2			
7	*(Name Illegible)*	Dead	*(Illegible)*	Liza *(Illegible)*		Dead	Chickasaw Roll
8	No. 1			No. 2			

(NOTES)

No. 5 on Chickasaw roll as Jessie
No. 3 transferred to Chickasaw Card #1577 eith his wife Gincy Conner Dec. 15, 1902.
No. 6 proof of birth received and filed Oct. 15, 1902   *(No. 6 Dawes' Roll No. 4635)*
No. 4 on 1897 Chickasaw Roll as Lizzie Wesley

Sept. 6/98.

RESIDENCE: Pontotoc COUNTY						CARD NO.		
POST OFFICE: Conner, Ind. Ter.						FIELD NO.		

NAME	RELATION-SHIP TO PERSON FIRST NAMED	AGE	SEX	BLOOD	TRIBAL ENROLLMENT		
					YEAR	COUNTY	PAGE
1 Thomas, Shonayea		90	F	Full	1897	Pontotoc	55
2 Nail, Harrison	Nephew	20	M	"	1897	"	55
3 Wisdom, Felix	(Ward)	15	"	"	1897	"	55

TRIBAL ENROLLMENT OF PARENTS

NAME OF FATHER	YEAR	COUNTY	NAME OF MOTHER	YEAR	COUNTY
1 *(Name Illegible)*	Dead	Chickasaw Roll	*(Name Illegible)*	Dead	Chickasaw Roll
2 Dave Nail	"	" "	Hattie	"	" "
3 Geo. Wisdom	1897	Pontotoc	Lizzie	"	Pontotoc

(NOTES)

No. 3 Also on Page 12, as Henderson Nail, Pickens County
No. 2 is in the Pennitentiary at Ft. Leavenworth, Kansas March 16, 1901
No. 1 Died April 17, 1901. Proof of Death filed Nov. 8, 1902.

Sept. 6/98.

RESIDENCE: Pontotoc COUNTY						CARD NO.		
POST OFFICE: Conner, Ind. Ter.						FIELD NO.		

NAME	RELATION-SHIP TO PERSON FIRST NAMED	AGE	SEX	BLOOD	TRIBAL ENROLLMENT		
					YEAR	COUNTY	PAGE
1 Alexander, Esias		30	M	Full	1897	Pontotoc	56
2 " Jane	Wife	25	F	"	1897	"	56
3 " Luelia	Dau	8	"	"	1897	"	56

49

Chickasaw Enrollment Cards 1898-1914
Chickasaw by Blood   Volume II

4	"	Elias	Son	4	M	"	1897		"	56
5	"	Iverson	"	2	"	"	1897		"	56
6	"	Sarah	Dau	5mo	F	"				

TRIBAL ENROLLMENT OF PARENTS

	NAME OF FATHER	YEAR	COUNTY	NAME OF MOTHER	YEAR	COUNTY
1	Calvin Alexander	Dead	Pontotoc	Betsey Alexander	1897	Pontotoc
2	*(Name Illegible)*	"	"	Agnes	Dead	"
3	No. 1			No. 2		
4	No. 1			No. 2		
5	No. 1			No. 2		
6	No. 1			No. 2		

(NOTES)

No. 6 Born Feb. 7ᵗʰ 1902. Enrolled July 3ʳᵈ 1902.

Sept. 6/98.

RESIDENCE: Pontotoc COUNTY						CARD NO.			
POST OFFICE: Hurd, Ind. Ter,						FIELD NO.			

	NAME	RELATION-SHIP TO PERSON FIRST NAMED	AGE	SEX	BLOOD	TRIBAL ENROLLMENT		
						YEAR	COUNTY	PAGE
1	Factor, Isteph Ifyaka		65	F	Full	1897	Pontotoc	45
2	Dyar, Annie	Gr. Niece	18	"	"	1897	"	45
3	Porter, Jackson	Son of No. 2	18mo	M	"			
4	Dyar, Katesy	Dau of No. 2	2mo	F	"			

TRIBAL ENROLLMENT OF PARENTS

	NAME OF FATHER	YEAR	COUNTY	NAME OF MOTHER	YEAR	COUNTY
1	A?hoinechettubby	Dead	Chickasaw Roll	Aajakachhojo	Dead	Chickasaw Roll
2	Allen Leader	"	Pontotoc	*(Name Illegible)*	"	Pontotoc
3	Wisdom B. Porter		Chickasaw Roll	No. 2		
4	Jos. Dyar	1897	Pontotoc	No. 2		

(NOTES)

No. 3 Enrolled June 5, 1900

No. 3 Illegitimate Son of Wisdom B. Porter and Annie Leader
    Wisdom B. Porter on Chickasaw Card 241.

No. 2 is now the wife of Jos. Dyar on Chickasaw Card #169. See affidavit of
    George Colbert filed July 31, 1902.

No. 4 Born May 18, 1902. Enrolled July 31, 1902.

Sept. 6/98.

Chickasaw Enrollment Cards 1898-1914
Chickasaw by Blood   Volume II

RESIDENCE: Choctaw Nation   COUNTY   CARD NO.

POST OFFICE: Sitre, Ind. Ter.   FIELD NO.

NAME	RELATION-SHIP TO PERSON FIRST NAMED	AGE	SEX	BLOOD	TRIBAL ENROLLMENT		
					YEAR	COUNTY	PAGE
1 Jones, Nancy		30	F	Full	1897	Pontotoc	44
2 Smith, Malisie	Dau	10	"	"	1897	"	44
3 Koey, Ida	"	6	"	"	1897	"	44

TRIBAL ENROLLMENT OF PARENTS

	NAME OF FATHER	YEAR	COUNTY	NAME OF MOTHER	YEAR	COUNTY
1	Nicholas	Dead	Chickasaw Roll	(Illegible) Brown	1897	Pontotoc
2	Wesley Smith	1897	Pontotoc	No. 1		
3	Billy Koey	1897	"	No. 1		

(NOTES)

This family now (illegible word) in Choctaw Nation 3rd District.
No. 1 On Chickasaw Roll as Nancy Jones
No. 3 "   "   "   " Ida Koey.

Sept. 6/98.

RESIDENCE: Choctaw Nation   COUNTY   CARD NO.

POST OFFICE: Oconee, Ind. Ter.   FIELD NO.

NAME	RELATION-SHIP TO PERSON FIRST NAMED	AGE	SEX	BLOOD	TRIBAL ENROLLMENT		
					YEAR	COUNTY	PAGE
1 Guynes, Margarett		37	F	3/4	1897	Chick residing in Choctaw N. 3rd Dist.	75
2 Allen, Ishmeal	Son	11	M	7/8	1897	" " " "	75
3 Guynes, Charles Monson	"	1	M	5/8			
4 " David J.	"	3mo	"	5/8			

TRIBAL ENROLLMENT OF PARENTS

	NAME OF FATHER	YEAR	COUNTY	NAME OF MOTHER	YEAR	COUNTY
1	Booker James	Dead	Chickasaw Roll	Martha James	Dead	Chickasaw Roll
2	James Allen	1897	Chick residing in Choctaw N. 3rd Dist.	No. 1		
3	William Guynes		Choctaw Roll	No. 1		
4	" "		" "	No. 1		

(NOTES)

No. 1 wife of William Guynes, Choctaw Roll Card No. ?
No. 3 on Choctaw Census Roll No. 2, Page ?
No. 4 Born Sept 25/99. Affidavit received but irregular.
    Returned for correction Dec. 14/99. Filed Dec. 19/99.

51

Evidence of birth of No. 3 received and filed March 31, 1902.

P.O. Seems now to be Coalgate, I.T. 3/27/02.

RESIDENCE: Pontotoc ***COUNTY***					***CARD NO.***			
POST OFFICE: Stonewall, Ind. Ter.					***FIELD NO.***			
	NAME	**RELATIONSHIP TO PERSON FIRST NAMED**	**AGE**	**SEX**	**BLOOD**	**TRIBAL ENROLLMENT**		
						YEAR	**COUNTY**	**PAGE**
1	Burris, Amy		38	F	Full	1897	Pontotoc	52
2	" Mack	Son	19	M	"	1897	"	52
3	Watkins, Lula	Dau	5	F	"	1897	"	52
4	McCurtin, Buster	Son	1	M	"			

TRIBAL ENROLLMENT OF PARENTS

	NAME OF FATHER	**YEAR**	**COUNTY**	**NAME OF MOTHER**	**YEAR**	**COUNTY**
1	Weel	Dead	Chickasaw Roll	*(Name Illegible)*	Dead	Chickasaw Roll
2	Bob Burris	"	Tishomingo	No. 1		
3	James Watkins	1897	Pontotoc	No. 1		
4	Zeno McCurtin	1897	"	No. 1		

(NOTES)

No. 1 On Chickasaw Roll as Annie Burris
No. 3 " " " " Babe "
No. 4 Proof of birth received and filed Oct. 28, 1902. *(No. 4 Dawes' Roll No. 4634)*
No. 3 Died about Sept. 14, 1899. Proof of death filed Nov. 12, 1902.
No. 1 is wife of No. 6 on Chickasaw Card 175. 11/10/02.
(Additional notations illegible)

Nos. 1 and 4 P.O. Franks, I.T. 11/10/02. Sept. 6/98.

RESIDENCE: Pontotoc ***COUNTY***					***CARD NO.***			
POST OFFICE: Stonewall, Ind. Ter.					***FIELD NO.***			
	NAME	**RELATIONSHIP TO PERSON FIRST NAMED**	**AGE**	**SEX**	**BLOOD**	**TRIBAL ENROLLMENT**		
						YEAR	**COUNTY**	**PAGE**
1	Keel, Hagan		46	M	Full	1897	Pontotoc	53
2	" Emely	Wife	55	F	"	1897	"	53
3	" Minnie	Dau	10	"	"	1897	"	54
4	Blunt, Galloway	Nephew	10	m	"	1897	"	54

TRIBAL ENROLLMENT OF PARENTS						
NAME OF FATHER	YEAR	COUNTY	NAME OF MOTHER	YEAR	COUNTY	
1 Co-su?-ley	Dead	Tishomingo	Sho-k??-?ey	Dead	Chickasaw Roll	
2 Sho-wau-key	"	Chickasaw Roll	*(Name Illegible)*	"	"	"
3 No. 1			*(Name Illegible)*	"	Pontotoc	
4 Simon Blunt	Dead	Pontotoc	*(Name Illegible)*	1897	"	

(NOTES)

No. 3 Died Feby 5th 1900. Proof of death filed Oct. 14th 1902.

Sept. 6/98.

RESIDENCE: Choctaw Nation	COUNTY				CARD NO.		
POST OFFICE: Oconee, Ind. Ter.					FIELD NO.		

NAME	RELATION-SHIP TO PERSON FIRST NAMED	AGE	SEX	BLOOD	TRIBAL ENROLLMENT		
					YEAR	COUNTY	PAGE
1 Allen, James	FIRST NAMED	39	M	1/2	1897	Chick residing in Choctaw N. 3rd Dist.	75
2 " Ella	Wife	30	F	Full	"	" " " "	75
3 " George	Son	6	M	3/4	"	" " " "	75
4 " Kitty	Dau	2	F	3/4	"	" " " "	75
5 " Mattie	"	2mo	"	3/4	"	" " " "	75
6 " Thomas J.	Son	1mo	M	3/4			

TRIBAL ENROLLMENT OF PARENTS						
NAME OF FATHER	YEAR	COUNTY	NAME OF MOTHER	YEAR	COUNTY	
1 Sam Allen	Dead	Non-Citizen	Nancy Allen	Dead	Chick residing in Choctaw N. 3rd Dist.	
2 Jesse Brown	"	Chickasaw Roll	Malinda Brown	1897	Pontotoc	
3 No. 1			No. 2			
4 No. 1			No. 2			
5 No. 1			No. 2			
6 No. 1			No. 2			

(NOTES)

No. 1 On Chickasaw Roll as J.?. Brown

No. 6 Enrolled Oct. 31, 1900

No. 5 Died May 29, 1899. proof of death filed March 11, 1902.

No. 6 Died January, 1901. Proof of death filed Nov. 22, 1902.

Sept. 6/98.

RESIDENCE: Pontotoc COUNTY

POST OFFICE: Stonewall, Ind. Ter.

CARD NO.

FIELD NO.

NAME	RELATION-SHIP TO PERSON FIRST NAMED	AGE	SEX	BLOOD	TRIBAL ENROLLMENT		
					YEAR	COUNTY	PAGE
1 Conohotubby, Susana		45	F	Full	1897	Pontotoc	45
2 Jones, Johnie	Son	1	M	1/2	1897	"	90

TRIBAL ENROLLMENT OF PARENTS

NAME OF FATHER	YEAR	COUNTY	NAME OF MOTHER	YEAR	COUNTY
1 Conohotubby	Dead	Chickasaw Roll	(Name Illegible)	Dead	Chickasaw Roll
2 Gipson Jones	1897	Seminole Roll	No. 1		

(NOTES)

No. 1 on Chickasaw Roll as Susana Koey

No. 2 (notation illegible)

Sept. 6/98.

RESIDENCE: Pontotoc COUNTY

POST OFFICE: Oakman, Ind. Ter.

CARD NO.

FIELD NO.

NAME	RELATION-SHIP TO PERSON FIRST NAMED	AGE	SEX	BLOOD	TRIBAL ENROLLMENT		
					YEAR	COUNTY	PAGE
1 Bean, Felin		25	M	1/2	1897	Pontotoc	45

TRIBAL ENROLLMENT OF PARENTS

NAME OF FATHER	YEAR	COUNTY	NAME OF MOTHER	YEAR	COUNTY
1 Nicholas Bean	Dead	Choctaw Roll	Doney Bean	Dead	Pontotoc

(NOTES)

Sept. 6/98.

RESIDENCE: Pontotoc COUNTY

POST OFFICE: Ada, Ind. Ter.

CARD NO.

FIELD NO.

NAME	RELATION-SHIP TO PERSON FIRST NAMED	AGE	SEX	BLOOD	TRIBAL ENROLLMENT		
					YEAR	COUNTY	PAGE
1 Killcrease, Betty		30	F	1/2	1897	Pontotoc	59
2 " Sim	Son	10	M	1/2	1897	"	59
3 " Lavay	Dau	4	F	1/2	1897	"	59
4 " Emma	"	1	"	1/2	1897	"	80
5 " Nelson	Son	9	M	1/2	1897	"	59
6 " Dixon	"	6mo	"	1/2			

	TRIBAL ENROLLMENT OF PARENTS						
	NAME OF FATHER	YEAR	COUNTY	NAME OF MOTHER	YEAR	COUNTY
1	Morris Mance	Dead	Choctaw Roll	Holchoke	Dead	Chickasaw Roll
2	Wade Killcrease		Creek Roll	No. 1		
3	" "		" "	No. 1		
4	" "		" "	No. 1		
5	" "		" "	No. 1		
6	" "		" "	No. 1		

(NOTES)

No. 1 William Wade Killcrease on Chickasaw Roll Pontotoc County
    Page 59 transferred to Creek Roll by Dawes Com
No. 4 On Chickasaw roll as Ema Killcrease
No. 5 and No. 3 is also on Chickasaw roll Page No. 75 as Nelson Killcrease and
    on pay roll Pontotoc County page 59, as Lavay Killcrease by testimony of Wade Killcrease. June 5, 1900.
    Present P.O. is *(illegible)*
    Wade Killcrease; husband of No. 1 on Chickasaw Roll
No. 3 Cancelled June 5, 1900. *(Remainder illegible)*
No. 6 Enrolled June 5, 1900.
No. 4 Born Dec. 25, 1897. Proof of birth filed Oct. ?/03.

RESIDENCE: Pontotoc *COUNTY*   *CARD NO.*
POST OFFICE: Ada, Ind. Ter.   *FIELD NO.*

	NAME	RELATION-SHIP TO PERSON FIRST NAMED	AGE	SEX	BLOOD	TRIBAL ENROLLMENT		
						YEAR	COUNTY	PAGE
1	Perry, Simon	NAMED	22	M	Full	1897	Pontotoc	45
2	" Ci?en	Wife	17	F	"	1897	"	45
3	" Lucy	Dau	1/2	"	"			
4	" Edward	Son	5mo	M	"			

	TRIBAL ENROLLMENT OF PARENTS						
	NAME OF FATHER	YEAR	COUNTY	NAME OF MOTHER	YEAR	COUNTY
1	Billy Perry	1897	Pontotoc	Eliza Perry	1897	Pontotoc
2	Nicholas Bean	Dead	Choctaw	Doney Bean	Dead	"
3	No. 1			No. 2		
4	No. 1			No. 2		

(NOTES)

No. 2 on Chickasaw roll as *(illegible)* Bean
No. 4 Enrolled June 18, 1901.

                          No. 3 Enrolled May 20/??

RESIDENCE: Pontotoc **COUNTY**					**CARD NO.**			
POST OFFICE: Ada, Ind. Ter.					**FIELD NO.**			
	NAME	**RELATIONSHIP TO PERSON FIRST NAMED**	**AGE**	**SEX**	**BLOOD**	**TRIBAL ENROLLMENT**		
						YEAR	**COUNTY**	**PAGE**
1	Perry, Thomas		20	M	1/2	1897	Pontotoc	40
2	" Rittie Peddycourt	Wife	17	F	I.W.			
3	" Zelda Marie	Dau	6mo	"	1/4			
4	" Benjamin Brandon	Son	2mo	M	1/4			

TRIBAL ENROLLMENT OF PARENTS

	NAME OF FATHER	**YEAR**	**COUNTY**	**NAME OF MOTHER**	**YEAR**	**COUNTY**
1	Frank Perry	Dead	Pontotoc	Margaret Perry	1897	Pontotoc
2	Frank Peddycourt		Non Citizen	Mary Peddycourt		Non Citizen
3	No. 1			No. 2		
4	No. 1			No. 2		

(NOTES)

No. 1 on Chickasaw roll as Tom Perry
No. 2 Not on Chickasaw Roll *(remainder illegible)*
No. 4 Born September 6, 1901. and enrolled *(illegible)*

Oct. 20, 02 P.O.
Jussy[sic], I.T.

Sept. 6/98.
No. 3 Enrolled Nov. 6/99.

RESIDENCE: Pontotoc **COUNTY**					**CARD NO.**			
POST OFFICE: Stonewall, Ind. Ter.					**FIELD NO.**			
	NAME	**RELATIONSHIP TO PERSON FIRST NAMED**	**AGE**	**SEX**	**BLOOD**	**TRIBAL ENROLLMENT**		
						YEAR	**COUNTY**	**PAGE**
1	Pettigrew, *(Illegible)*		29	M	Full	1897	Pontotoc	53
2	" *(Illegible)*	Wife	20	F	"	1897	"	53
3	" Lou	Dau	1	"	"			
4	" Tennessee	Mother	47	"	"	1897	Pontotoc	54
5	" Eliza?ene	Dau	4	F	"			

TRIBAL ENROLLMENT OF PARENTS

	NAME OF FATHER	**YEAR**	**COUNTY**	**NAME OF MOTHER**	**YEAR**	**COUNTY**
1	Solomon Pettigrew	Dead	Pontotoc	Tennessee Pettigrew	1897	Pontotoc
2	Jackson Reed	"	"	Mary Reed	Dead	"
3	No. 1			No. 2		
4	*(Name Illegible)*	Dead	Chickasaw Roll	La-ha-na	Dead	Chickasaw Roll
5	No. 1	Dead[sic]		No. 2		

Chickasaw Enrollment Cards 1898-1914
Chickasaw by Blood   Volume II

(NOTES)

No. 3 Died May 20, 1901; Evidence of death filed Jan. 8, 1902.
No. 4 " Dec. 8, 1900; " " " " Jan. 8, 1902.
No. 5 Born May 12, 1900. Enrolled November 24, 1902.

P.O. Connerville, I.T.

	NAME	RELATIONSHIP TO PERSON FIRST NAMED	AGE	SEX	BLOOD	TRIBAL ENROLLMENT		
						YEAR	COUNTY	PAGE
1	Clopton, R.M.		47	M	I.W.	1897	Pontotoc	81
2	" Susie	Wife	38	F	3/4	1897	"	64
3	" Fannie	Dau	8	"	3/8	1897	"	64
4	" Maggie	"	5	"	3/8	1897	"	64
5	" Susie	"	3	"	3/8	1897	"	64
6	" Luella	"	1	"	3/8	~~1897~~	"	~~88~~
7	Berkett, Jennie	Step Dau	17	"	3/8	1897	Pontotoc	64
8	" George	" Son	13	M	3/8	1897	"	64
9	" Eddie	" "	11	"	3/8	1897	"	64
10	Clopton, Thomas W,	Son	3mo	"	3/8			
11	" Sopha Easter	Dau	2mo	F	3/8			

RESIDENCE: Pontotoc COUNTY
POST OFFICE: Newcastle, Ind. Ter.
CARD NO.
FIELD NO.

TRIBAL ENROLLMENT OF PARENTS

	NAME OF FATHER	YEAR	COUNTY	NAME OF MOTHER	YEAR	COUNTY
1	Abner Clopton	Dead	Non Citizen	Margaret Clopton	Dead	Non Citizen
2	Ah-co-yet-ly Brown	"	Chickasaw Roll	Minerva Brown	"	Chickasaw Roll
3	No. 1			No. 2		
4	No. 1			No. 2		
5	No. 1			No. 2		
6	No. 1			No. 2		
7	Jonathan Berkett	Dead	Non Citizen	No. 2		
8	" "	"	" "	No. 2		
9	" "	"	" "	No. 2		
10	No. 1			No. 2		
11	No. 1			No. 2		

(NOTES)

No. 2 on Chickasaw roll as Susie Cloppon   (No. 1 Dawes' Roll No. 87)
No. 5 " " " " Sisie J. "
No. 6 registered under Act of Legislature (remainder illegible)   (No. 6 Dawes' Roll No. 4632)

(Illegible entry)
Marriage of R.M. Clopton and Mr. Mollie Cooper in November 1884 and *(illegible)*
Marriage license issued by the Judge
No. 5 Died in July 1901. Proof of death filed May 1, 1902.   No. 1 enrolled Sept. 8/98.
No. 11 Born March 30, 1902. Enrolled May 23, 1902.   All others Sept. 6/98

RESIDENCE:	Pontotoc	COUNTY				CARD NO.			
POST OFFICE:	Waldon, Ind. Ter.					**FIELD NO.**			

	NAME	RELATION-SHIP TO PERSON FIRST NAMED	AGE	SEX	BLOOD	TRIBAL ENROLLMENT		
						YEAR	COUNTY	PAGE
1	Rice, O.E.		33	M	I.W.	1897	Pontotoc	81
2	" Serena M	Wife	23	F	3/4	1897	"	64
3	" Kittie Jane	Dau	3	"	3/8	1897	"	64
4	" Susie Meruda	"	1	"	3/8			
5	" Lizzie Evaline	Dau	7mo	F	3/8			

	TRIBAL ENROLLMENT OF PARENTS						
	NAME OF FATHER	YEAR	COUNTY	NAME OF MOTHER	YEAR	COUNTY	
1	Marshall E. Rice	Dead	Non Citizen	Kittie Jane Rice		Non Citizen	
2	Ah-co-yet-ly Brown	"	Chickasaw Roll	Menerva Brown	Dead	Chickasaw Roll	
3	No. 1			No. 2			
4	No. 1			No. 2			
5	No. 1			No. 2			

(NOTES)
No. 1 will forward marriage certificate to Muskogee office. Received Oct. 31/98.
No. 2 on Chickasaw Roll as S.M.
No. 3 "   "   " " K.J.
No. 5 Enrolled August 1, 1901
      Evidence of birth of No. 4 received and filed March 11, 1902
      All additional testimony *(illegible)* taken Oct. 15, 1902.

Sept. 6/98.

RESIDENCE:	Choctaw Nation	COUNTY				CARD NO.			
POST OFFICE:	Owl, Ind. Ter.					**FIELD NO.**			

	NAME	RELATION-SHIP TO PERSON FIRST NAMED	AGE	SEX	BLOOD	TRIBAL ENROLLMENT		
						YEAR	COUNTY	PAGE
1	Benton, Louis		34	M	Full	1897	Chick residing in Choctaw N. 3rd Dist.	73
2	" Ellen	Wife	24	F	"	1897	Pontotoc	51

58

3	Gipson, Liza	Dau	18	"	"	1897	Chick residing in Choctaw N. 3rd Dist.	73
4	Benton, Nora	"	14	"	"	1897	" " " "	73
5	" James L	Son	7	M	"	1897	" " " "	73
6	Gipson, Martha	Neice[sic]	14	F	"	1897	Pickens	19
7	Benton, Adaline	Dau	3mo	F	"			
8	Gipson, Ethel May	Gr. Dau	2	F	"			
9	" Murtley	Gr. Dau	8mo	F	"			

TRIBAL ENROLLMENT OF PARENTS

	NAME OF FATHER	YEAR	COUNTY	NAME OF MOTHER	YEAR	COUNTY
1	Fuk-nl-by	Dead	Chickasaw Roll	Jensey	Dead	Chickasaw Roll
2	Roman Monroe	"	Pontotoc	Martha	"	Pontotoc
3	No. 1			Frances	"	
4	No. 1			"	"	"
5	No. 1			"	"	"
6	Gipson	Dead	Chickasaw Roll	Nicey	"	Chickasaw Roll
7	No. 1			No. 2		
8	Wilburn Gipson	1897	Pontotoc	No. 3		
9	" "	"	"	No. 3		

(NOTES)

No. 1 on Chickasaw Roll as Lomvey Benton
No. 2 "   "   "   " Ellen Monroe
No. 7 Enrolled November 24th 1900
No. 3 is now the wife of Wilburn Gipson on Chickasaw Card #264. See
affidavit of Wilburn Gipson filed Jany 8, 1902.
No. 8 Born Jany 24, 1900. Enrolled Jany 8, 1902.
No. 9 Born May 28 1901   " Jany 8, 1902.
No. 1 is the father of Sloan Roberts pm Choc. card No. 5474.

Sept. 5/98.

RESIDENCE: Pontotoc COUNTY		CARD NO.	
POST OFFICE: Pontotoc, Ind. Ter.		FIELD NO.	

	NAME	RELATION-SHIP TO PERSON FIRST NAMED	AGE	SEX	BLOOD	TRIBAL ENROLLMENT		
						YEAR	COUNTY	PAGE
1	Wolfe, Lucy		70	F	Full	1897	Pontotoc	55
2	Greenwood, Robert	G. Son	14	M		1897	"	55

TRIBAL ENROLLMENT OF PARENTS

	NAME OF FATHER	YEAR	COUNTY	NAME OF MOTHER	YEAR	COUNTY
1	(Name Illegible)	Dead	Chickasaw Roll	Sallie	Dead	Chickasaw Roll

2	Sim Greenwood	"	Ppmtptpc	Caroline	1897	Pontotoc

(NOTES)

No. 1 Died April 5, 1901. Proof of death filed July 18, 1901.
No. 2 is a full blood Chickasaw. Testimony of Hogan Greenwood *(illegible)* *(No. 2 Dawes' Roll No. 747)*
Sept. 5/98.

RESIDENCE: Pontotoc COUNTY						CARD NO.		
POST OFFICE: Hart, Ind. Ter.						FIELD NO.		
	NAME	RELATIONSHIP TO PERSON FIRST NAMED	AGE	SEX	BLOOD	TRIBAL ENROLLMENT		
						YEAR	COUNTY	PAGE
1	Purtle, Kitty		26	F	1/2	1897	Pontotoc	48
2	" John Allen	Son	6	M	1/4	1897	"	48

	NAME OF FATHER	YEAR	COUNTY	NAME OF MOTHER	YEAR	COUNTY
1	John Davis	Dead	Cherokee Roll	Harriet Bumett	1897	Pontotoc
2	J.A. Purtle		Non Citizen	No. 1		

(NOTES)

No. 2 on Chickasaw Roll John Purtle.

RESIDENCE: Pontotoc COUNTY						CARD NO.		
POST OFFICE: Stonewall, Ind. Ter.						FIELD NO.		
	NAME	RELATIONSHIP TO PERSON FIRST NAMED	AGE	SEX	BLOOD	TRIBAL ENROLLMENT		
						YEAR	COUNTY	PAGE
1	Becca		54	F	Full	1897	Pontotoc	45

TRIBAL ENROLLMENT OF PARENTS

	NAME OF FATHER	YEAR	COUNTY	NAME OF MOTHER	YEAR	COUNTY
1	E-mi-nun-tubby	Dead	Chickasaw Roll	Ma--so-wah-tu	Dead	Chickasaw Roll

(NOTES)

No. 1 died in October 1900.

Sept. 5/98.

RESIDENCE: Pontotoc COUNTY						CARD NO.		
POST OFFICE: Roff, Ind. Ter.						FIELD NO.		
	NAME	RELATIONSHIP TO PERSON FIRST NAMED	AGE	SEX	BLOOD	TRIBAL ENROLLMENT		
						YEAR	COUNTY	PAGE
1	Thomas, Joe L.		33	M	1/4	1897	Pontotoc	47
2	" Mattee	Wife	28	F	I.W.	1897	"	80

3	" Mamie	Dau	10	"	1/8	1897	"	48

TRIBAL ENROLLMENT OF PARENTS

	NAME OF FATHER	YEAR	COUNTY	NAME OF MOTHER	YEAR	COUNTY
1	Tom Thomas	Dead	Non Citizen	Susan Thomas	Dead	Pickens
2	Joseph Bassett		" "	Linda Bassett		Non Citizen
3	No. 1			No. 2		

(NOTES)

No. 1 on Chickasaw Roll as J.L. Thomas
No. 2 "   "   "   " Mollie   "   *(No. 2 Dawes' Roll No. 85)*
No. 3 "   "   "   " Mainy   "

Sept. 5/98.

RESIDENCE: Pontotoc COUNTY		CARD NO.	
POST OFFICE: Hart, Ind. Ter.		FIELD NO.	

NAME	RELATION-SHIP TO PERSON FIRST NAMED	AGE	SEX	BLOOD	TRIBAL ENROLLMENT		
					YEAR	COUNTY	PAGE
1 Davis, Samuel C.	NAMED	29	M	1/4	1897	Pontotoc	48
2 " Linnie R.	Wife	22	F	I.W.	1897	"	80
3 " Julia B.	Dau	9dys	"	1/8			
4 " Matilda F	Dau	2mo	"	1/8			
5 " Arvilla	Dau	1mo	F	1/8			

TRIBAL ENROLLMENT OF PARENTS

	NAME OF FATHER	YEAR	COUNTY	NAME OF MOTHER	YEAR	COUNTY
1	John L. Davis	Dead	Cherokee Citz.	Harriet I. Burnett	1897	Pontotoc
2	John Mantou	"	Non Citizen	Elizabeth Mantou		Non Citizen
3	No. 1			No. 2		
4	No. 1			No. 2		
5	No. 1			No. 2		

(NOTES)

No. 1 on Chickasaw roll as Sam Davis
No. 2 "   "   "   " L.R.   "   *(No. 2 Dawes' Roll No. 84)*
No. 3 Died July 22 1900. proof of death filed March 25, 1902.
No. 5 Born Feby 18, 1902. enrolled March 25, 1902.

Sept. 5/98.
No. 4 Enrolled Dec. 13/ *(illegible)*

Chickasaw Enrollment Cards 1898-1914
Chickasaw by Blood   Volume II

RESIDENCE: Pontotoc   COUNTY

POST OFFICE: Conner, Ind. Ter.

CARD NO.

FIELD NO.

	NAME	RELATIONSHIP TO PERSON FIRST NAMED	AGE	SEX	BLOOD	TRIBAL ENROLLMENT		
						YEAR	COUNTY	PAGE
1	Alexander, Davidson	NAMED	28	M	Full	1897	Pontotoc	53
2	" Mary	Wife	31	F	"	1897	"	53
3	" Eliza	Dau	5	"	"	1897	"	53
4	" Clayton	Bro	16	M	"	1897	"	55

TRIBAL ENROLLMENT OF PARENTS

	NAME OF FATHER	YEAR	COUNTY	NAME OF MOTHER	YEAR	COUNTY
1	Wall Alexander	Dead	Pontotoc	E-la-hok-te	Dead	Pontotoc
2	Ca-nish-ma-tubby	"	Chickasaw Roll	Ta-wal-ke	"	Chickasaw Roll
3	No. 1			No. 2		
4	Wall Alexander	Dead	Pontotoc	E-la-hok-te	Dead	Pontotoc

(NOTES)

RESIDENCE: Pontotoc   COUNTY

POST OFFICE: Allen, Ind. Ter.

CARD NO.

FIELD NO.

	NAME	RELATIONSHIP TO PERSON FIRST NAMED	AGE	SEX	BLOOD	TRIBAL ENROLLMENT		
						YEAR	COUNTY	PAGE
1	Sealy, Lela	NAMED	40	F	Full	1897	Pontotoc	39

TRIBAL ENROLLMENT OF PARENTS

	NAME OF FATHER	YEAR	COUNTY	NAME OF MOTHER	YEAR	COUNTY
1	Byd-han-na	Dead	Chickasaw Roll	Chim-ho-te	Dead	Chickasaw Roll

(NOTES)

No. 1 Died Dec. 15, 1901. Evidence of death filed July 3rd 1902.

Sept. 5/98.

RESIDENCE: Choctaw Nation (3rd Dist)   COUNTY

POST OFFICE: Owl, Ind. Ter.

CARD NO.

FIELD NO.

	NAME	RELATIONSHIP TO PERSON FIRST NAMED	AGE	SEX	BLOOD	TRIBAL ENROLLMENT		
						YEAR	COUNTY	PAGE
1	Frazier. Kiliza	NAMED	48	f	1/2			
2	" Louiza	Dau	3	"	1/4			

	NAME OF FATHER	YEAR	COUNTY	NAME OF MOTHER	YEAR	COUNTY
1	On-na-pul-ley	Dead	Choctaw Roll	Salley	Dead	Chickasaw Roll

2	Solomon Frazier		" "	No. 1		

(NOTES)

No. 1 Wife of Solomon Frazier Choctaw Roll Card No. 36
No. 1 on Choctaw Census Record No. 2, Page 191. and on Choctaw roll, 1896
    Ataka County No. 4480.
    Evidence of birth of No. 2 received and filed Feby 26, 1902.

Sept. 5/98.

RESIDENCE: Choctaw Nation   **COUNTY**   **CARD NO.**

POST OFFICE: Gurtie, Ind. Ter.   **FIELD NO.**

	NAME	RELATION-SHIP TO PERSON FIRST NAMED	AGE	SEX	BLOOD	TRIBAL ENROLLMENT		
						YEAR	COUNTY	PAGE
1	Story, James C.		26	M	1/8	1897	Chick residing in Choctaw N. 1st Dist.	68
2	" Corbett	Son	5	M	1/16	1897	" " " "	68
3	" Elleen	Dau	3	F	1/16	1897	" " " "	68
4	" Jake	Son	8mo	M	1/16			
5	" Eliza	Wife	27	F	I.W.	1897	Chick residing in Choctaw N. 1st Dist.	82

TRIBAL ENROLLMENT OF PARENTS

	NAME OF FATHER	YEAR	COUNTY	NAME OF MOTHER	YEAR	COUNTY
1	Allen Storey	Dead	Non Citizen	Sally Corbert	Dead	Chickasaw Roll
2	No. 1			Eliza Storey		Non Citizen
3	No. 1			" "		" "
4	No. 1			" "		" "
5	Jake Pegg		Non Citz.	Louisa Pegg		Non Citz.

(NOTES)

No. 1 on Chickasaw Roll as James Storey
No. 3 " " " " Maggie "
No. 5 is Mother of Nos. 2-3-4.   *(No. 5 Dawes' Roll No. 83)*
No. 5 on Chickasaw Roll as Lizzie Storey
    Evidence of birth of No. 4 received and filed May 6, 1902.
No. 5 Enrolled Aug. 9/99.

Sept. 5/98.

RESIDENCE: Pontotoc ***COUNTY*** ***CARD NO.***
POST OFFICE: Jeff, Ind. Ter. ***FIELD NO.***

	NAME	RELATION-SHIP TO PERSON FIRST NAMED	AGE	SEX	BLOOD	TRIBAL ENROLLMENT		
						YEAR	COUNTY	PAGE
1	Huckloontubby		60	M	Full	1897	Pontotoc	54
2	" Mary	Wife	45	F	"	1897	"	54
3	Tyson, Joe	Gr G.Son	13	M	"	1897	Pickens	18

TRIBAL ENROLLMENT OF PARENTS

	NAME OF FATHER	YEAR	COUNTY	NAME OF MOTHER	YEAR	COUNTY
1	I-ok-la-tubby	Dead	Chickasaw Roll	*(Name Illegible)*	Dead	Chickasaw Roll
2	Pe-sub-by	"	" "	No-ma-lo-ke	"	" "
3	Cubbash Tyson	"	Tishomingo	Missey	"	Pontotoc

(NOTES)

No. 1 is Dead. Evidence of death requested 12/20/ *(illegible)*

Sept. 5/98.

RESIDENCE: Pontotoc ***COUNTY*** ***CARD NO.***
POST OFFICE: Jeff, Ind. Ter. ***FIELD NO.***

	NAME	RELATION-SHIP TO PERSON FIRST NAMED	AGE	SEX	BLOOD	TRIBAL ENROLLMENT		
						YEAR	COUNTY	PAGE
~~1~~	~~Williams, Simon~~		~~35~~	~~M~~	~~Full~~	~~1897~~	~~Pontotoc~~	~~54~~
~~2~~	~~" Angeline~~	~~Wife~~	~~30~~	~~F~~	~~"~~	~~1897~~	~~"~~	~~57~~
3	Williams, Sophia	Dau	11	"	"	1897	"	54
4	" Sylvia	"	8	"	"	1897	"	57
5	" Silas	Son	7	M	"	1897	"	57
6	" Boyle	"	3	"	"	1897	"	57

TRIBAL ENROLLMENT OF PARENTS

	NAME OF FATHER	YEAR	COUNTY	NAME OF MOTHER	YEAR	COUNTY
~~1~~	~~William Williams~~	~~Dead~~	~~Chickasaw Roll~~	~~Kittie~~	~~Dead~~	~~Chickasaw Roll~~
~~2~~	~~To-she-ah~~	~~"~~	~~" "~~	~~Mary~~	~~1897~~	~~Pontotoc~~
3	No. 1			No. 2		
4	No. 1			No. 2		
5	No. 1			No. 2		
6	No. 1			No. 2		

(NOTES)

No. 1 Died November 27, 1899, Evidence of death filed May 6, 1901.
No. 2 " May 30, 1899. " " " " May 6, 1901.

Sept. 5/98.

Chickasaw Enrollment Cards 1898-1914
Chickasaw by Blood   Volume II

RESIDENCE: Pontotoc *COUNTY*					*CARD NO.*			
POST OFFICE: Pontotoc, Ind. Ter.					*FIELD NO.*			

	NAME	RELATION-SHIP TO PERSON FIRST NAMED	AGE	SEX	BLOOD	TRIBAL ENROLLMENT		
						YEAR	COUNTY	PAGE
1	Anderson, William B.	NAMED	46	M	1/2			
2	" Rosa	Dau	14	F	3/4			
3	" Bessie	Gr.Dau	8	"	7/8			

TRIBAL ENROLLMENT OF PARENTS

	NAME OF FATHER	YEAR	COUNTY	NAME OF MOTHER	YEAR	COUNTY
1	Reuben Anderson	Dead	Choctaw Roll	Hettie Anderson	Dead	Chick residing in Choctaw N 3rd Dist.
2	No. 1			Lizzie Anderson	"	Chickasaw Roll
3	Tom Anderson		Chickasaw now on Choctaw Roll	Mary McCann		Chickasaw now on Choctaw roll

(NOTES)

No. 1 on Choctaw Census Record No. 2, Page 21.
No. 2 "   "   "   "   " 2.   " 21
No. 3 "   "   "   "   " 2,   " 21
No. 1 husband of Elsie Anderson Choctaw Roll Card No. 35.

No. 1 on Choctaw Roll 1896 Jack Fork County No. 511.
No. 2 "   "   " 1896 "   "   "   No. 513
No. 3 "   "   " 1896 "   "   "   No. 514
      All transferred to Chickasaw Roll by Dawes Com.

Sept. 5/98.

RESIDENCE: Pontotoc *COUNTY*					*CARD NO.*			
POST OFFICE: Pontotoc, Ind. Ter.					*FIELD NO.*			

	NAME	RELATION-SHIP TO PERSON FIRST NAMED	AGE	SEX	BLOOD	TRIBAL ENROLLMENT		
						YEAR	COUNTY	PAGE
1	Anderson, Sampson	NAMED	42	M				

TRIBAL ENROLLMENT OF PARENTS

	NAME OF FATHER	YEAR	COUNTY	NAME OF MOTHER	YEAR	COUNTY
1	Reuben Anderson	Dead	Choctaw Roll	Hettie Anderson	Dead	Chick residing in Choctaw N 3rd Dist.

(NOTES)

No. 1 on Choctaw Census Record No. 2 page 21 on Choctaw roll 1896, Jack Fork Co. No. 527
Husband of Lizzie Anderson, Choctaw Roll Card No. 34.

Sept. 5/98.

RESIDENCE: Pontotoc COUNTY   CARD No.

POST OFFICE: Walker, Ind. Ter.   FIELD No.

	NAME	RELATION-SHIP TO PERSON FIRST NAMED	AGE	SEX	BLOOD	TRIBAL ENROLLMENT		
						YEAR	COUNTY	PAGE
~~1~~	~~James, Suel~~	NAMED	~~39~~	~~M~~	~~Full~~	~~1897~~	~~Pontotoc~~	~~41~~
2	" Mary	Wife	23	F	"	1897	"	41
3	" Walter	Son	7mo	M	"			
4	" Arthur	"	15	"	"	1897	Pontotoc	41
5	" Johnson	"	13	"	"	1897	"	41

TRIBAL ENROLLMENT OF PARENTS

	NAME OF FATHER	YEAR	COUNTY		NAME OF MOTHER	YEAR	COUNTY
~~1~~	~~James~~	~~Dead~~	~~Chickasaw Roll~~		~~Sahl-ho-ye~~	~~Dead~~	~~Chickasaw Roll~~
2	Chi-ki-ke-Brown	"	"	"	Annie Brown	1897	Pontotoc
3	No. 1				No. 2		
4	No. 1				Josephine	Dead	Pontotoc
5	No. 1				"	"	"

(NOTES)

No. 1 Died March 22nd 1901. Proof of death filed June 14, 1901.
Evidence of birth of No. 3 received and filed Feby 20, 1902.

Sept. 5/98.

RESIDENCE: Pontotoc COUNTY   CARD No.

POST OFFICE: Stonewall, Ind. Ter.   FIELD No.

	NAME	RELATION-SHIP TO PERSON FIRST NAMED	AGE	SEX	BLOOD	TRIBAL ENROLLMENT		
						YEAR	COUNTY	PAGE
1	Brown, Halison	NAMED	35	M	Full	1897	Pontotoc	53
2	" Ellen	Wife	23	F	Full	1897	"	53

TRIBAL ENROLLMENT OF PARENTS

	NAME OF FATHER	YEAR	COUNTY	NAME OF MOTHER	YEAR	COUNTY
1	Harris Brown	1897	Pontotoc	Eickie	Dead	Chickasaw Roll
2	Wright Alexander	Dead	"	Jane	"	Pontotoc

(NOTES)

No. 2 Also on 1897 roll page 93. Pontotoc Co.   *(No. 2 Dawes' Roll No. 4031)*
No. 2 is Full blood. See affidavit of Annie Perry. filed Oct. 2, 1902.

Sept. 5/98.

Chickasaw Enrollment Cards 1898-1914
Chickasaw by Blood   Volume II

RESIDENCE: Pontotoc COUNTY						CARD NO.		
POST OFFICE: Franks, Ind. Ter.						FIELD NO.		

	NAME	RELATION-SHIP TO PERSON FIRST NAMED	AGE	SEX	BLOOD	TRIBAL ENROLLMENT		
						YEAR	COUNTY	PAGE
1	Jackson, William H	NAMED	46	M	I.W.	1897	Pontotoc	81
2	" Annie D.	Wife	36	F	1/2	1897	"	52
3	" ~~Viola~~	~~Dau~~	~~21~~	~~"~~	~~1/4~~	~~1897~~	~~"~~	~~52~~
4	" ~~Colbert H~~	~~Son~~	~~20~~	~~M~~	~~1/4~~	~~1897~~	~~"~~	~~52~~
5	" Lizzie	Dau	18	F	1/4	1897	"	52
6	" Crudip	Son	17	M	1/4	1897	"	52
7	" Zenobin	Dau	14	F	1/4	1897	"	52
8	" Thomas P.	Son	11	M	1/4	1897	"	52
9	" Wm Byrd	"	10	"	1/4	1897	"	52
10	" Juanita	Dau	8	F	1/4	1897	"	52
11	" Wynona	"	7	"	1/4	1897	"	52
12	" Othelo	Son	3	M	1/4	1897	"	52
13	" Jerold W.	Gr.Son	2mo	M	1/8			

TRIBAL ENROLLMENT OF PARENTS

	NAME OF FATHER	YEAR	COUNTY	NAME OF MOTHER	YEAR	COUNTY
1	James M. Jackson		Non Citizen	Elizabeth Jackson		Non Citizen
2	Thos Donovan	Dead	" "	Salina Matubby	Dead	Pontotoc
3	No. 1			No. 2		
4	No. 1			No. 2		
5	No. 1			No. 2		
6	No. 1			No. 2		
7	No. 1			No. 2		
8	No. 1			No. 2		
9	No. 1			No. 2		
10	No. 1			No. 2		
11	No. 1			No. 2		
12	No. 1			No. 2		
13	No. 6			Essie M. Jackson		Non Citizen

(NOTES)

No. 1 married Sept. 5/74.   *(No. 1 Dawes' Roll No. 199)*
No. 10 on Chickasaw roll as Waneta
No. 11 "   "   " " Nona W.
No. 12 "   "   " " Ptjeta D/
No. 6 is now the husband of Essie M. Jackson, non citizen. Evidence of marriage filed May 13, 1902.
No. 13 Born March 14, 1902, enrolled May 13, 1902.
No. 4 Died Nov. 18, 1899. Proof of death filed Nov. 6, 1902.

No. 1 on Chickasaw Roll as W.H. Jackson
No. 4 "   "   " " Colbert Jackson
No. 9 "   "   " " William B. Jackson
No. 3 Transferred to Chickasaw Card #886 with husband Hindman H. Burris, Dec. 21, 1900.

P.O. Viola, IT 10/31/02.   Sept. 5/98.

	NAME	RELATION-SHIP TO PERSON FIRST NAMED	AGE	SEX	BLOOD	TRIBAL ENROLLMENT		
RESIDENCE: Pontotoc COUNTY						CARD NO.		
POST OFFICE: Stonewall, Ind. Ter.						FIELD NO.		
						YEAR	COUNTY	PAGE
1	Rowe, Leticia	NAMED	21	F	3/8	1897	Pontotoc	49
2	" Rena	Dau	3mo	"	3/16			

TRIBAL ENROLLMENT OF PARENTS

	NAME OF FATHER		YEAR	COUNTY	NAME OF MOTHER	YEAR	COUNTY
1	Wood Smith	(I.W.)	1897	Pontotoc	Rena Smith	1897	Pontotoc
2	Clyde Rowe			White man	No. 1		

(NOTES)

on Chickasaw Roll as Leticia Smith
Transferred to Choctaw Card #11935. This *(remainder illegible)*
29th Nov 1899 by order of the Commission.

Sept. 5/98.
No. 2 Enrolled Nov. 3/99.

	NAME	RELATION-SHIP TO PERSON FIRST NAMED	AGE	SEX	BLOOD	TRIBAL ENROLLMENT		
RESIDENCE: Choctaw Nation (3rd Dist.) COUNTY						CARD NO.		
POST OFFICE: Lehigh, Ind. Ter.						FIELD NO.		
						YEAR	COUNTY	PAGE
1	Roberts, Becca	NAMED	50	F	Full	1897	Chick residing in Choctaw N. 3rd Dist.	74
2	Burris, Noah	Son	9	M	"	1897	" " " "	74
3	" Edmund	G. "	18	"	"			
4	Roberts. Josephine	G.Dau	4	F	1/2			

TRIBAL ENROLLMENT OF PARENTS

	NAME OF FATHER	YEAR	COUNTY	NAME OF MOTHER	YEAR	COUNTY
1	*(Name Illegible)*	Dead	Chickasaw Roll	O-na-ho-ye	Dead	Chickasaw Roll
2	Harmon Burris	"	" "	No. 1		

3	John Burris	"	"	"	Rhoda Burris	Dead	Chick residing in Choctaw N. 3rd Dist.
4	Sampson Roberts		Choctaw Roll		Sallie Roberts	"	"	" " "

(NOTES)

No. 1 on Chickasaw Roll as Becca Frazier
No. 3 on Choctaw Census Record No. 2 Page 71. Also Choctaw Roll 1896, Ataka Co. No. 1736.
No. 4 "   "   "   " No. 2 " 415. " "   " 1896 " " No. 10984.
(Remainder illegible)

Sept. 5/98.

RESIDENCE: Pontotoc   COUNTY   CARD NO.
POST OFFICE: Stonewall, Ind. Ter.   FIELD NO.

	NAME	RELATION-SHIP TO PERSON FIRST NAMED	AGE	SEX	BLOOD	TRIBAL ENROLLMENT		
						YEAR	COUNTY	PAGE
1	Porter, Oshway	NAMED	44	M	Full	1897	Pontotoc	59
2	" Betsey	Wife	46	F	"	1897	"	59
3	" Chetona	Dau	9	"	"	1897	"	59

TRIBAL ENROLLMENT OF PARENTS

	NAME OF FATHER	YEAR	COUNTY	NAME OF MOTHER	YEAR	COUNTY
1	*(Illegible)* Porter	Dead	Pontotoc	*(Name Illegible)*	Dead	Chickasaw Roll
2	*(Name Illegible)*		Chickasaw Roll	*(Name Illegible)*		" "
3	No. 1			No. 2		

(NOTES)

(All notations illegible)

RESIDENCE: Pontotoc   COUNTY   CARD NO.
POST OFFICE: Pontotoc, Ind. Ter.   FIELD NO.

	NAME	RELATION-SHIP TO PERSON FIRST NAMED	AGE	SEX	BLOOD	TRIBAL ENROLLMENT		
						YEAR	COUNTY	PAGE
1	Sealy, Watson	NAMED	42	M	Full	1897	Pontotoc	55
2	" Jane	Wife	34	F	"	1897	"	55
3	" Grayson	Son	9	M	"	1897	"	55
4	" Daniel	"	3	"	"	1897	"	55

TRIBAL ENROLLMENT OF PARENTS

	NAME OF FATHER	YEAR	COUNTY	NAME OF MOTHER	YEAR	COUNTY
1	Par-son-we-a	Dead	Chickasaw Roll	Eliza	Dead	Chickasaw Roll
2	Wall Lewis	1897	Tishomingo	Lucy Wolfe	1897	Pontotoc
3	No. 1			No. 2		

4	No. 1			No. 2		

(NOTES)

No. 2 Died Feb, 1901. Proof of death filed Nov. 10, 1902.
No. 4 Died May 1901. Proof of death filed Nov. 10, 1902.

Sept. 5/98.

RESIDENCE: Choctaw Nation **COUNTY**   **CARD NO.**

POST OFFICE: Coalgate, Ind. Ter.   **FIELD NO.**

	NAME	RELATION-SHIP TO PERSON FIRST NAMED	AGE	SEX	BLOOD	TRIBAL ENROLLMENT		
						YEAR	COUNTY	PAGE
1	Burris, Cyrilla	NAMED	22	F	1/2			
2	" Wellington	Son	11mo	M	1/4			

TRIBAL ENROLLMENT OF PARENTS

	NAME OF FATHER	YEAR	COUNTY	NAME OF MOTHER	YEAR	COUNTY
1	Michael Smallwood	Dead	Chickasaw Roll	Lucy Smallwood	Dead	Non Citizen
2	M.W. Burris	1896	Ataka County Choctaw Roll	No. 1		

(NOTES)

Both on Choctaw Census record No. 2, page 75.
No. 1 wife of M.W. Burris, Choctaw Card #4395
No. 1 on 1896 Ataka County as Crilla Smallwood
transferred to Chickaaw Roll by Dawes Com
No. 1 Died April 6, 1901. Proof of death filed Oct. 10, 1902.
No. 2 Died June 16, 1899. Proof of death filed Oct. 10, 1902.

Sept. 5/98.

RESIDENCE: Pontotoc **COUNTY**   **CARD NO.**

POST OFFICE: Conway, Ind. Ter.   **FIELD NO.**

	NAME	RELATION-SHIP TO PERSON FIRST NAMED	AGE	SEX	BLOOD	TRIBAL ENROLLMENT		
						YEAR	COUNTY	PAGE
1	Wade, George	NAMED	45	M	Full	1897	Pontotoc	46
2	" Eliza	Dau	3	F	"	1897	"	46

TRIBAL ENROLLMENT OF PARENTS

	NAME OF FATHER	YEAR	COUNTY	NAME OF MOTHER	YEAR	COUNTY
1	John Wade	Dead	Pontotoc	Rhoda Perry	1897	Pontotoc
2	No. 1			Lizzie Wade	Dead	"

(NOTES)

Sept. 5/98.

Chickasaw Enrollment Cards 1898-1914
Chickasaw by Blood   Volume II

RESIDENCE: Pontotoc COUNTY					CARD NO.			
POST OFFICE: Viola, Ind. Ter.					FIELD NO.			

NAME	RELATION-SHIP TO PERSON FIRST NAMED	AGE	SEX	BLOOD	TRIBAL ENROLLMENT			
					YEAR	COUNTY		PAGE
1 Dyer, Bennie	NAMED	20	M	Full	1897	Pontotoc		55

TRIBAL ENROLLMENT OF PARENTS							
NAME OF FATHER	YEAR	COUNTY	NAME OF MOTHER		YEAR	COUNTY	
1 Safron Dyer	Dead	Pontotoc	Lizzie Dyer		Dead	Pontotoc	

(NOTES)

No. 1 on Chickasaw roll as Benney Dyer.
No. 1 Died May 1, 1902. Proof of death filed May 2nd 1902.

Sept. 5/98.

RESIDENCE: Pontotoc COUNTY					CARD NO.			
POST OFFICE: Stonewall, Ind. Ter.					FIELD NO.			

NAME	RELATION-SHIP TO PERSON FIRST NAMED	AGE	SEX	BLOOD	TRIBAL ENROLLMENT			
					YEAR	COUNTY		PAGE
1 Brown, Allen	NAMED	32	M	Full	1897	Pontotoc		53
2 " Betsey	Wife	38	F	3/4	1897	"		57

TRIBAL ENROLLMENT OF PARENTS							
NAME OF FATHER	YEAR	COUNTY	NAME OF MOTHER		YEAR	COUNTY	
1 Harris Brown	1897	Pontotoc	Eiskie		Dead	Pontotoc	
2 Humphrey Colbert	1897	"	Elminey		"	"	

(NOTES)

No. 2 on Chickasaw Roll as Betsey Colbert

Sept. 5/98.

RESIDENCE: Pontotoc COUNTY					CARD NO.			
POST OFFICE: Stonewall, Ind. Ter.					FIELD NO.			

NAME	RELATION-SHIP TO PERSON FIRST NAMED	AGE	SEX	BLOOD	TRIBAL ENROLLMENT			
					YEAR	COUNTY		PAGE
1 Immohotichey, Jesse	NAMED	22	M	Full	1897	Pontotoc		53

TRIBAL ENROLLMENT OF PARENTS							
NAME OF FATHER	YEAR	COUNTY	NAME OF MOTHER		YEAR	COUNTY	
1 Jackson	Dead	Pontotoc	Jane		Dead	Pontotoc	

(NOTES)

on Chickasaw Roll as Jessie Immotichey

Also "   "   "   "   Jessie Jackson, Page 94
No. 1 is the husband of Lena Undersood on Chick Card No. 877. See test. Gibson T. Grayson *(illegible)*

Sept. 5/98.

	NAME	RELATION-SHIP TO PERSON FIRST NAMED	AGE	SEX	BLOOD	TRIBAL ENROLLMENT		
						YEAR	COUNTY	PAGE
1	Roberts, Wilson	FIRST NAMED	27	M	Full	1897	Chick residing in Choctaw N. 3rd Dist.	75
2	" Elsie	Wife	25	F	"	1897	" " " "	75
3	" Josephine	Dau	2mo	"	"			

RESIDENCE: Choctaw Nation   *COUNTY*   *CARD NO.*
POST OFFICE: Nixon, Ind. Ter.   *FIELD NO.*

TRIBAL ENROLLMENT OF PARENTS

	NAME OF FATHER	YEAR	COUNTY	NAME OF MOTHER	YEAR	COUNTY
1	Lawson Roberts	Dead	Chickasaw Roll	Eliza Roberts	1897	Chick residing in Choctaw N. 3rd Dist.
2	Noah Walton	"	" "	Siley	Dead	Chickasaw Roll
3	No. 1			No. 2		

(NOTES)

No. 2 on Chickasaw Roll as Elsie Brown
Evidence of birth of No. 3 received and filed May 27, 1902.
No. 2 is mother of Margaret Brown on Chickasaw card #28. See letter G.O.F. #8537. 1902.

Sept. 5/98.

RESIDENCE: Pontotoc   *COUNTY*   *CARD NO.*
POST OFFICE: Allen   *FIELD NO.*

	NAME	RELATION-SHIP TO PERSON FIRST NAMED	AGE	SEX	BLOOD	TRIBAL ENROLLMENT		
						YEAR	COUNTY	PAGE
1	Shield, Simon	NAMED	24	M	1/2	1897	Pontotoc	46

TRIBAL ENROLLMENT OF PARENTS

	NAME OF FATHER	YEAR	COUNTY	NAME OF MOTHER	YEAR	COUNTY
1	Willis Shield	Dead	Choctaw Roll	Epsie Alexander	1897	Pontotoc

(NOTES)

No. 1 pm 1897 Chickasaw Roll as Simon Shields.

Sept. 5/98.

Chickasaw Enrollment Cards 1898-1914
Chickasaw by Blood   Volume II

RESIDENCE: Pontotoc COUNTY   CARD NO.

POST OFFICE: Allen, Ind. Ter.   FIELD NO.

	NAME	RELATION-SHIP TO PERSON FIRST NAMED	AGE	SEX	BLOOD	TRIBAL ENROLLMENT		
						YEAR	COUNTY	PAGE
1	Alexander, Epsie		42	F	Full	1897	Pontotoc	44
2	" Sena	Dau	15	"	1/2	1897	"	44
3	" Russell	Son	12	M	1/2	1897	"	44
4	" Willie	"	9	"	1/2	1897	"	44
5	" Wat	"	8	"	1/2	1897	"	43
6	" Casey	Dau	7	F	1/2	1897	"	43
7	" Carrie	"	5	"	1/2	1897	"	43
8	" Jeff	Son	3	M	1/2	1897	"	43
9	" Julia	Dau	1	F	1/2			
10	Stick, Morris	Gr.Dau[sic]	3	M	3/4			

TRIBAL ENROLLMENT OF PARENTS

	NAME OF FATHER	YEAR	COUNTY	NAME OF MOTHER	YEAR	COUNTY
1	Simon Wolfe	1897	Pontotoc	Me-ho-key	Dead	Pontotoc
2	John Alexander		Chick Freedman	No. 1		
3	" "		" "	No. 1		
4	" "		" "	No. 1		
5	" "		" "	No. 1		
6	" "		" "	No. 1		
7	" "		" "	No. 1		
8	" "		" "	No. 1		
9	" "		" "	No. 1		
10	Albert Stick	1897	Pontotoc	(Name Illegible)		

(NOTES)

No. 4 Also on Chickasaw roll page 93   (No. 9 Dawes' Roll No. 4956)

John Alexander husband of No. 1 and father of children hereon is a Chickasaw freedman on Chickasaw freedman Card #133.

No. 4 born April, 1897. Proof of birth filed May 10, 1905.

No. 10 born Oct. 13, 1899. Application recd May 1, 1905[sic], under Act of Congress approved March 3, 1905. Father of No. 10 is Albert Stick, No. 2 on Chickasaw Card #122.

Sept. 5/98.

Chickasaw Enrollment Cards 1898-1914
Chickasaw by Blood   Volume II

RESIDENCE: Pontotoc COUNTY   CARD NO.

POST OFFICE: Jeff, Ind. Ter.   FIELD NO.

NAME	RELATION-SHIP TO PERSON FIRST NAMED	AGE	SEX	BLOOD	TRIBAL ENROLLMENT		
					YEAR	COUNTY	PAGE
1 Hucklochubby, Robertson	NAMED	28	M	Full	1897	Pontotoc	54

TRIBAL ENROLLMENT OF PARENTS						
NAME OF FATHER	YEAR	COUNTY	NAME OF MOTHER	YEAR	COUNTY	
1 Wm Hucklochubby	Dead	Pontotoc	Cha-mi-key	Dead	Pontotoc	

(NOTES)

P.O. Jesse, I.T.   Sept, 5/98.

RESIDENCE: Pontotoc COUNTY   CARD NO.

POST OFFICE: Ada, Ind. Ter.   FIELD NO.

NAME	RELATION-SHIP TO PERSON FIRST NAMED	AGE	SEX	BLOOD	TRIBAL ENROLLMENT		
					YEAR	COUNTY	PAGE
1 Walton, Josiah S.	NAMED	41	M	Full	1897	Pontotoc	43
2 " Emely	Wife	44	F	"	1897	"	43
3 " Maggie	Dau	4	F	"	1897	"	43
4 Folsom, Minerva	StepDau	16	F	"	1897	"	43
5 Byrd, Louisa	Step Gr.Dau	2	F	"	1897	"	43
6 Brown, Alley	StepDau	13	F	Full	1897	"	43
7 Johnson, Jincy	Mother	50	F	"	1897	"	42
8 Walton, Carney	Son	4mo	M	"			
9 Byrd, Timmie	Step Gr.Son	4mo	M	1/2			
10 Folsom, Jefferson	Son of No. 4	2mo	m	3/4			

TRIBAL ENROLLMENT OF PARENTS						
NAME OF FATHER	YEAR	COUNTY	NAME OF MOTHER	YEAR	COUNTY	
1 Joe Walton	1897	Pontotoc	Jinsey	1897	Pontotoc	
2 Edmon McGee	Dead	Chickasaw	Elsey	Dead	Chickasaw Roll	
3 No. 1			No. 2			
4 Benj. Harris	Dead	Chickasaw Roll	No. 2			
5 John Byrd	1897	Seminole	No. 4			
6 Robinson Brown	1897	Pontotoc	No. 2			
7 Conway Killcrease	Dead	Chickasaw Roll	Tohkey	1897	Pontotoc	
8 No. 1			No. 2			

74

9	John Byrd	1897	Seminole Roll	No. 4			
10	Mulbert Folsom	1897	Pontotoc	No. 4			

(NOTES)

No. 1 on Chickasaw Roll as J.S. Walron

No. 4   "   "   "   " "M"   *(No. 4 Dawes' Roll No. 4628)*

No. 5   "   "   "   " "L"

No. ? Enrolled Feby 26th 1900.

No. 4 was formerly wife of John Byrd: Seminole 1897 Roll. They were divorced in May 1901. No. 4 then married Mulbert Folsom on Chickasaw Card #156. Evidence of divorce and marriage filed Nov. 4, 1902.

No. 10 Born Aug. 15, 1902. enrolled Nov. 4, 1902.   *(No. 10 Dawes' Roll No. 4630)*

No. 9 is a male. Change made under Departmental instructions of July 30, 1904. *(No. 9 Dawes' Roll No. 4629)*

No. 8 enrolled Jany 17/00.

Sept. 5/98.

RESIDENCE: Pontotoc **COUNTY**   **CARD NO.**

POST OFFICE: Conway, Ind. Ter.   **FIELD NO.**

	NAME	RELATION-SHIP TO PERSON FIRST NAMED	AGE	SEX	BLOOD	TRIBAL ENROLLMENT		
						YEAR	COUNTY	PAGE
1	Johnson, Isaac	NAMED	28	M	Full	1897	Pontotoc	45

TRIBAL ENROLLMENT OF PARENTS

	NAME OF FATHER	YEAR	COUNTY	NAME OF MOTHER	YEAR	COUNTY
1	Ma-ah-mon-tubby	Dead	Pontotoc	Fo-ti-ke	Dead	Pontotoc

(NOTES)

RESIDENCE: Pontotoc **COUNTY**   **CARD NO.**

POST OFFICE: Allen, Ind. Ter.   **FIELD NO.**

	NAME	RELATION-SHIP TO PERSON FIRST NAMED	AGE	SEX	BLOOD	TRIBAL ENROLLMENT		
						YEAR	COUNTY	PAGE
1	Johnson, Jimmie	NAMED	42	M	Full	1897	Pontotoc	45
2	" Nancy	Wife	40	F	"	1897	"	45
3	" Thompson	Son	23	M	"	1897	"	45
4	" Lucy	Dau	21	F	"	1897	"	45
5	" Frances	"	15	"	"	1897	"	45
6	" Solomon	Son	10	M	"	1897	"	45
7	" George	"	7	"	"	1897	"	45
8	Edwards, Birum	G.Son	2	"	"	1897	"	45
9	Shield, Watson	G. "	1mo	"	"			
10	" Mary Jane	Gr.Dau	?mo	F	"			

11	Colbert, Jessie		Son of No. 5	6mo	M	"				

TRIBAL ENROLLMENT OF PARENTS

	NAME OF FATHER	YEAR	COUNTY	NAME OF MOTHER	YEAR	COUNTY
1	Sah-ka-tub-by	Dead	Chickasaw Roll	Mulcey	Dead	Chickasaw Roll
2	Daniel Harris	1897	Pontotoc	*(Name Illegible)*	"	
3	No. 1			No. 2		
4	No. 1			No. 2		
5	No. 1			No. 2		
6	No. 1			No. 2		
7	No. 1			No. 2		
8	John Edwards	Dead	Pontotoc	No. 4		
9	Simeon Shield	1897	"	No. 4		
10	" "	"	"	No. 4		
11	Edmon Colbert on Choctaw	Card	#287. Illegitimate	No. 5		

(NOTES)

No. 1 Evidence of death filed June 30, 1902. Died March 4th 1900
No. 10 Enrolled June 5, 1900
No. 10 Illegitemate[sic] child
Evidence of birth of No. 9 received and filed March 5, 1902.
No. 11 Illegitemate[sic] child born Dec[r] 23, 1901. Enrolled June 30, 1902.

Sept. 5/98.

RESIDENCE: Pontotoc COUNTY				CARD NO.			
POST OFFICE: Connor, Ind. Ter.				FIELD NO.			

	NAME	RELATION-SHIP TO PERSON FIRST NAMED	AGE	SEX	BLOOD	TRIBAL ENROLLMENT		
						YEAR	COUNTY	PAGE
1	Wisdom, George		56	M	Full	1897	Pontotoc	55
2	" Caroline	Wife	36	F	"	1897	"	55
3	" Linhey	Dau	9	"	"	1897	"	55
4	" Lem	Son	7	M	"	1897	"	55
5	" Frances	Dau	5	F	"	1897	"	55
6	" Cleveland	Son	2	M	"	1897	"	55
7	" George	Son	4mo	M	"			

TRIBAL ENROLLMENT OF PARENTS

	NAME OF FATHER	YEAR	COUNTY	NAME OF MOTHER	YEAR	COUNTY
1	Na-ho-kla-nub-by	Dead	Chickasaw Roll	E-ma-sa-ho-wa	Dead	Chickasaw Roll
2	Wall Lewis	1897	Tishomingo	Lucy Wolfe	1897	Pontotoc
3	No. 1			No. 2		

4	No. 1			No. 2		
5	No. 1			No. 2		
6	No. 1			No. 2		
7	No. 1			No. 2		

(NOTES)

No. 7 Enrolled May 25, 1900.

Sept. 5/98.

RESIDENCE: Choctaw Nation *COUNTY* CARD NO.

POST OFFICE: Newburg, Ind. Ter. FIELD NO.

NAME	RELATION-SHIP TO PERSON FIRST NAMED	AGE	SEX	BLOOD	TRIBAL ENROLLMENT		
					YEAR	COUNTY	PAGE
1 Love, Slone		43	M	1/4	1897	Chick residing in Choctaw N. 1st Dist.	68
2 Dawkins, Minnie	Dau	16	F	1/8	1897	" " " "	68
3 Love, Edmon P	Son	14	M	1/8	1897	" " " "	68
4 " Grace	Dau	11	F	1/8	1897	" " " "	68
5 " Claude	Son	8	"[sic]	1/8	1897	" " " "	68
6 " Eunice	"[sic]	6	"	1/8	1897	" " " "	68
7 " Addie	"	3	"	1/8	1897	" " " "	68
8 Dawkins, Wallace	Grand Son	3mo	M	1/16			
9 " Lonnie E.	Gr.Son	7mo	M	1/16			

TRIBAL ENROLLMENT OF PARENTS

	NAME OF FATHER	YEAR	COUNTY	NAME OF MOTHER	YEAR	COUNTY
1	Calvin Love	Dead	Pickens	Sallie Love	Dead	Pickens
2	No. 1			Loley Love		Non Citizen
3	No. 1			" "		" "
4	No. 1			" "		" "
5	No. 1			" "		" "
6	No. 1			" "		" "
7	No. 1			" "		" "
8	L.G. Dawkins		Non Citizen	No. 2		
9	Graham L. Dawkins		" "	No. 2		

(NOTES)

No. 2 is now the wife of L.G. Dawkins
No. 7 on Chickasaw Roll as "Eddie"
Evidence of marriage of Slone Love and Loley Love furnished Jany 30th 1900
    Loley Love is now Dead

No. 8 Enrolled June 15, 1900
No. 9 Born Oct. 17, 1901. enrolled June 5, 1902.

Sept. 5/98.

RESIDENCE: Pontotoc COUNTY					CARD NO.			
POST OFFICE: Stonewall, Ind. Ter.					FIELD NO.			
NAME	RELATION-SHIP TO PERSON FIRST NAMED	AGE	SEX	BLOOD	TRIBAL ENROLLMENT			
					YEAR	COUNTY	PAGE	
1 James, William	NAMED	48	M	Full	1897	Pontotoc	54	
2 " Annie	Wife	46	F	"	1897	"	54	
3 " Mulbert	Son	14	M	"	1897	"	54	
4 " Daniel	"	9	"	"	1897	"	54	
5 " Joe	"	6	"	"	1897	"	54	

TRIBAL ENROLLMENT OF PARENTS

	NAME OF FATHER	YEAR	COUNTY	NAME OF MOTHER	YEAR	COUNTY
1	John James	Dead	Chickasaw Roll	Jane	Dead	Chickasaw Roll
2	La-po-nub-by	"	" "	She-pa-hak-te	"	" "
3	No. 1			No. 2		
4	No. 1			No. 2		
5	No. 1			No. 2		

(NOTES)

No. 3 Died Feby 21, 1902. Proof of death filed July 8, 1902.

Sept. 5/98.

RESIDENCE: Choctaw Nation COUNTY					CARD NO.			
POST OFFICE: Savannah, Ind. Ter.					FIELD NO.			
NAME	RELATION-SHIP TO PERSON FIRST NAMED	AGE	SEX	BLOOD	TRIBAL ENROLLMENT			
					YEAR	COUNTY	PAGE	
4 ~~Coleman, William R.~~	NAMED	~~63~~	~~M~~	~~I.W.~~	~~1897~~	~~Chick residing in Choctaw N. 1st Dist~~	~~82~~	
2 " Louisa	Wife	70	F	Full	1897	Chick residing in Choctaw N. 1st Dist	70	
3 Nolatubbee, Ella	G.Dau	20	"	"	1897	" " " "	70	
4 " James	" Son	18	M	"	1897	" " " "	70	
5 Lewis, Alvin	" "	21	M	1/2	1897	" " " "	70	
6 Thurston, Davd Jeff	Gr.Neph	13	"	1/2	1897	" " " "	70	
7 Proce. :pivoma	GG.Niece	16	F	Full	1897	" " " "	70	

Chickasaw Enrollment Cards 1898-1914
Chickasaw by Blood   Volume II

8	Price, Katie	Dau of No. 7	7m	F	1/2			
9	Nolatubbee, Bessie	Wife of No. 4	18	"	I.W.			

TRIBAL ENROLLMENT OF PARENTS

	NAME OF FATHER	YEAR	COUNTY	NAME OF MOTHER	YEAR	COUNTY
1	~~(Name Illegible)~~	~~Dead~~	~~Non Citizen~~	~~(Name Illegible)~~	~~Dead~~	~~Non Citizen~~
2	La-co-chub-by	"	Chickasaw Roll	Sally	"	Chickasaw Roll
3	James Nolatubbee	"	" "	Sally Nolatubbee	"	" "
4	" "	"	" "	" "	"	" "
5	Eastman Lewis	"	" "	Frances Lewis	"	Non Citizen
6	Dave Thurston	"	Non Citizen	Kizzie Thurston	"	Chickasaw Roll
7	Wilburn Moore	"	Chickasaw Roll	Sissie Moore	"	" "
8	E.H. Price		Non Citizen	No. 7		
9	Ike Blevins	Dead	" "	Margaret Blevins	Dead	Non Citz

(NOTES)

No. 3 on Chickasaw roll as Ella Coleman
No. 4   "   "   " " Jennie "
No. 6   "   "   " " David I. Thurston
No. 7   "   "   " " Nadian Cotledge
No. 8 Born Dec. 31, 1901. Enrolled July 14, 1902.
No. 7 Now the wife of E.H. Price non citizen. Evidence of marriage filed July 14, 1902.
No. 1 died July 25, 1900.
No. 9 originally listed for enrollment on Chickasaw Card #D-450 Dec. 24, 1902, transferred
     to this card May 15, 1905. See decision of April 1, 1905.

Sept. 29/98.

RESIDENCE: Pontotoc *COUNTY*						*CARD NO.*		
POST OFFICE: Stonewall, Ind. Ter.						*FIELD NO.*		

	NAME	RELATION-SHIP TO PERSON FIRST NAMED	AGE	SEX	BLOOD	TRIBAL ENROLLMENT		
						YEAR	COUNTY	PAGE
1	James, Gipson	NAMED	39	M	Full	1897	Pontotoc	53
2	" Nellie	Wife	30	F	"	1897	"	53
3	" Alba	Step Dau	8	"	"	1897	"	53
4	" Sylva	"	6	"	"	1897	"	53
5	" Lavin	Son	4	M	"	1897	"	53

TRIBAL ENROLLMENT OF PARENTS

	NAME OF FATHER	YEAR	COUNTY	NAME OF MOTHER	YEAR	COUNTY
1	Puk-na-tubby	Dead	Chickasaw Roll	Cha-las-te	Dead	Chickasaw Roll

2	Cha-ta-be	"	"	"	Slauth-le		1897	Pontotoc
3	Wesley James				No. 2			
4	No. 1				No. 2			
5	No. 1				No. 2			

(NOTES)

No. 4 Also on Page 94, Pontotoc Co. as Alma James.

No. 2 Died *(Month difficult to read - looks like June - date and year illegible).*

Sept. 5/98.

RESIDENCE: Choctaw Nation	COUNTY				CARD NO.			
POST OFFICE: South McAlester, Ind. Ter.					FIELD NO.			

NAME	RELATION-SHIP TO PERSON FIRST NAMED	AGE	SEX	BLOOD	TRIBAL ENROLLMENT		
					YEAR	COUNTY	PAGE
1 Prola, John		36	M	I.W.	18797	Chick residing in Choctaw N. 1st Dist.	82

TRIBAL ENROLLMENT OF PARENTS

	NAME OF FATHER	YEAR	COUNTY	NAME OF MOTHER	YEAR	COUNTY
1	Peter Prola		Non Citizen	Clara Prola		Non Citizen

(NOTES)

On Chickasaw Roll as John Proler

"will send certificate to Dawes Com - from Nat Secy Choctaw Nation"

Certificate received Sept. 15/98.

Dec. 6/99 Admitted by Dawes Commission as an intermarried citizen of Choctaw Nation Case No. 610.

Sept. 5/98.

RESIDENCE: Pontotoc	COUNTY				CARD NO.			
POST OFFICE: Conway, Ind. Ter.					FIELD NO.			

NAME	RELATION-SHIP TO PERSON FIRST NAMED	AGE	SEX	BLOOD	TRIBAL ENROLLMENT		
					YEAR	COUNTY	PAGE
1 Nelson, Cornelius	NAMED	21	M	1/2	1897	Pontotoc	47
2 " Linty	Wife	20	F	Full	1897	"	44
3 " Minnie	Dau	1mo	"	34			

TRIBAL ENROLLMENT OF PARENTS

	NAME OF FATHER	YEAR	COUNTY	NAME OF MOTHER	YEAR	COUNTY
1	Chilly Nelson	1897	Pontotoc	Betsey Nelson	Dead	Pontotoc
2	John McLain	"	"	Kilsey	"	"
3	No. 1			No. 2		

(NOTES)

Chilly Nelson on Choctaw Card No. 22
No. 3 born Aug. 17, 1898; proof of birth filed July 14, 1904.

Sept. 5/98.

RESIDENCE: Pontotoc   **COUNTY**   **CARD NO.**

POST OFFICE: Allen, Ind. Ter.   **FIELD NO.**

	NAME	RELATION-SHIP TO PERSON FIRST NAMED	AGE	SEX	BLOOD	TRIBAL ENROLLMENT		
						YEAR	COUNTY	PAGE
1	Haynes, Julia		50	F	3/4	1897	Chick residing in Choctaw N. It Dist.	68
2	Williams, Isum	Son	13	M	1/2	1897	Pontotoc	97
3	Haynes, Peter	Husband	57	"	I.W.			

	NAME OF FATHER	YEAR	COUNTY	NAME OF MOTHER	YEAR	COUNTY
1	Winchester Colbert	Dead	Chickasaw Roll	Rhoda Perry	Dead	Chickasaw Roll
2	Edward Williams	"	" "	No. 1		
3	Elisha Haynes	"	Non. Citiz	Ruthie Haynes	Dead	Non citiz

(NOTES)

No. 2 is on Choctaw Census record No. 2 page 484   *(No. 2 Dawes' Roll No. ?666)*
No. 2 on Choctaw Roll 1896 Ataka County No. 14029, as Isom Williams.
   transferred to Chickasaw Roll by Dawes Com. -
Oct. 4/99: No. 1 Also on Choctaw 1896 Roll, Tobuckey Co. page 131 #5363.   *(No. 1 Dawes' Roll No. ?665)*
No. 2 Also on 1897 Roll as Isom Williams
No. 1 Also on page 94, 1897 Chickasaw roll as Julia Hames.
No. 3 enrolled Aug. 9/99.
(Entry illegible)
No. 3 died August 1, 1900. Proof of death filed January 5, 1905.

DISMISSED stamped on card.

Sept. 5/98.

RESIDENCE: Pontotoc   **COUNTY**   **CARD NO.**

POST OFFICE: Allen, Ind. Ter.   **FIELD NO.**

	NAME	RELATION-SHIP TO PERSON FIRST NAMED	AGE	SEX	BLOOD	TRIBAL ENROLLMENT		
						YEAR	COUNTY	PAGE
1	Harjo, Lucy		40	F	Full	1897	Pontotoc	44
2	" Alice	Dau	12	F	1/2	1897	"	44
3	" Lem	Son	9	M	1/2	1897	"	44
4	" Lewis	"	6	"	1/2	1897	"	44

Chickasaw Enrollment Cards 1898-1914
Chickasaw by Blood Volume II

5	" Mattie	Dau	2	F	1/2	1897	"		44
6	Wade, Nancy	Neice[sic]	15	"	Full	1897	"		44
7	" Missie	"	13	"	"	1897	"		44
8	" Nannie	"	9	"	"	1897	"		44

TRIBAL ENROLLMENT OF PARENTS

	NAME OF FATHER	YEAR	COUNTY	NAME OF MOTHER	YEAR	COUNTY
1	John Wade	Dead	Chickasaw Roll	Rhoda Wade	Dead	Chickasaw Roll
2	Contulle Harjo		Seminole Roll	No. 1		
3	" "		" "	No. 1		
4	" "		" "	No. 1		
5	" "		" "	No. 1		
6	William Wade	Dead	Pontotoc	Sukey Wade	Dead	Pontotoc
7	" "	"	"	" "	"	"
8	" "	"	"	" "	"	"

(NOTES)

No. 1 on Chickasaw Roll as Lucy Wade.
As to amount of Chickasaw blood on No.s 6-7-8, See affidavits of Lucy Harjo
   and Samson Johnson filed Sept. 12, 1902.

(No. 6 Dawes' Roll No. 4025)
(No. 7 Dawes' Roll No. 4026)
(No. 8 Dawes' Roll No. 4027)

Sept. 5/98.

RESIDENCE: Pontotoc **COUNTY**   **CARD NO.**
POST OFFICE: Franks, Ind. Ter.   **FIELD NO.**

	NAME	RELATION-SHIP TO PERSON FIRST NAMED	AGE	SEX	BLOOD	TRIBAL ENROLLMENT		
						YEAR	COUNTY	PAGE
1	Brown, Gabrel	NAMED	42	M	Full	1897	Pontotoc	49
2	" Lucy	Wife	45	F	"	1897	"	49
3	" Susan	Dau	11	"	"	1897	"	49
4	Isaac, William	Nephew	4	M	1/2	1897	"	49

TRIBAL ENROLLMENT OF PARENTS

	NAME OF FATHER	YEAR	COUNTY	NAME OF MOTHER	YEAR	COUNTY
1	Jesse Brown	Dead	Chickasaw Roll	Lucy Brown	1897	Pontotoc
2	Solomon	"	" "	Druthie	Dead	Chickasaw Roll
3	No. 1			No. 2		
4	Williams		Non Citizen	Lizzie	1897	Tishomingo

(NOTES)

No. 3 Died January 28, 1901. Proof of death filed July 16, 1901.

Sept. 5/98.

RESIDENCE: Pontotoc COUNTY					CARD NO.		
POST OFFICE: Franks, Ind. Ter.					FIELD NO.		
NAME	RELATION-SHIP TO PERSON FIRST NAMED	AGE	SEX	BLOOD	TRIBAL ENROLLMENT		
					YEAR	COUNTY	PAGE
1 Brown, Lucy		60	F	Full	1897	Pontotoc	50
2 Killcrease, Cena	Dau	36	"	"	1897	"	50
3 " Nancy	"	32	"	"	1897	"	50
4 Brown, Mason	"	23	"	"	1897	"	50
5 " Willie	Son	16	M	"	1897	"	50
6 " James	G.Son	16	"	"	1897	"	50
7 Wilson, Elsie	G.Dau	11	F	"	1897	"	50
8 Killcrease, Filmore	G.Son	4mo	M	"			

TRIBAL ENROLLMENT OF PARENTS

	NAME OF FATHER	YEAR	COUNTY	NAME OF MOTHER	YEAR	COUNTY
1	Bem Russell	Dead	Chickasaw Roll	Do 'a-Sey'	Dead	Chickasaw Roll
2	Jesse Brown	"	" "	No. 1		
3	" "	"	" "	No. 1		
4	" "	"	" "	No. 1		
5	" "	"	" "	No. 1		
6	Wallace Underwood	"	Pontotoc	No. 2		
7	George Wilson	1897	"	No. 2		
8	Eastman Killcrease		"	No. 2		

(NOTES)

No. 3 Also on 1897 roll page 93, Pontotoc Co.
No. 2 is now the wife of Eastman Killcrease on Chickasaw Care #168.
No. 8 Enrolled February 4, 1901. Evidence of birth to bne supplied
No. 3 is the wife of Galoway Lewis on Chickasaw Card #19. See notation on that card.
No. 3 transferred to Chickasaw Card #19 with her husband Galloway Lewis: Nov. 11th 1901.
Evidence of birth of No. 8 received and filed May 19, 1902.
No. 6 was married in March, 1903, *(remainder illegible)*
No. 6 is husband of No. 1 on Chickasaw card 229; wife says name is James Underwood 11/10/02.

Sept. 5/98.

RESIDENCE: Pontotoc COUNTY					CARD NO.		
POST OFFICE: Roff, Ind. Ter.					FIELD NO.		
NAME	RELATION-SHIP TO PERSON FIRST NAMED	AGE	SEX	BLOOD	TRIBAL ENROLLMENT		
					YEAR	COUNTY	PAGE
1 Paul, Columbus W.		43	M	1/4	1897	Pontotoc	60

| 2 | " | Nettie May | Dau | 16mo | F | 1/8 | ~~1897~~ | | " | | ~~88~~ |
| 3 | " | Charles Henry | Son | 3wks | M | 1/8 | | | | | |

TRIBAL ENROLLMENT OF PARENTS

	NAME OF FATHER	YEAR	COUNTY	NAME OF MOTHER	YEAR	COUNTY
1	John Paul		Non Citizen	Kittie Paul	Dead	Panola
2	No. 1			Emily P. Paul		Non Citizen
3	No. 1			" " "		" "

(NOTES)

No. 2 on Chickasaw Roll as Netta. Registered under Act of Legislature July 31/98. page 89   No.
No. 1 Died Aug 28, 1899. proof of death filed May 10, 1902.
No. 3 Died June 28, 1900. proof of death filed May 10, 1902.
No. 2 Evidence of birth received and filed Sept. 14, 1902.   *(No. 2 Dawes' Roll No. 4024)*
No. 3 Enrolled Oct. 21/98.

P.O. Fitzhugh, I.T.   Sept. 5/98.

RESIDENCE:	Pontotoc	COUNTY				CARD NO.			
POST OFFICE:	Conway, Ind. Ter.					FIELD NO.			

NAME		RELATION-SHIP TO PERSON FIRST NAMED	AGE	SEX	BLOOD	TRIBAL ENROLLMENT		
						YEAR	COUNTY	PAGE
1	Richardson, Walton		15	M	1/2	1897	Pontotoc	44
2	" Stephen	Bro	10	"	1/2	1897	"	44
3	" Dora	Sister	9	F	1/2	1897	"	44
4	" Frank	Bro	4	M	1/2	1897	"	44

TRIBAL ENROLLMENT OF PARENTS

	NAME OF FATHER	YEAR	COUNTY	NAME OF MOTHER	YEAR	COUNTY
1	Si Richardson		Chick Freedman	Jennie Frazier	Dead	Pontotoc
2	" "		" "	" "	"	"
3	" "		" "	" "	"	"
4	" "		" "	" "	"	"

(NOTES)

No. 1 on Chickasaw Roll as Walter

RESIDENCE:	Pontotoc	COUNTY				CARD NO.			
POST OFFICE:	Stonewall, Ind. Ter.					FIELD NO.			

NAME		RELATION-SHIP TO PERSON FIRST NAMED	AGE	SEX	BLOOD	TRIBAL ENROLLMENT		
						YEAR	COUNTY	PAGE
1	McLeon, Julia		50	F	Full	1897	Pontotoc	51

Chickasaw Enrollment Cards 1898-1914
Chickasaw by Blood   Volume II

	TRIBAL ENROLLMENT OF PARENTS					
	NAME OF FATHER	YEAR	COUNTY	NAME OF MOTHER	YEAR	COUNTY
1	*(Name Illegible)*	Dead	Chickasaw Roll	Sin-ta-thlyk-ey	Dead	Chickasaw Roll

(NOTES)

On Chickasaw roll as Julia McCloud

Sept. 5/98.

RESIDENCE: Pontotoc   **COUNTY**   **CARD NO.**

POST OFFICE: Conway   **FIELD NO.**

	NAME	RELATION-SHIP TO PERSON FIRST NAMED	AGE	SEX	BLOOD	TRIBAL ENROLLMENT		
						YEAR	COUNTY	PAGE
1	Pettigrew, Mose	NAMED	22	M	Full	1897	Pontotoc	44
2	" Louvinia	Wife	16	F	"	1897	"	44
3	" Bynum	Son	2	M	"			

	TRIBAL ENROLLMENT OF PARENTS					
	NAME OF FATHER	YEAR	COUNTY	NAME OF MOTHER	YEAR	COUNTY
1	Foster Pettigrew	Dead	Tishomingo	Jennie Pettigrew	Dead	Pontotoc
2	Morrison Carr	"	Pontotoc	Litch-e-say	"	"
3	No. 1			No. 2		

(NOTES)

No. 1 In Ardmore Jail awaiting trial

No. 3 born Oct. 15, 1900. Application received May 8, 1905.   *(No. 3 Dawes' Roll No. 4966)*
  under Act of Congress approved March *(illegible)*

Sept. 5/98.

RESIDENCE: Pontotoc   **COUNTY**   **CARD NO.**

POST OFFICE: Stonewall, Ind. Ter.   **FIELD NO.**

	NAME	RELATION-SHIP TO PERSON FIRST NAMED	AGE	SEX	BLOOD	TRIBAL ENROLLMENT		
						YEAR	COUNTY	PAGE
1	Frazier, Eastman	NAMED	48	M	Full	1897	Pontotoc	43
2	" Mollie	Wife	23	F	"	1897	"	43
3	" Colsen	Son	8	M	"	1897	"	43
4	" Elizabeth	Step neice[sic]	7	F	"	1897	"	43

	TRIBAL ENROLLMENT OF PARENTS					
	NAME OF FATHER	YEAR	COUNTY	NAME OF MOTHER	YEAR	COUNTY
1	Ben Frazier	Dead	Chickasaw Roll	Betsey Frazier	Dead	Chickasaw Roll
2	Ke-lo Brown	1897	Pontotoc	Eley	"	Pontotoc

3	No. 1			No. 2			
4	Allen Tealey	Dead	Pontotoc	Upsey		1897	Chick residing in Choctaw N. 1st Dist.

(NOTES)

Sept. 5/98.

RESIDENCE: Pontotoc COUNTY						CARD NO.		
POST OFFICE: Ada, Ind. Ter.						FIELD NO.		

	NAME	RELATION- SHIP TO PERSON FIRST NAMED	AGE	SEX	BLOOD	TRIBAL ENROLLMENT		
						YEAR	COUNTY	PAGE
1	Dyar, Calvin	NAMED	32	M	Full	1897	Pontotoc	46
2	" Sallie	Wife	23	F	"	1897	"	46
3	" Canton	Son	10mo	M	"			
4	" Fannie	Mother	65	F	"	1897	"	46
5	" Susan	Sister	23	"	"	1897	"	46
6	" Joe	Bro	25	M	"	1897	"	46
7	Perry, Jacob	Nephew	11mo	"	"			
8	Walker, Amy	Neice[sic]	13	F	"	1897	"	46
9	" Amon	Nephew	11	M	"	1897	"	46

TRIBAL ENROLLMENT OF PARENTS

	NAME OF FATHER	YEAR	COUNTY	NAME OF MOTHER	YEAR	COUNTY
1	John Dyar	Dead	Pontotoc	Fannie Dyar	1897	Pontotoc
2	Daniel Harris	1897	"	Susanna Harris	1897	"
3	No. 1			No. 2		
4	(Name Illegible)	Dead	Chickasaw Roll	Salvina Dyar	Dead	Chickasaw Roll
5	John Dyar	Dead	Pontotoc	No. 4		
6	" "	"	"	No. 4		
7	Albert Perry	1897	"	No. 5		
8	Joe Walker	Dead	"	Joy Walker	Dead	Pontotoc
9	" "	"	"	" "	"	"

(NOTES)

No. 4 Also on Chickasaw roll page 94 as Cholscie Dyar   *(No. 5 Dawes' Roll No. 4623)*

No. 9 Also on Chickasaw roll page 94   June 5, 1900.
    as Ammond Dyer.

No. 3 Died June 30" 1899. Evidence of death filed July 22nd 1902.

No. 6 is now the husband of Annie Leader on Chickasaw Card #232, July 31, 1902.

No. 7 born Sept. 2, 1897. Proof of birth filed Sept 2, 1903.   *(No. 7 Dawes' Roll No. 4746)*

Sept. 5/98.

Chickasaw Enrollment Cards 1898-1914
Chickasaw by Blood   Volume II

RESIDENCE: Pontotoc COUNTY   CARD NO.
POST OFFICE: Franks, Ind. Ter.   FIELD NO.

NAME	RELATION-SHIP TO PERSON FIRST NAMED	AGE	SEX	BLOOD	TRIBAL ENROLLMENT		
					YEAR	COUNTY	PAGE
1 Killcrease, Eastman	NAMED	35	M	Full	1897	Pontotoc	49
2 " Robin	Son	6	"	"	1897	"	49
3 " Agnes	Dau	4	F	"	1897	"	49

TRIBAL ENROLLMENT OF PARENTS

	NAME OF FATHER	YEAR	COUNTY	NAME OF MOTHER	YEAR	COUNTY
1	Sim Killcrease	Dead	Pontotoc	Lina Killcrease	Dead	Pontotoc
2	No. 1			Frances Killcrease	"	"
3	No. 1			" "	"	"

(NOTES)

No. 2 on Chickasaw Roll as Reubin Killcrease
No. 1 is now the husband of Cena Brown
On Chickasaw Card 175, February 4, 1901.

Sept. 5/98.

RESIDENCE: Pontotoc COUNTY   CARD NO.
POST OFFICE: Stonewall, Ind. Ter.   FIELD NO.

NAME	RELATION-SHIP TO PERSON FIRST NAMED	AGE	SEX	BLOOD	TRIBAL ENROLLMENT		
					YEAR	COUNTY	PAGE
1 Porter, Ben	NAMED	32	M	Full	1893	Pontotoc	183
2 " Sis	Wife	23	F	"	1897	"	89
3 " Mamie	Dau	5	"	"	1897	"	89

TRIBAL ENROLLMENT OF PARENTS

	NAME OF FATHER	YEAR	COUNTY	NAME OF MOTHER	YEAR	COUNTY
1	Henderson Porter	Dead	Chickasaw Roll	Mollie Porter	1897	Pontotoc
2	(Name Illegible)	"	" "	Liz	Dead	Chickasaw Roll
3	No. 1			No. 2		

(NOTES)

All registered under Act of Legislature July 31/97, page 89 of roll
No. 2 Died June 12, 1900. Evidence of death filed May 16, 1901.   *(No. 1 Dawes' Roll No. 4822)*
No. 3 appears on 1893 Chickasaw Payroll No. 2, 183 as Cicy Porter   *(No. 3 Dawes' Roll No. 4565)*
    See letter of Jan 10 filed herein.

Sept. 5/98.

Chickasaw Enrollment Cards 1898-1914
Chickasaw by Blood Volume II

RESIDENCE: Pontotoc COUNTY   CARD NO.

POST OFFICE: Conway, Ind. Ter.   FIELD NO.

	NAME	RELATION-SHIP TO PERSON FIRST NAMED	AGE	SEX	BLOOD	TRIBAL ENROLLMENT		
						YEAR	COUNTY	PAGE
1	~~Walton, Malinda~~	NAMED	~~46~~	~~F~~	~~Full~~	~~1897~~	~~Pontotoc~~	~~45~~
2	" Simon	Son	22	M	"	1897	"	45
3	" Wisdom	"	20	"	"	1897	"	45
4	Williams, Sukey	Dau	12	F	"	1897	"	45

TRIBAL ENROLLMENT OF PARENTS

	NAME OF FATHER	YEAR	COUNTY	NAME OF MOTHER	YEAR	COUNTY
1	Esh-so-no	Dead	Chickasaw Roll	Cha-ta-ne-cha	Dead	Chickasaw Roll
2	Pa-sa-co-min-tubby	"	Pontotoc	No. 1		
3	"	"	"	No. 1		
4	Simon Williams	1897	"	No. 1		

(NOTES)

No. 3 Evidence of death filed June 30, 1902. Died Oct. 10, 1898
No. 2 is now the husband of Minnie Stick on Chickasaw Card #165. Oct. 9, 1902.

Sept. 5/98.

RESIDENCE: Pontotoc COUNTY   CARD NO.

POST OFFICE: Conway. Ind. Ter.   FIELD NO.

	NAME	RELATION-SHIP TO PERSON FIRST NAMED	AGE	SEX	BLOOD	TRIBAL ENROLLMENT		
						YEAR	COUNTY	PAGE
1	Stick, Rogers	NAMED	36	M	Full	1897	Pontotoc	47
2	" Lucy	Wife	34	F	"	1897	"	47
3	" Minnie	Dau	14	F	"	1897	"	47
4	" Amosin	Son	12	M	"	1897	"	47
5	" Mary	Dau	10	F	"	1897	"	47
6	" Lottie	"	6	"	"	1897	"	47
7	" Charles	Son	3	M	"	1897	"	47
8	" Nora	Dau	6mo	F	"			
9	" Linton	Son	8	M	"	1897	"	47
10	Walton, Virgie	Gr.Dau	7mo		"			

TRIBAL ENROLLMENT OF PARENTS

	NAME OF FATHER	YEAR	COUNTY	NAME OF MOTHER	YEAR	COUNTY
1	Charley Stick	Dead	Chickasaw Roll	Mary Stick	Dead	Pontotoc
2	Clark Homan	"	" "	Snu-a-ka-ke	"	"
3	No. 1			No. 2		

Chickasaw Enrollment Cards 1898-1914
Chickasaw by Blood   Volume II

4	No. 1			No. 2			
5	No. 1			No. 2			
6	No. 1			No. 2			
7	No. 1			No. 2			
8	No. 1			No. 2			
9	No. 1			Lizzie Factor		Dead	Pontotoc
10	Simon Walton	1897		No. 3			

(NOTES)

No. 2 Also on Chickasaw Roll page 94, as Lucinda Hamen
No. 3 "   "   "   "   "   "   " Minnie "
No. 4 "   "   "   "   "   "   " Amos "
No. 5 "   "   "   "   "   "   " Mary "
No. 2 Died June 10, 1900. Proof of death filed March 5, 1902.
No. 3 is now the wife of Simon Walton on Chickasaw Card #166. See copy of letter from W.H. Allison as to marriage. Filed Oct. 9, 1902.
No. 10 Born March 7, 1902, enrolled Oct. 9, 1902.   *(No. 10 Dawes' Roll No. 4621)*
Evidence of birth of No. 8 received and filed April 3, 1902.

Sept. 5/98.

RESIDENCE: Pontotoc COUNTY   CARD NO.
POST OFFICE: Stonewall, Ind. Ter.   FIELD NO.

	NAME	RELATIONSHIP TO PERSON FIRST NAMED	AGE	SEX	BLOOD	TRIBAL ENROLLMENT		
						YEAR	COUNTY	PAGE
1	Brown, Angeline		35	F	Full	1897	Pontotoc	42
2	Parmacher, Titas	Son	12	M	"	1897	"	42
3	Liley, Dotson	"	6	"	"	1897	"	42
4	~~Perry, Jane~~	~~Dau~~	~~22~~	~~F~~	~~"~~	~~1897~~	~~"~~	~~42~~
5	~~Parmacher, William~~	~~G.Son~~	~~Ima~~	~~M~~	~~"~~			

TRIBAL ENROLLMENT OF PARENTS

	NAME OF FATHER	YEAR	COUNTY	NAME OF MOTHER	YEAR	COUNTY
1	Ki-o-chi-che Brown	Dead	Chickasaw Roll	So-wa-na-ha	Dead	Chickasaw Roll
2	Robison Parmacher	1897	Pontotoc	No. 1		
3	Wallie Liley	Dead	"	No. 1		
4	~~Walton Gaines~~	~~"~~	~~"~~	~~No. 1~~		
5	~~Robison Parmacher~~	~~1786~~	~~"~~	~~No. 4~~		

(NOTES)

No. 3 on Chickasaw Roll as Dotson Lasey
No. 4 was also known as Jane Gaines. See letter of Ben Porter filed July 3, 1901.
No. 4 Died February 6, 1899. Proof of death filed July 3, 1901.
" 3 is now living with Wilson Tohan *(remainder illegible)*

89

Chickasaw Enrollment Cards 1898-1914
Chickasaw by Blood   Volume II

No. 1 died Sept. 15, 1899, Proof of death filed Feby 15, 1904.
No. 5 died Jany 5, 1899, proof of death filed *(remainder illegible)*

Sept. 5/98.

	NAME	RELATION-SHIP TO PERSON FIRST	AGE	SEX	BLOOD	TRIBAL ENROLLMENT		
						YEAR	COUNTY	PAGE
1	Colbert, Dougherty C	NAMED	26	M	1/2	1897	Pontotoc	41
2	" Nettie Rowe	Wife	20	F	I.W.	1897	"	86
3	" Liza Lessie	Dau	2	"	1/4	1897	"	41
4	" Harley Humphrey	Son	9mo	M	1/4			
5	" Donovo A.	"	2mo	"	1/4			
6	" Zeno Penner	Son	2mo	M	1/4			

RESIDENCE: Pontotoc   COUNTY   CARD NO.
POST OFFICE: Stonewall, Ind. Ter.   FIELD NO.

TRIBAL ENROLLMENT OF PARENTS

	NAME OF FATHER	YEAR	COUNTY	NAME OF MOTHER	YEAR	COUNTY
1	Humphrey Colbert	1897	Pontotoc	Elminey	Dead	Pontotoc
2	Wm Henry Rowe		Non Citizen	Liza L. Rowe		Non Citizen
3	No. 1			No. 2		
4	No. 1			No. 2		
5	No. 1			No. 2		
6	No. 1			No. 2		

(NOTES)

Nos. 2 and 3 were admitted by Dawes Commission Case No. 132.
and No appeal taken.
No. 1 on Chickasaw Roll as D.C. Colbert
No. 3 "   "   " " L.L. "
No. 6 Enrolled May 15, 1901.
Evidence of birth of No. 4 received and filed Feby 10, 1902.
No. 5 Enrolled 7/1/99.

(No. 2 Dawes' Roll No. 250)
(No. 3 Dawes' Roll No. 4020)

Mill Creek, IT 11/10/02

Sept. 5/98.

RESIDENCE: Pontotoc   COUNTY   CARD NO.
POST OFFICE: Wayne, Ind. Ter.   FIELD NO.

	NAME	RELATION-SHIP TO PERSON FIRST	AGE	SEX	BLOOD	TRIBAL ENROLLMENT		
						YEAR	COUNTY	PAGE
1	Hopping, Augustus	NAMED	55	M	I.W.	1897	Pontotoc	84

2	"	Rosa Ella	Wife	43	F	1/4	1897	"	59
3	"	Augustus M	Son	21	M	1/8	1897	"	59
4	"	Gordon	"	19	M	1/8	1897	"	59

TRIBAL ENROLLMENT OF PARENTS

	NAME OF FATHER	YEAR	COUNTY	NAME OF MOTHER	YEAR	COUNTY
1	E.S. Hopping	Dead	Non Citizen	Parmelia A. Hopping	Dead	Non citizen
2	John McIntosh	"	Chickasaw Roll	Esun McIntosh	"	Chickasaw Roll
3	No. 1			No. 2		
4	No. 1			No. 2		

(NOTES)

No. 2 on Chickasaw roll as Rosa S. Hopping.   *(No. 1 Dawes' Roll No. 82)*

Sept.5/98.

RESIDENCE: Pontotoc   COUNTY   CARD NO.

POST OFFICE: Ada, Ind. Ter.   FIELD NO.

	NAME	RELATION-SHIP TO PERSON FIRST NAMED	AGE	SEX	BLOOD	TRIBAL ENROLLMENT		
						YEAR	COUNTY	PAGE
1	Walton, Tecumseh	NAMED	22	M	Full	1897	Pontotoc	39
2	" Holmes	Son	7	"	"	1897	"	39

TRIBAL ENROLLMENT OF PARENTS

	NAME OF FATHER	YEAR	COUNTY	NAME OF MOTHER	YEAR	COUNTY
1	Joe Walton	1897	Pontotoc	Jinsey Walton	1894	Pontotoc
2	No. 1			Mary Walton	Dead	"

(NOTES)

Sept. 5/98.

RESIDENCE: Pontotoc   COUNTY   CARD NO.

POST OFFICE: Ada, Ind. Ter.   FIELD NO.

	NAME	RELATION-SHIP TO PERSON FIRST NAMED	AGE	SEX	BLOOD	TRIBAL ENROLLMENT		
						YEAR	COUNTY	PAGE
1	Grayson, Acey	NAMED	19	F	Full	1897	Pontotoc	42

TRIBAL ENROLLMENT OF PARENTS

	NAME OF FATHER	YEAR	COUNTY	NAME OF MOTHER	YEAR	COUNTY
1	Tom Grayson	Dead	Creek Citz	Patsey	Dead	Pontotoc

(NOTES)

On Chickasaw Roll as Annie Folsom

Sept. 5/98.

91

RESIDENCE: Pontotoc COUNTY					CARD NO.			
POST OFFICE: Stonewall, Ind. Ter.					FIELD NO.			

	NAME	RELATION-SHIP TO PERSON FIRST NAMED	AGE	SEX	BLOOD	TRIBAL ENROLLMENT		
						YEAR	COUNTY	PAGE
1	Bourland, Frances	NAMED	33	F	1/2	1897	Pontotoc	43
2	Hatcher, Mary Ellen	Dau	15	"	1/4	1897	"	43
3	Hatcher, Lillie May	"	13	"	1/4	1897	"	43
4	Bourland, Norman Dale	Son	10	M	1/4	1897	"	43
5	" Estelle Valeria	Dau	10	F	1/4	1897	"	43
6	Hatcher, Lula May	Gr.Dau	4mo	F	1/8			
7	" Hampton Bourland	Gr.Son	3wks	M	1/8			
8	" Robert Norman	Gr.Son	2wks	M	1/8			
9	" Andrew J.	Husband of No. 2	22	M	I.W.			

TRIBAL ENROLLMENT OF PARENTS

	NAME OF FATHER	YEAR	COUNTY	NAME OF MOTHER	YEAR	COUNTY
1	Wm Harrison	Dead	Pontotocx	Mary Harrison	Dead	Pontotoc
2	Wm Hampton Bourland	"	non citizen	No. 1		
3	" " "	"	" "	No. 1		
4	" " "	"	" "	No. 1		
5	" " "	"	" "	No. 1		
6	H.J. Hatcher		" "	No. 2		
7	" "		" "	No. 2		
8	R.F. Hatcher		" "	No. 3		
9	Jas. F. Hatcher		" "	Cath F. Hatcher		non citizen

(NOTES)

No. 1 on 1897 Choctaw roll as Francis Bourland
No. 2 on Chickasaw roll as W.F. Bourland
No. 3 "   "   "   " L.M. "
No. 4 "   "   "   " N. "
No. 5 "   "   "   " E.V. "
No. 2 is now wife of Andrew J. Hatcher, Feby 19, 1900.
No. 6 enrolled May 24, 1900.
No. 7 Born Nov. 12, 1901, enrolled Dec. 4, 1901.
No. 2 Died Nov. 19, 1901. See affidavit of Geo. H. Truas filed Dec. 4, 1901.
    Proof of death of No. 2 filed Dec. 12, 1901.
Andrew J. Hatcher father of No. 6 and 7 on Chickasaw card #D275.
No. 3 is now wife of R.E. Hatcher, non-citizen, evidence of marriage requested May 12, 1902. Filed May 29, 1902.
No. 8 Born April 30, 1902; enrolled May 12, 1902
No. 7 Died Aug 31, 1902. Proof of death filed Nov. 13, 1902.

No. 9 transferred from Chickasaw card #D275 March 29, 1903.
   See decision of March 13, 1903.

Sept. 5/98.

RESIDENCE: Pontotoc COUNTY					CARD No.			
POST OFFICE: Stonewall, Ind. Ter.					FIELD No.			
NAME	RELATION-SHIP TO PERSON FIRST NAMED	AGE	SEX	BLOOD	TRIBAL ENROLLMENT			
					YEAR	COUNTY	PAGE	
1 Hawkins, Nelson	NAMED	24	M	Full	1897	Pontotoc	42	
2 " Milie	Wife	26	F	"	1897	"	42	
3 Greenwood, Tom	Step-Son	4	M	"	1897	"	42	
4 Davis, Henry	" "	2	"	"	1897	"	42	
5 Underwood, Jane	Cousin in Law	25	F	"	1897	"	42	
6 Hawkins, Lewis	Son	3mo	M	"				
7 " Patsey	Dau	10mo	F	"				

TRIBAL ENROLLMENT OF PARENTS

	NAME OF FATHER	YEAR	COUNTY	NAME OF MOTHER	YEAR	COUNTY
1	Jallis Hawkins	1897	Pontotoc	Kissie Hawkins	Dead	Pontotoc
2	William Brown	Dead	"	Susie Brown	"	"
3	Henry Greenwood	1897	Tishomingo	No. 2		
4	Newton Davis	Dead	Pontotoc	No. 2		
5	Houston Hunderwood	Dead	Tishomingo	Wicey	Dead	Tishomingo
6	No. 1			No. 2		
7	No. 1			No. 2		

(NOTES)

No. 2 on Chickasaw Roll as Millie
No. 7 Born Feby 8, 1901; Enrolled Nov. 18, 1901.
No. 5 Died in Feby 1900. Proof of death filed Nov. 12, 1902.
No. 6 Enrolled Aug 9/99.

Sept. 5/98.

RESIDENCE: Pontotoc COUNTY					CARD No.			
POST OFFICE: Ada. Ind. Ter.					FIELD No.			
NAME	RELATION-SHIP TO PERSON FIRST NAMED	AGE	SEX	BLOOD	TRIBAL ENROLLMENT			
					YEAR	COUNTY	PAGE	
1 Elementoner	NAMED	72	F	Full	1897	Pontotoc	39	

	TRIBAL ENROLLMENT OF PARENTS						
	NAME OF FATHER	YEAR	COUNTY	NAME OF MOTHER	YEAR	COUNTY
1	I-a-kay-da	Dead	Chickasaw Roll	Im-a-hok-te	Dead	Chickasaw Roll

(NOTES)

Sept. 5/98.

RESIDENCE: Pontotoc   **COUNTY**

POST OFFICE: Ada, Ind. Ter.

CARD NO.

FIELD NO.

	NAME	RELATION-SHIP TO PERSON FIRST NAMED	AGE	SEX	BLOOD	TRIBAL ENROLLMENT		
						YEAR	COUNTY	PAGE
1	Folsom, Lyman	NAMED	39	M	Full	1897	Pontotoc	46
2	" Jane	Wife	42	F	"	1897	"	42
3	" Mulbert	Son	19	M	"	1897	"	46
4	" Clicy	Dau	6	F	"	1897	"	46

	TRIBAL ENROLLMENT OF PARENTS						
	NAME OF FATHER	YEAR	COUNTY	NAME OF MOTHER	YEAR	COUNTY
1	Shu-mil	Dead	Pontotoc	She-ma-hok-te	Dead	Pontotoc
2	Edmund McGee	"	Chickasaw Roll	Eley	"	Chickasaw Roll
3	No. 1			Siney	"	Pontotoc
4	No. 1			"	"	"

(NOTES)

No. 3 is now the husband of Minerva Harris on Chickasaw Card #188. Nov. 4, 1902.
Correct spelling of surname of family on this card is Fulsom. See statement of
No. 3 filed Nov. 4, 1902 in Chickasaw #188.
Surname of Nos 1, 3 and 4 on 1897 Chickasaw roll as "Fulsome"

Sept. 5/98.

RESIDENCE: Pontotoc   **COUNTY**

POST OFFICE: Conway, Ind. Ter.

CARD NO.

FIELD NO.

	NAME	RELATION-SHIP TO PERSON FIRST NAMED	AGE	SEX	BLOOD	TRIBAL ENROLLMENT		
						YEAR	COUNTY	PAGE
1	Elmy	NAMED	72	F	Full	1897	Pontotoc	40
2	Rhoda	Dau	25	F	"	1897	"	40
3	Mitchell, Agnes	G.Dau	12	"	"	1897	"	40
4	Stick, Henry	" Son	5	M	"	1897	"	40

	TRIBAL ENROLLMENT OF PARENTS						
	NAME OF FATHER	YEAR	COUNTY	NAME OF MOTHER	YEAR	COUNTY
1	(Name Illegible)	Dead	Chickasaw Roll	(Name Illegible)	Dead	Chickasaw Roll

2	*(Name Illegible)*	"	"	"		No. 1		
3	Thompsey Mitchell		"	"	Rhoda		Dead	Pontotoc
4	Rogers Stick	1897	Pontotoc	*(Illegible)* Factor			"	"

(NOTES)

No. 1 on Chickasaw Roll as Elmy Walker
No. 2 on Chickasaw roll as Rhoda Walker   *(No. 2 Dawes' Roll No. 4943)*
No. 3 "   "   " " Agnes Mitchell
No. 4 "   "   " " Henry Steck

Sept. 5/98.

RESIDENCE: Pontotoc COUNTY   CARD NO.
POST OFFICE: Conway, Ind. Ter.   FIELD NO.

NAME	RELATION-SHIP TO PERSON FIRST NAMED	AGE	SEX	BLOOD	TRIBAL ENROLLMENT		
					YEAR	COUNTY	PAGE
1 Wall, Billie	NAMED	57	M	Full	1897	Pontotoc	40

TRIBAL ENROLLMENT OF PARENTS

	NAME OF FATHER	YEAR	COUNTY	NAME OF MOTHER	YEAR	COUNTY
1	Wall	Dead	Chickasaw Roll	Sim-hok-te	Dead	Chickasaw Roll

(NOTES)

Sept. 5/98.

RESIDENCE: Pontotoc COUNTY   CARD NO.
POST OFFICE: McGee, Ind. Ter.   FIELD NO.

	NAME	RELATION-SHIP TO PERSON FIRST NAMED	AGE	SEX	BLOOD	TRIBAL ENROLLMENT		
						YEAR	COUNTY	PAGE
1	Burris, Isaac A.	NAMED	46	M	Full	1897	Pontotoc	48
2	" Celia J	Wife	39	F	1/2	1897	"	48
3	" Mary C	Dau	15	"	3/4	1897	"	48
4	" Maude C.	"	12	"	3/4	1897	"	48
5	" Colbert A. Jr.	Son	10	M	3/4	1897	"	48
6	" Walter P.H.	"	6	"	3/4	1897	"	48

TRIBAL ENROLLMENT OF PARENTS

	NAME OF FATHER	YEAR	COUNTY	NAME OF MOTHER	YEAR	COUNTY
1	Judge Burris	1897	Pontotoc	*(Name Illegible)*	Dead	Pontotoc
2	W.F. Harrison	Dead	Non Citizen	Mary Harrison	"	"
3	No. 1			No. 2		
4	No. 1			No. 2		
5	No. 1			No. 2		

6	No. 1	·		No. 2		

(NOTES)

No. 6 Walter Peyton Harrison Burris on Chickasaw Roll as Peyton Burris

No. 1 On Chickasaw Roll as I.A. Burris

No. 2 " " " " C.J. "

No. 3 " " " " M.C. "

No. 4 " " " " Maude "

No. 5 " " " " C.A. Burris, Jr.

No. 6 " " " " Peyton Burris.

No. 6 Died in Aug 1899, Proof of death filed Nov. 7, 1902.

Sept 5/98.

RESIDENCE: Pontotoc **COUNTY**   **CARD NO.**

POST OFFICE: Stonewall, I.T.   **FIELD NO.**

	NAME	RELATION-SHIP TO PERSON FIRST NAMED	AGE	SEX	BLOOD	TRIBAL ENROLLMENT		
						YEAR	COUNTY	PAGE
1	Puller, Charles	NAMED	38	M	Full	1897	Pontotoc	41
2	" Peter	Son	18	"	"	1897	"	41
3	" Thomas	"	8	"	"	1897	"	41
4	" Mike	"	7	"	"	1897	"	41
5	" Nieby	Dau	4	F	"	1897	"	41

TRIBAL ENROLLMENT OF PARENTS

	NAME OF FATHER	YEAR	COUNTY	NAME OF MOTHER	YEAR	COUNTY
1	Puller	Dead	Chickasaw Roll	Se-na-no-ye	Dead	Chickasaw Roll
2	No. 1			Lo-ne-nay	"	Pontotoc
3	No. 1			Bettie	"	"
4	No. 1			"	"	"
5	No. 1			"	"	"

(NOTES)

No. 5 on Chickasaw Roll as Naby.

Sept. 5/98.

RESIDENCE: Pontotoc **COUNTY**   **CARD NO.**

POST OFFICE: Stonewall, Ind. Ter.   **FIELD NO.**

	NAME	RELATION-SHIP TO PERSON FIRST NAMED	AGE	SEX	BLOOD	TRIBAL ENROLLMENT		
						YEAR	COUNTY	PAGE
1	Ford, Robert P.	NAMED	32	M	I.W.	1897	Pontotoc	80
2	" Sallie	Wife	21	F	Full	1897	"	48

3	" Willie	Dau	2	"	1/2	1897	"	48
4	" Nannie	"	1mo	"	1/2			
5	" Mary	Dau	6mo	F	1/2			

TRIBAL ENROLLMENT OF PARENTS

	NAME OF FATHER	YEAR	COUNTY	NAME OF MOTHER	YEAR	COUNTY
1	Pleas Ford	Dead	Non Citizen	Maggie Ford		Non Citizen
2	Martin Carney	1897	Pontotoc	Liza Russell	Dead	Chickasaw roll
3	No. 1			No. 2		
4	No. 1			No. 2		
5	No. 1			No. 2		

(NOTES)

No. 1 on Chickasaw Roll as R.P. Ford   (No. 1 Dawes' Roll No. 81)
No. 5 Enrolled Aug. 19, 1901.
No. 4 Enrolled May 6/99.

P.O. Ada, I.T. 11/2/02   Sept. 5/98.

RESIDENCE: Pontotoc COUNTY						CARD NO.		
POST OFFICE: Conway, Ind. Ter.						FIELD NO.		

NAME	RELATIONSHIP TO PERSON FIRST NAMED	AGE	SEX	BLOOD	TRIBAL ENROLLMENT		
					YEAR	COUNTY	PAGE
1 Folsom, Eli	NAMED	26	M	Full	1897	Pontotoc	42
2 " Frank	Son	6	"	"	1897	"	42

TRIBAL ENROLLMENT OF PARENTS

	NAME OF FATHER	YEAR	COUNTY	NAME OF MOTHER	YEAR	COUNTY
1	Joe Folsom	Dead	Chick residing in Choctaw N. 1st Dist	Hattie Folsom	Dead	Pontotoc
2	No. 1			Asay	1897	"

(NOTES)

No. 1 is now the husband of Sina Sealy on Chickasaw Card 144;
No. 1 is on 1897 Chickasaw Roll as Eli Fulsome.
" 2 " " " " " Frank "

Sept. 5/98.

RESIDENCE: Pontotoc COUNTY						CARD NO.		
POST OFFICE: Conway, Ind. Ter.						FIELD NO.		

NAME	RELATIONSHIP TO PERSON FIRST NAMED	AGE	SEX	BLOOD	TRIBAL ENROLLMENT		
					YEAR	COUNTY	PAGE
1 Johnson, Louisa	NAMED	60	F	Full	1897	Pontotoc	44

2	" Gipson		Son	15	M	"	"		"	44

TRIBAL ENROLLMENT OF PARENTS

	NAME OF FATHER	YEAR	COUNTY	NAME OF MOTHER	YEAR	COUNTY
1	Lagua	Dead	Pontotoc	*(Name Illegible)*	Dead	Chickasaw Roll
2	Chambers Johnson		Pontotoc	No. 1		

(NOTES)

Louisa Johnson on roll as Laza Johnson.

RESIDENCE: Pontotoc   *COUNTY*   *CARD NO.*

POST OFFICE: Coal Gate Ind. Ter.   *FIELD NO.*

NAME	RELATION-SHIP TO PERSON FIRST NAMED	AGE	SEX	BLOOD	TRIBAL ENROLLMENT		
					YEAR	COUNTY	PAGE
1 Mayer, Bruno		25	M	I.W.			

TRIBAL ENROLLMENT OF PARENTS

	NAME OF FATHER	YEAR	COUNTY	NAME OF MOTHER	YEAR	COUNTY
1	Bruno Mayer		Non citizen	Regine Mayer	Dead	Non Citizen

(NOTES)

Married May 25, 1898.   *(No. 1 Dawes' Roll No. 381)*

Name not on Chickasaw Roll

No. 1 is husband of Cornelia Walker on Choctaw Card #3.

   and Father of child; thereon No. 11 on Final roll. Approved Decr 12 '02

See decision of June 13 '01

P.O. Conway, IT 10/9/??   Sept. 5/98.

RESIDENCE: Pontotoc   *COUNTY*   *CARD NO.*

POST OFFICE: Jeff, Ind. Ter.   *FIELD NO.*

	NAME	RELATION-SHIP TO PERSON FIRST NAMED	AGE	SEX	BLOOD	TRIBAL ENROLLMENT		
						YEAR	COUNTY	PAGE
4	~~Perry, J.D.~~		~~35~~	~~M~~	~~Full~~	~~1897~~	~~Pontotoc~~	~~54~~
2	" Annie Keel	Wife	40	F	"	1897	"	54
3	" Theodore	Son	8	M	"	1897	"	43
4	" Annie	Mother	52	F	"	1897	"	54
5	" Mary	Sister	17	"	"	1897	"	54
6	Browne, Alice	Cousin	25	"	1/2	1897	"	54
7	Immoticha, Clarisa	Neice[sic]	11	"	Full	1897	"	54
8	James, Emmet	Ward	10	M	"	1897	"	54
9	Gipson, William	Cousin	22	"	"	1897	Pickens	18

10	Monroe, William	"	14	"	"	1897	"	18
11	" Sarah	"	16	F	"	1897	"	19
12	Dyer, Frances	"	1mo	F	"			
13	Monroe, Lizzie	"	15	F	"	1897	Pickens	19

TRIBAL ENROLLMENT OF PARENTS

	NAME OF FATHER	YEAR	COUNTY	NAME OF MOTHER	YEAR	COUNTY
1	~~Isaac Perry~~	~~Dead~~	~~Pontotoc~~	~~Annie Perry~~	~~1897~~	~~Pontotoc~~
2	A-chak-a-tom-by	"	"	(Name Illegible)	"	"
3	No. 1			Sallie	"	"
4	Wm Ok-lo-chubby	Dead	Chickasaw roll	(Name Illegible)	"	Chickasaw Roll
5	Isaac Perry	Dead	Pontotoc	Annie Perry	1897	Pontotoc
6	John Brown	"	Pottawatomie Indian	Caroline	Dead	Chickasaw Roll
7	Robert Immoticha	1897	Pontotoc	Mattie Immoticha	1897	Pontotoc
8	Isom James	Dead	"	Missey	Dead	"
9	William Gipson	"	"	Sallie	"	"
10	Loman Monroe	"	"	Nancy	"	"
11	" "	"	"	"	"	"
12	Burney Dyer	1897	"	No. 11		
13	Loman Monroe	Dead	"	Nancy	Dead	Pontotoc

(NOTES)

No. 7 on 1897 Roll page 94 Pontotoc Co. as Clarence Immoticha
No. 1 Died November 12th 1899. Evidence of death filed May 1, 1901.
No. 2 Died May 31, 1901; proof of death filed July 6, 1901.
No. 12 Died March 16, 1901; proof of death filed July 23, 1901.
No. 6 now the wife of WA Spencer Non-cit. Evidence of mar. requested 11/10/02.
No. 9 now husband of No. 3 on Chick card No. 11. 11/10/02

Sept. 5/98.

RESIDENCE: Pontotoc COUNTY   CARD NO.
POST OFFICE: Stonewall, Ind. Ter.   FIELD NO.

	NAME	RELATIONSHIP TO PERSON FIRST NAMED	AGE	SEX	BLOOD	TRIBAL ENROLLMENT		
						YEAR	COUNTY	PAGE
1	Dickerson, L.D.	NAMED	31	M	I.W.	1897	Pontotoc	80
2	" Lillie	Wife	23	F	1/4	1897	"	42
3	" Cecil R.	Son	3	M	1/8	1897	"	42
4	" Leo. Earl	"	2mo	"	1/8			
5	" Robert R.	"	1mo	M				

99

			TRIBAL ENROLLMENT OF PARENTS			
NAME OF FATHER	YEAR	COUNTY	NAME OF MOTHER	YEAR	COUNTY	
1	Kinsey Dickenson[sic}	Dead	Non Citizen	Mary A. Dickenson[sic]		Non Citizen
2	B.F. Byrd	1897	Pontotoc	Molsey E. Byrd	Dead	Pontotoc
3	No. 1			No. 2		
4	No. 1			No. 2		
5	No. 1			No. 2		

(NOTES)

Nos. 1 and 3 admitted by Dawes Commission in 1896.   *(No. 1 Dawes' Roll No. 249)*
  Chickasaw Case #39 No Appeal.   *(No. 3 Dawes' Roll No. 4049)*
No. 5 Enrolled May 29, 1901.
  See additional testimony of No. 1 taken Oct. 20, 1902.
No. 4 Enrolled Mar. 15/99.
  See additional testimony of No. 1 taken Oct. 20, 1902.

P.O. Purcell I.T. 10-20-02   Sept. 3/98.

RESIDENCE: Pontotoc *COUNTY*   *CARD NO.*

POST OFFICE: Conway, Ind. Ter.   *FIELD NO.*

	NAME	RELATIONSHIP TO PERSON FIRST NAMED	AGE	SEX	BLOOD	TRIBAL ENROLLMENT		
						YEAR	COUNTY	PAGE
1	Brown, Luffie	NAMED	42	M	Full	1897	Pontotoc	45
2	" Sallie	Wife	34	F	"	1897	"	45
3	" Julia	Dau	19	"	"	1897	"	45
4	" Louie	Son	16	M	"	1897	"	45
5	" Elum	"	9	"	"	1897	"	45
6	Johnson, Millie	G.Dau	4	F	"	1897	"	45
7	Wolf, Josephine	G.Dau	1	"	"	~~1897~~	~~"~~	~~90~~

				TRIBAL ENROLLMENT OF PARENTS			
	NAME OF FATHER	YEAR	COUNTY	NAME OF MOTHER	YEAR	COUNTY	
1	Is-ta-go-nuk	Dead	Chickasaw Roll	Sa-ta-ne-cha	Dead	Chickasaw roll	
2	I-is-ha-be	"	" "	Ima	"	" " "	
3	No. 1			No. 2			
4	No. 1			No. 2			
5	No. 1			No. 2			
6	Thompson Johnson	1897	Pontotoc	No. 3			
7	Jesse Wolf	1897	"	No. 3			

(NOTES)

No. 5 Evidence of death filed June 30" 1902. Died April 15, 1901.
No. 7 on Chickasaw roll as Josephine Wolfe.   *(No. 7 Dawes' Roll No. 4048)*

Chickasaw Enrollment Cards 1898-1914
Chickasaw by Blood   Volume II

No. 2   Also on 1897 roll page 93, Pontotoc Co.
No. 7   Proof of birth received and filed Oct. 22, 1902
No. 4   on 1897 Chickasaw Roll as Louisa Brown.

Sept. 3/98.

RESIDENCE: Pontotoc COUNTY   CARD NO.
POST OFFICE: Conway, Ind. Ter.   FIELD NO.

	NAME	RELATION-SHIP TO PERSON FIRST NAMED	AGE	SEX	BLOOD	TRIBAL ENROLLMENT		
						YEAR	COUNTY	PAGE
1	Johnson, Sampson	NAMED	37	M	Full	1897	Pontotoc	39
2	" Jane	Wife	35	F	"	1897	"	39
3	Fulsome, Sina	Dau	18	"	"	1897	"	39
4	Sealy, Elizabeth	G. "	7mo	"	"			
5	Fulsome, Pharo	Grand-Dau	4mo	"	"			

TRIBAL ENROLLMENT OF PARENTS

	NAME OF FATHER	YEAR	COUNTY	NAME OF MOTHER	YEAR	COUNTY
1	Shutchorikey	Dead	Chickasaw roll	Fulotike	Dead	Chickasaw Roll
2	Chepaney	"	" "	(Name Illegible)	"	" "
3	No. 1			No. 2		
4	Eli Fulsome	1897	Pontotoc	No. 3		
5	" "	"	"	No. 3		

(NOTES)
No. 3 is the wife of Eli Folsom on Chickasaw Card #150.
No. 5 Enrolled May 25, 1900.

Sept. (date illegible)

RESIDENCE: Pontotoc COUNTY   CARD NO.
POST OFFICE: Stonewall, Ind. Ter.   FIELD NO.

	NAME	RELATION-SHIP TO PERSON FIRST NAMED	AGE	SEX	BLOOD	TRIBAL ENROLLMENT		
						YEAR	COUNTY	PAGE
1	Immotichey, Robert	NAMED	31	M	Full	1897	Pontotoc	53
2	" Molliean	Wife	30	F	"	1897	"	53
3	" Holmes	Son	8	M	"	1897	"	53
4	" Barton	"	4	"	"	1897	"	53
5	" Harriet	"	4	"	"	1897	"	53
6	Thomas, Enus	StepSon	12	"	"	1897	"	53
7	Ayakatubby, Ida	Ward	7	F	"	1897	"	53

	TRIBAL ENROLLMENT OF PARENTS						
	NAME OF FATHER	YEAR	COUNTY	NAME OF MOTHER	YEAR	COUNTY	
1	Labon	Dead	Chickasaw Roll	Betsey	Dead	Chickasaw Roll	
2	Wall Alexander	"	" "	E-la-nok-te	"	" "	
3	No. 1			No. 2			
4	No. 1			No. 2			
5	No. 1			No. 2			
6	John Thomas	Dead	Chickasaw Roll	No. 2			
7	Esias Ayakatubby	1897	Pontotoc	Patsey	Dead	Chickasaw Roll	

(NOTES)

No. 7 on 1897 roll, page 94, as Ida Iyakatuby
No. 6 Died Feby 9, 1902. Proof of death filed July 8, 1902.
No. 4 Died Sept. 22, 1900. Proof of death filed Nov. 14, 1902.
No. 5 is on 1897 Chickasaw Roll as Harritt Immotichey.

Sept. 3/98.

RESIDENCE: Pontotoc COUNTY					CARD NO.			
POST OFFICE: Ada, Ind. Ter.					FIELD NO.			

	NAME	RELATION-SHIP TO PERSON FIRST NAMED	AGE	SEX	BLOOD	TRIBAL ENROLLMENT		
						YEAR	COUNTY	PAGE
1	Killcrease, Thompson	NAMED	40	M	Full	1897	Pontotoc	58
2	" Tooko	Wife	49	F	"	1897	"	58
3	" Tohkey	Mother	70	F	"	1897	"	58
4	" Melton	1/2 Bro	18	M	"	1897	"	58
5	Melville, Frances	Ward	12	F	1/2	1897	"	58
6	Melville, Leon	Son of No. 5	3mo	M	1/2			

	TRIBAL ENROLLMENT OF PARENTS						
	NAME OF FATHER	YEAR	COUNTY	NAME OF MOTHER	YEAR	COUNTY	
1	Con-no-we Killcrease	Dead	Chickasaw Roll	Tohkey	1897	Pontotoc	
2	Ka-to-he	"	" "	Tennessee	Dead	Chickasaw Roll	
3	Abomowar	"	" "	Shalukachar	"	" "	
4	Con-no-ne Killcrease	"	" "	Betsey	"	" "	
5	Newton Johnson	1897	Pontotoc	Seanna	"	" "	
6	Samuel C. Melville	1897	"	No. 5			

(NOTES)

No. 1 is now the husband Emaline Carney on Chickasaw Card #279, March 25, 1902.
No. 4 Died in Jan. 1899. proof of death filed Nov. 12, 1902.
Sept 30/98. Newton Johnson the father of Frances Johnson states that the mother of Frances Johnson, (Seanna) was a Seminole Indian. That Frances Johnson is on the Seminole roll at the present time and that she

draws her annuity money every year.
No. 5 is now the wife of Samuel C. Melville on Chick Card #47.
Evidence of marriage filed March 12, 1902.
No. 6 Born Dec. 9, 1901. Enrolled March 12, 1902.
No. 2 Died Jany 27, 1899. See affidavits of Martin Carney andThompson Killcrease filed March 25, 1902.
No. 5 is not on Seminole Rolls

Sept. 3/98.

RESIDENCE: Pontotoc   **COUNTY**   **CARD NO.**
POST OFFICE: Stonewall, Ind. Ter.   **FIELD NO.**

	NAME	RELATION-SHIP TO PERSON FIRST NAMED	AGE	SEX	BLOOD	TRIBAL ENROLLMENT		
						YEAR	COUNTY	PAGE
1	Brown, Harris	NAMED	56	M	Full	1897	Pontotoc	53
2	" Foamie	Wife	35	F	"	1897	"	53
3	" Daniel	Son	11	M	"	1897	"	53
4	" Epsie	Dau	10	F	"	1897	"	53
5	" Willis	Son	5	M	"	1897	"	53
6	" Eddie	Dau	3	F	"	1897	"	53
7	" Calberson	Son	25	M	"	1897	"	53
8	" Nanna	Dau	3mos	F	"			

TRIBAL ENROLLMENT OF PARENTS

	NAME OF FATHER	YEAR	COUNTY	NAME OF MOTHER	YEAR	COUNTY
1	Nin-na-ko-che	Dead	Chickasaw Roll	Wa-he-key	Dead	Chickasaw Roll
2	Cha-da-he-ka-me	"	" "	Se-ne-ho-ke	1897	Pontotoc
3	No. 1			No. 2		
4	No. 1			No. 2		
5	No. 1			No. 2		
6	No. 1			No. 2		
7	No. 1			Kilsey	Dead	Chickasaw Roll
8	No. 1			No. 2		

(NOTES)

No. 4 Also on 1897 roll page 93 Pontotoc Co.
No. 7 " " 1897 " " 88 Tishomingo Co.
No. 7 on Chickasaw roll Page 53 as Alberson Brown
No. 7 " " " " 88 " Culberson "
No. 4 " " " " 93 " Epsy Brown.
No. 7 Died March 1st 1902. Enrolled July 14th 1902
Nos. 1 and 2 are the parents of Dinton Brown on Chickasaw Card #48
See copy of letter from No. 1 filed herein Aug. 20, 1902.
No. 8 Enrolled Aug 7/99.

Chickasaw Enrollment Cards 1898-1914
Chickasaw by Blood   Volume II

No. 2 died in December 1898. Enrollment cancelled by Department Dec. 28, 1904
No. 8 "   " September 1898.   "   "   "   "   Dec. 28, 1904.

P.O. Hogan, I.T. 7/14/02   Sept. 3/98.

RESIDENCE: Pontotoc COUNTY   CARD NO.

POST OFFICE: Ada, Ind. Ter.   FIELD NO.

	NAME	RELATION-SHIP TO PERSON FIRST NAMED	AGE	SEX	BLOOD	TRIBAL ENROLLMENT		
						YEAR	COUNTY	PAGE
1	Wilson, George T.	NAMED	53	M	Full	1897	Pontotoc	40
2	" Ruth	Dau	5	F	"	1897	"	40
3	Thomas, Bob	StepSon	14	M	"	1897	"	40

TRIBAL ENROLLMENT OF PARENTS

	NAME OF FATHER	YEAR	COUNTY	NAME OF MOTHER	YEAR	COUNTY
1	Wm Wilson	Dead	Chickasaw Roll	Siney Wilson	Dead	Chickasaw Roll
2	No. 1			Mary Wilson	"	Pontotoc
3	Isaac Thomas	Dead	Chickasaw Roll	" "	"	"

(NOTES)

Sept. 3/98.

RESIDENCE: Pontotoc COUNTY   CARD NO.

POST OFFICE: Viola, Ind. Ter.   FIELD NO.

	NAME	RELATION-SHIP TO PERSON FIRST NAMED	AGE	SEX	BLOOD	TRIBAL ENROLLMENT		
						YEAR	COUNTY	PAGE
1	Cravatt, Katie	NAMED	36	F	Full	1897	Pontotoc	54
2	" Angeline	Dau	17	F	1/2	1897	"	54
3	" Maggie	"	11	F	1/2	1897	"	54
4	" Lila	"	9	F	1/2	1897	"	54
5	" Ina	"	5	F	1/2	1897	"	54
6	" ~~John~~	~~Son~~	~~1~~	~~M~~	~~1/2~~			
7	" Clarence	StepSon	21	M	1/2	1897	Pontotoc	54
8	Alexander, Odelia	orphan	10	F	Full	1897	"	54
9	" Ella	"	8	"	"	1897	"	54
10	" Cornelius	"	6	M	"	1897	"	54

TRIBAL ENROLLMENT OF PARENTS

	NAME OF FATHER	YEAR	COUNTY	NAME OF MOTHER	YEAR	COUNTY
1	Shulkey	1897	Pontotoc	Susan	1897	Pontotoc

2	Allen W. Cravatt	"	Card #21 Choctaw Roll	No. 1			
3	" " "	"	" "	No. 1			
4	" " "	"	" "	No. 1			
5	" " "	"	" "	No. 1			
6	~~" " "~~	~~"~~	~~" "~~	~~No. 1~~			
7	" " "	"	" "	Bicey	Dead	Chickasaw Roll	
8	Charlie Alexander	Dead	Chickasaw	Sibbey	"	"	"
9	" "	"	"	"	"	"	"
10	" "	"	"	"	"	"	"

(NOTES)

First 7 names Wife nd chilcren of Allen W. Cravatt, Choctaw Roll Card No. 26
No. 8 on Chickasaw Roll Pickens County page 18,
No. 9 "   "   "   "   "   "   " as Elbe Alexander.
No. 6 Died November 7, 1899. Evidence of death filed March 30, 1901.
No. 9 Died April 8, 1901. Proof of death filed July 13, 1901.
No. 8 Died June 5, 1902. Proof of death filed Nov. 10, 1902.
No. 10 is a male. Correction made under Dept. letter of Jan. 26, 1904. (D.C. #3478-1904)

Sept. 3/98.

RESIDENCE: Pontotoc   COUNTY   CARD NO.

POST OFFICE: Stonewall, Ind. Ter.   FIELD NO.

	NAME	RELATION-SHIP TO PERSON FIRST NAMED	AGE	SEX	BLOOD	TRIBAL ENROLLMENT		
						YEAR	COUNTY	PAGE
1	Carney, Martin	NAMED	50	M	Full	1897	Pontotoc	41
2	" Lottie	Wife	30	F	"	1897	"	41
3	" Bina	Dau	10	F	"	1897	"	41
4	" Jimpson	Son	12	M	"	1897	"	41
5	" Lee	"	7	"	"	1897	"	41
6	" Morris	"	5	"	"	1897	"	41
7	" Lucy	Dau	3	F	"	1897	"	41
8	" Maltsie	"	1	"	"			
9	~~Shimohoke~~	~~Mother~~	~~103~~	~~"~~	~~"~~	~~1897~~	~~Pontotoc~~	
10	Carney, Mary McC	Dau	3wks	"	"			

TRIBAL ENROLLMENT OF PARENTS

	NAME OF FATHER	YEAR	COUNTY	NAME OF MOTHER	YEAR	COUNTY
1	Cha-te-he	Dead	Chickasaw Roll	Shi-moho-ke	1897	Pontotoc
2	Ish-ta-noon-tubby	"	" "	I-ho-che	Dead	Chickasaw
3	No. 1			No. 2		

4	No. 1			No. 2		
5	No. 1			No. 2		
6	No. 1			No. 2		
7	No. 1			No. 2		
8	No. 1			No. 2		
9	~~Si-ne-wa~~	~~Dead~~	~~Chickasaw Roll~~	~~Par-se-ho-ye~~	~~Dead~~	~~Chickasaw Roll~~
10	No. 1			No. 2		

(NOTES)

No. 1 Also on Chickasaw roll, page 89, as Maude Carney
No. 3 " " " " " 41 " Bennie "
Dec. 13/99 Daughter of Nos. 1-2 on Card No. D.296.
No. 9 Died in December 1900. Proof of death recd and filed Nov. 15, 1902.
No. 10 Born Nov. 21, 1899. transferred to this card February 1, 1902.
No. 10 Died in Sept 1900. Proof of death filed Nov. 13, 1902.
No. 8 born June 28, 1897, proof of birth filed *(illegible)*

Sept. 3/98.

RESIDENCE: Pontotoc ***COUNTY*** ***CARD NO.***
POST OFFICE: Stonewall, Ind. Ter. ***FIELD NO.***

	NAME	RELATION-SHIP TO PERSON FIRST NAMED	AGE	SEX	BLOOD	TRIBAL ENROLLMENT		
						YEAR	COUNTY	PAGE
1	Duke, Billy		40	M	Full	1897	Chick residing in Choctaw N. 3rd Dist.	73
2	" Lena	Wife	25	F	"	1897	" " " "	73
3	" Lankford	Son	6	M	"	1897	" " " "	73
4	" Lillian	Dau	6mo	F	"			
5	" Tip Graham	Son	1mo	M	"			

TRIBAL ENROLLMENT OF PARENTS

	NAME OF FATHER	YEAR	COUNTY	NAME OF MOTHER	YEAR	COUNTY
1	Shucky	Dead	Chickasaw Roll	Is-ta-ma-ye	Dead	Chickasaw Roll
2	Lawson	"	" "	Ke-li-sey	1897	Chick residing in Choctaw N. 3rd Dist.
3	No. 1			No. 2		
4	No. 1			No. 2		
5	No. 1			No. 2		

(NOTES)

No. 1 on Chickasaw roll as Billy Shucky
No. 2 " " " " Lena "
No. 3 " " " " Lankford "
No. 4 Died October 20, 1898. Proof of death filed June 29, 1901

No. 2 Died Jany 16, 1902. Proof of death filed March 17, 1902.
No. 5 enrolled Nov. 3/99.

Sept. 3/98.

RESIDENCE: Pontotoc   **COUNTY**   **CARD NO.**
POST OFFICE: Jeff, Ind. Ter.   **FIELD NO.**

	NAME	RELATION-SHIP TO PERSON FIRST NAMED	AGE	SEX	BLOOD	TRIBAL ENROLLMENT		
						YEAR	COUNTY	PAGE
1	Albertson, Robert	NAMED	30	M	Full	1897	Pontotoc	52
2	" ~~Frances~~	~~Wife~~	~~20~~	~~F~~	~~"~~	~~1897~~	~~"~~	~~52~~
3	" John	Son	10	M	"	1897	"	52
4	" David	Son	6	"	"	1897	"	52
5	" Salina	Dau	3	F	"	1897	"	52
6	" Sina	"	3	F	"	1897	"	52
7	" Nicy	Mother	70	"	"	1897	"	52

TRIBAL ENROLLMENT OF PARENTS

	NAME OF FATHER	YEAR	COUNTY	NAME OF MOTHER	YEAR	COUNTY
1	Elijah	Dead	Chickasaw Roll	Nicey	1897	Pontotoc
2	~~Thompson~~	~~"~~	~~" "~~	~~Mason~~	~~Dead~~	~~Chickasaw Roll~~
3	No. 1			Wicey	"	" "
4	No. 1			No. 2		
5	No. 1			No. 2		
6	No. 1			No. 2		
7	*(Name Illegible)*	Dead	Chickasaw Roll	*(Name Illegible)*	Dead	Chickasaw Roll

(NOTES)

No. 7 Died Sept 17, 1902. Proof of death filed Oct. 17, 1902.
No. 2 on 1897 Chickasaw roll as Francis.
No. 2 died March 5, 1902; proof of death filed *(illegible)*

P.O. Jesse, I.T.   Sept. 3/98.

RESIDENCE: Pontotoc   **COUNTY**   **CARD NO.**
POST OFFICE: Stonewall, Ind. Ter.   **FIELD NO.**

	NAME	RELATION-SHIP TO PERSON FIRST NAMED	AGE	SEX	BLOOD	TRIBAL ENROLLMENT		
						YEAR	COUNTY	PAGE
1	Johnson, Newton	NAMED	50	M	Full	1897	Pontotoc	57
2	" Adaline	Wife	29	F	"	1897	"	57
3	" Markey	Dau	7	F	"	1897	"	57

4	" Elum	Ward	18	M	"	1897	"	57
5	Hawkins, Lena	Neice[sic]	16	F	"	1897	"	58
6	Wilson, Salan	Ward	3	M	"	1897	"	58
7	Futischa, Wincy	"	15	F	"	1897	"	40
8	Edwards, Esias	StepSon	13	M	"	1897	"	58
9	Futischa, Joe	Son of No. 7	4mo	M	3/4			
10	Johnson, Mary	Dau	1mo	F	Full			
~~11~~	~~Futischa, Maud~~	~~Dau of No. 7~~	~~1p~~	~~F~~	~~3/4~~			

TRIBAL ENROLLMENT OF PARENTS

	NAME OF FATHER	YEAR	COUNTY	NAME OF MOTHER	YEAR	COUNTY
1	Lewis	Dead	Chickasaw Roll	Tennessee	Dead	Chickasaw Roll
2	*(Name Illegible)*	"	" "	Liley	"	" "
3	No. 1			No. 2		
4	Ish-ta-ki-yo	Dead	Chickasaw Roll	Missey	Dead	Chickasaw Roll
5	Charles Hawkins	1897	Pontotoc	Casie	"	" "
6	Geo. Wilson	1897	"	Mary	"	Pontotoc
7	John Edwards	Dead	Chickasaw Roll	Betsey	"	Chickasaw Roll
8	" "	"	" "	No. 2		
9	Johnnie Futischa		" "	No. 7		
10	No. 1			No. 2		
~~11~~	~~Johnnie Futischa~~	~~1897~~	~~Chickasaw roll~~	~~No. 7~~		

(NOTES)

No. 3 on Chickasaw roll as Morkey
No. 6 "   "   " " Salan Johnson
No. 7 is now the wife of Johnnie Futischa, on Chickasaw Card #46
No. 9 Enrolled Sept. 15th 1900
No. 10 Enrolled Aug. 12, 1901.
No. 11 Born Jany 24, 1902, enrolled March 11, 1902.
No. 11 Died June 20, 1902, proof of death filed Nov. 13, 1902.
No. 11 Died June 20, 1902. Enrollment cancelled by Dept. *(Illegible)*

P.O. of #7 is now Ada I.T.   Sept. 3/98.

RESIDENCE: Pontotoc *COUNTY*					*CARD No.*			
POST OFFICE: Stonewall, Ind. Ter					*FIELD No.*			
NAME	RELATION- SHIP TO PERSON FIRST NAMED	AGE	SEX	BLOOD	TRIBAL ENROLLMENT			
					YEAR	COUNTY	PAGE	
1 Peter, Jack	NAMED	22	M	Full	1897	Pontotoc	39	

Chickasaw Enrollment Cards 1898-1914
Chickasaw by Blood   Volume II

TRIBAL ENROLLMENT OF PARENTS						
NAME OF FATHER	YEAR	COUNTY	NAME OF MOTHER	YEAR	COUNTY
1 Bill Peter	Dead	Pontotoc	Di-o-ke	Dead	Pontotoc

(NOTES)

Sept. 3/98.

RESIDENCE: Pontotoc   COUNTY   CARD NO.

POST OFFICE: Conway. Ind. Ter.   FIELD NO.

NAME	RELATION-SHIP TO PERSON FIRST NAMED	AGE	SEX	BLOOD	TRIBAL ENROLLMENT		
					YEAR	COUNTY	PAGE
1 Johnson, Scott	NAMED	47	M	Full	1897	Pontotoc	46
2 Smith, Kittie	Dau	18	F	"	1893	Pay Roll #2	124
3 " Winnie	G. "	3	F	1/2	1897	Pontotoc	90
4 Johnson, Holmes	Son	12	M	Full	1893	Pay Roll #2	124
5 " Carrie	Dau	7	F	"	1893	" " "	124
6 " Ebutamby	Son	2	M	"	?	Pontotoc	90
7 Smith, Hobart	G.Son	1	"	1/2			
8 " Martha	G.Dau	9mo	F	1/2			
9 " Esaw	G.Son	4mo	M	1/2			

TRIBAL ENROLLMENT OF PARENTS						
NAME OF FATHER	YEAR	COUNTY	NAME OF MOTHER	YEAR	COUNTY
1 Setch-ki-ke	Dead	Chickasaw Roll	Ful-o-ti-ke	Dead	Chickasaw Roll
2 No. 1			Ta-me-na	"	" " "
3 Wislin		Choctaw Roll	No. 2		
4 No. 1			Ta-me-na	Dead	Chickasaw Roll
5 No. 1		" " "		"	" " "
6 No. 1		" " "		"	" " "
7 Wislin		Choctaw Roll	No. 2		
8 Wesley Smith			No. 2		
9 " "			No. 2		

(NOTES)

Nos. 2-3-4-5 & 6 Registered under Act of Legislature Aug. 31/97   *(No. 2 Dawes' Roll No. 4917)*

See Roll page 90.   *(No. 3 Dawes' Roll No. 4918)* *(No. 4 Dawes' Roll No. 4919)* *(No. 5 Dawes' Roll No. 4920)*

No. 6 on Chickasaw Roll as Ebalubby   *(No. 6 Dawes' Roll No. 4921)*   *(No. 7 Dawes' Roll No. 4922)*

No. 8 Enrolled Oct. 30th 1900.   *(No. 8 Dawes' Roll No. 4923)*   *(No. 9 Dawes' Roll No. 4924)*

Evidence of birth of No. 7 received and filed May 31, 1902

No. 9 Born Jany 19, 1902; enrolled May 31, 1902.

Nos. 1,2,4 and 5 on 1893 Chickasaw Pay roll #2. All but No. 1 marked "don't pay by order, Geo. Wolfe"

Sept. 3/98.

RESIDENCE: Pontotoc   COUNTY   CARD NO.

POST OFFICE: Conway, Ind. Ter.   FIELD NO.

	NAME	RELATION-SHIP TO PERSON FIRST NAMED	AGE	SEX	BLOOD	TRIBAL ENROLLMENT		
						YEAR	COUNTY	PAGE
1	Johnson, Laban	NAMED	45	M	Full	1897	Pontotoc	46
2	" Mason	Wife	40	F	"	1897	"	46
3	" Hunas	Son	16	M	"	1897	"	46
4	" Henry	"	8	"	"	1897	"	46
5	" Willie	"	7	"	"	1897	"	46
6	" Esther	Dau	11/2	F	"	1897	"	90
7	" Arthur	Son	5mo	M	"			

TRIBAL ENROLLMENT OF PARENTS

	NAME OF FATHER	YEAR	COUNTY	NAME OF MOTHER	YEAR	COUNTY
1	Setch-o-ki-ke	Dead	Chickasaw Roll	Fil-o-ti-ge	Dead	Chickasaw Roll
2	We-wa	1897	Pontotoc	Ta-li-te	"	" "
3	No. 1			No. 2		
4	No. 1			No. 2		
5	No. 1			No. 2		
6	No. 1			No. 2		
7	No. 1			No. 2		

(NOTES)

No. 1 Evidence of death filed June 30, 1902. Died Jany 5, 1902.

No. 6 on Chickawa roll as Hester Johnson

No. 7 Enrolled Febry 24th 1900

No. 6 dismissed Jan *(illegible)*

No. 6 died priot to Sept. 25 *(illegible)* Proof of death filed Jan. *(illegible)*

Sept. 3/98.

RESIDENCE: Pontotoc   COUNTY   CARD NO.

POST OFFICE: Ada, Ind. Ter.   FIELD NO.

	NAME	RELATION-SHIP TO PERSON FIRST NAMED	AGE	SEX	BLOOD	TRIBAL ENROLLMENT		
						YEAR	COUNTY	PAGE
1	Bishop, Margaret	NAMED	52	F	3/4	1897	Pontotoc	40

TRIBAL ENROLLMENT OF PARENTS

	NAME OF FATHER	YEAR	COUNTY	NAME OF MOTHER	YEAR	COUNTY
1	*(Name Illegible)*	Dead	Chickasaw Roll	Silsey	Dead	Chickasaw Roll

(NOTES)

Sept. 3/98.

CANCELLED Stamped across card

Chickasaw Enrollment Cards 1898-1914
Chickasaw by Blood   Volume II

RESIDENCE: Pontotoc   COUNTY

POST OFFICE: Franks, Ind. Ter.

CARD NO.

FIELD NO.

	NAME	RELATION-SHIP TO PERSON FIRST NAMED	AGE	SEX	BLOOD	TRIBAL ENROLLMENT		
						YEAR	COUNTY	PAGE
1	Dearring, Richard	NAMED	70	M	Full	1897	Pontotoc	53
2	" Kilsie Collins	Wife	16	F	"	1897	"	40
3	~~" Nora~~	~~Dau~~	~~6mo~~	"	"			

TRIBAL ENROLLMENT OF PARENTS

	NAME OF FATHER	YEAR	COUNTY	NAME OF MOTHER	YEAR	COUNTY
1	A-to-nok-chi-bley	Dead	Chickasaw Roll	Se-ma-no-the	Dead	Chickasaw Roll
2	Isaac Collins	"	" "	Salena	1897	Pontotoc
3	~~No. 1~~			~~No. 2~~		

(NOTES)

(Entry illegible)

No. 2 on Chickasaw Roll as Kilsie Collins

No. 3 Born June 18/99. Affidavit received. Irregular and returned for correction Dec. 14/99. Returned corrected and filed April 6, 1900.

Nos. 1-2 and 3 should have been enrolled as Dearring their correct names. See affidavit attached April 6. 1900.

No. 3 Died Nov. 26, 1900. proof of death filed June 20, 1901.

RESIDENCE: Pontotoc   COUNTY

POST OFFICE: Stonewall, Ind. Ter.

CARD NO.

FIELD NO.

	NAME	RELATION-SHIP TO PERSON FIRST NAMED	AGE	SEX	BLOOD	TRIBAL ENROLLMENT		
						YEAR	COUNTY	PAGE
1	~~Sealy, Harkin~~	NAMED	~~66~~	~~M~~	~~Full~~	~~1897~~	~~Pontotoc~~	~~50~~
2	~~" Margaret~~	~~Wife~~	~~42~~	~~F~~	"	~~1897~~	"	~~50~~

TRIBAL ENROLLMENT OF PARENTS

	NAME OF FATHER	YEAR	COUNTY	NAME OF MOTHER	YEAR	COUNTY
1	~~Ton-tub-by~~	~~Dead~~	~~Chickasaw Roll~~	~~Is-ta-ma-ye~~	~~Dead~~	~~Chickasaw Roll~~
2	~~Po-ok-ta~~	"	" "	~~O-na-ho-ye~~	"	" "

(NOTES)

No. 1 died in January 1899. Enrollment cancelled by Department Dec. 28, 1900

No. 2 "   "   "   1900. *(Remainder illegible)*

Sept. 3/98.

111

RESIDENCE: Pontotoc COUNTY					CARD NO.			
POST OFFICE: Conway, Ind. Ter.					FIELD NO.			

NAME	RELATION-SHIP TO PERSON FIRST NAMED	AGE	SEX	BLOOD	TRIBAL ENROLLMENT		
					YEAR	COUNTY	PAGE
1 Perry, Geo. H	NAMED	28	M	1/4	1897	Pontotoc	47

TRIBAL ENROLLMENT OF PARENTS

NAME OF FATHER	YEAR	COUNTY	NAME OF MOTHER	YEAR	COUNTY
1 Frank Perry	Dead	Chickasaw Roll	Peggy Perry	1897	Pontotoc

(NOTES)

No. 1 is the husband of Annie Perry and father of the children on Choctaw Card #25.

No. 1 is on Chickasaw 1897 Roll as G.H. Perry.

Sept. 3/98.

RESIDENCE: Pontotoc COUNTY					CARD NO.			
POST OFFICE: Conway, Ind. Ter.					FIELD NO.			

NAME	RELATION-SHIP TO PERSON FIRST NAMED	AGE	SEX	BLOOD	TRIBAL ENROLLMENT		
					YEAR	COUNTY	PAGE
1 Levi, Lem	NAMED	28	M	Full	1897	Tishomingo	27

TRIBAL ENROLLMENT OF PARENTS

NAME OF FATHER	YEAR	COUNTY	NAME OF MOTHER	YEAR	COUNTY
1 Levi Po-can-tubby	Dead	Chickasaw Roll	(Name Illegible)	Dead	Chickasaw Roll

(NOTES)

RESIDENCE: Pontotoc COUNTY					CARD NO.			
POST OFFICE: Stonewall, Ind. Ter.					FIELD NO.			

NAME	RELATION-SHIP TO PERSON FIRST NAMED	AGE	SEX	BLOOD	TRIBAL ENROLLMENT		
					YEAR	COUNTY	PAGE
1 Brown, Lizzie	NAMED	35	F	Full	1897	Pontotoc	51
2 " Clarence	Son	12	M	"	1897	"	51
3 " Joseph	"	10	"	"	1897	"	51
4 " Morgan	"	3	"	"	1897	"	51
5 " Lauvina	Dau	1	F	"	1897	"	51

TRIBAL ENROLLMENT OF PARENTS

NAME OF FATHER	YEAR	COUNTY	NAME OF MOTHER	YEAR	COUNTY
1 La-wa-tub-by	Dead	Chickasaw Roll	Aggie	Dead	Chickasaw Roll
2 Joe Brown	"	Pontotoc	No. 1		

3	" "	"	"	No. 1		
4	" "	"	"	No. 1		
5	" "	"	"	No. 1		

(NOTES)

No. 4 Died Dec. 30, 1899, proof of death filed Jany 25, 1902.
No. 5 died Nov. 6th 1899.   "   "   "   "   "   "   "
No. 1 now wife of *(Name Illegible),* Chickasaw 314.

P.O. Hogan, I.T.
P.O. Jesse I.T. 1/29-04   Sept. 3/98.

| RESIDENCE: Pontotoc COUNTY | | | | | CARD No. | | |
| POST OFFICE: Conway, Ind. Ter. | | | | | FIELD No. | | |

NAME	RELATION-SHIP TO PERSON FIRST NAMED	AGE	SEX	BLOOD	TRIBAL ENROLLMENT		
					YEAR	COUNTY	PAGE
1 Cass, Levi		25	M	Full	1897	Chick residing in Choctaw N. 1st Dist.	68

TRIBAL ENROLLMENT OF PARENTS

NAME OF FATHER	YEAR	COUNTY	NAME OF MOTHER	YEAR	COUNTY
1 Joe Cass	Dead	Chickasaw Roll	Sophia Wright	1897	Pontotoc

(NOTES)

In penitentiary at Detroit, Mich.

Sept. 3/98.

| RESIDENCE: Pontotoc COUNTY | | | | | CARD No. | | |
| POST OFFICE: Conway, Ind. Ter. | | | | | FIELD No. | | |

NAME	RELATION-SHIP TO PERSON FIRST NAMED	AGE	SEX	BLOOD	TRIBAL ENROLLMENT		
					YEAR	COUNTY	PAGE
1 Wright, Dillard		24	M	Full	1897	Pontotoc	46

TRIBAL ENROLLMENT OF PARENTS

NAME OF FATHER	YEAR	COUNTY	NAME OF MOTHER	YEAR	COUNTY
1 Hick-a-tub-by	Dead	Chickasaw Roll	Martha Wright	1897	Pontotoc

(NOTES)

No. 1 Died Sept. 25, 1902 at 3 P.M. Proof of death filed Nov. 13, 1902.

Sept. 3/98.

Chickasaw Enrollment Cards 1898-1914
Chickasaw by Blood   Volume II

RESIDENCE: Pontotoc   COUNTY   CARD NO.

POST OFFICE: Conway, Ind. Ter.   FIELD NO.

NAME	RELATIONSHIP TO PERSON FIRST NAMED	AGE	SEX	BLOOD	TRIBAL ENROLLMENT		
					YEAR	COUNTY	PAGE
1 Wright, Sophia	NAMED	40	F	Full	1897	Pontotoc	45
2 Stick, Albert	Son	11	M	"	1897	"	45
3 Blue, Rosce	Dau	10	F	1/2	1897	"	45

TRIBAL ENROLLMENT OF PARENTS

NAME OF FATHER	YEAR	COUNTY	NAME OF MOTHER	YEAR	COUNTY
1 Hick-a-tub-by	Dead	Chickasaw Roll	Martha Wright	1897	Pontotoc
2 Rogers Stick	1897	Pontotoc	No. 1		
3 Peter Blue		Chick Freedman	No. 1		

(NOTES)

No. 2 Also on Chickasaw roll, page 97 as Abbert Wright
No. 3   "   "   "   "   "   "   " Rose   "
(Entry illegible)

Sept. 3/98.

RESIDENCE: Pontotoc   COUNTY   CARD NO.

POST OFFICE: Conway, Ind. Ter.   FIELD NO.

NAME	RELATIONSHIP TO PERSON FIRST NAMED	AGE	SEX	BLOOD	TRIBAL ENROLLMENT		
					YEAR	COUNTY	PAGE
1 Nelson, Jynson	NAMED	15	M	1/2	1897	Pontotoc	46
2 " Silas	Bro	13	"	1/2	1897	"	46
3 " Albert	"	10	"	1/2	1897	"	46
4 " Maggie	Sister	9	F	1/2	1897	"	46
5 " Adeline	"	7	"	1/2	1897	"	46
6 " Cena	"	4	"	1/2	1897	"	46

TRIBAL ENROLLMENT OF PARENTS

NAME OF FATHER	YEAR	COUNTY	NAME OF MOTHER	YEAR	COUNTY
1 Chilly Nelson		Choctaw residing in Chickasaw District	Betsey Nelson	Dead	Pontotoc
2 " "		" "	" "	"	"
3 " "		" "	" "	"	"
4 " "		" "	" "	"	"
5 " "		" "	" "	"	"
6 " "		" "	" "	"	"

(NOTES)

No. 2 on Chickasaw Roll as *(Name Illegible)*

Father of above children is Chilly Nelson, Choctaw roll Card No. 22

Sept. 3/98.

	RESIDENCE: Pontotoc COUNTY					CARD NO.		
	POST OFFICE: Conway, Ind. Ter.					FIELD NO.		
	NAME	RELATION-SHIP TO PERSON FIRST NAMED	AGE	SEX	BLOOD	TRIBAL ENROLLMENT		
						YEAR	COUNTY	PAGE
1	Watters, Joe	NAMED	46	M	Full	1897	Pontotoc	47
2	" Susan	Wife	21	F	"	1897	"	47
3	" Evan	Son	6	M	"	1897	"	47
4	" Hamilton	"	4	"	"	1897	"	47
5	" McKinney	"	1	"	"	1897	"	90
6	" Polly	Dau	8	F	"	1897	Pontotoc	47

TRIBAL ENROLLMENT OF PARENTS

	NAME OF FATHER	YEAR	COUNTY	NAME OF MOTHER	YEAR	COUNTY
1	Bob Watters	Dead	Chickasaw Roll	Ah-la-ke	Dead	Chickasaw Roll
2	Stin-che-he-o	"	" "	Ta-ia-ne	"	" "
3	No. 1			No. 2		
4	No. 1			No. 2		
5	No. 1			No. 2		
6	No. 1			No. 2		

(NOTES)

No. 5 on Chickasaw Roll as McKinney Watters

No. 5 died Sept. 16, 1898, proof of death filed March 1, 1904.

	RESIDENCE: Choctaw Nation COUNTY					CARD NO.		
	POST OFFICE: Sitre, Ind. Ter.					FIELD NO.		
	NAME	RELATION-SHIP TO PERSON FIRST NAMED	AGE	SEX	BLOOD	TRIBAL ENROLLMENT		
						YEAR	COUNTY	PAGE
1	Wright, Jimpson	NAMED	26	M	Full	1897	Pontotoc	47

TRIBAL ENROLLMENT OF PARENTS

	NAME OF FATHER	YEAR	COUNTY	NAME OF MOTHER	YEAR	COUNTY
1	E-ka-tub-by	Dead	Pontotoc	Martha Wright	1897	Pontotoc

(NOTES)

P.O. Conway I.T. 2/19-04

RESIDENCE: Pontotoc	COUNTY				CARD NO.			
POST OFFICE:	Franks, Ind. Ter.				FIELD NO.			
	NAME	RELATION-SHIP TO PERSON FIRST NAMED	AGE	SEX	BLOOD	TRIBAL ENROLLMENT		
						YEAR	COUNTY	PAGE
1	Frazer. Robert		39	M	Full	1897	Pontotoc	50
2	" Maulsie	Wife	39	F	"	1897	"	50
3	Burris, Euas	StepSon	19	M	"	1897	"	50
4	" Maria	" Dau	7	F	"	1897	"	50

TRIBAL ENROLLMENT OF PARENTS

	NAME OF FATHER	YEAR	COUNTY	NAME OF MOTHER	YEAR	COUNTY
1	Frank Frazer	Dead	Chickasaw Roll	Sani-mi-he-cha	Dead	Chickasaw Roll
2	*(Name Illegible)*	"	" "	Liza	"	" "
3	Rollin Burris	"	" "	No. 2		
4	" "	"	" "	No. 2		

(NOTES)

No. 1 Died April 13, 1901. *(Remainder illegible)*
No. 4 Died about March 4, 1899, Proof of death filed Nov. 12, 1902.
No. 2 on 1897 Chickasaw Roll as Maulsie Frazier

Sept. 3/98.

RESIDENCE: Pontotoc	COUNTY				CARD NO.			
POST OFFICE:	Viola, Ind. Ter.				FIELD NO.			
	NAME	RELATION-SHIP TO PERSON FIRST NAMED	AGE	SEX	BLOOD	TRIBAL ENROLLMENT		
						YEAR	COUNTY	PAGE
1	Underwood, Burney		26	M	Full	1897	Pontotoc	56

TRIBAL ENROLLMENT OF PARENTS

	NAME OF FATHER	YEAR	COUNTY	NAME OF MOTHER	YEAR	COUNTY
1	Bond Underwood	Dead	Pontotoc	Susie	Dead	Pontotoc

(NOTES)

No. 1 is now the husband of Lemie Underwood on Chickasaw card #377.
(Entry illegible)

Sept. 3/98.

RESIDENCE: Choctaw Nation   **COUNTY**   **CARD NO.**

POST OFFICE: Owl, Ind. Ter.   **FIELD NO.**

	NAME	RELATION-SHIP TO PERSON FIRST NAMED	AGE	SEX	BLOOD	TRIBAL ENROLLMENT		
						YEAR	COUNTY	PAGE
1	Colley, William E.	FIRST NAMED	33	M	I.W.	1897	Chick residing in Choctaw N. 3rd Dist.	82
2	" Ella	Wife	21	F	Full	"	" " " "	75
3	" Lizzie	Dau	11	F	1/2	"	" " " "	75
4	" Lillie	"	2	"	1/2	"	" " " "	75
5	" Willie	Son	1	M	1/2			
6	" Lydia	Dau	6mo	F	1/2			
7	" John R.	Son	1mo	M	1/2			

TRIBAL ENROLLMENT OF PARENTS

	NAME OF FATHER	YEAR	COUNTY	NAME OF MOTHER	YEAR	COUNTY
1	Wm C. Colley	Dead	Non Citizen	Frances Colley		Non citizen
2	Albert Brown	"	Chickasaw Roll	Elizabeth Brown	Dead	Chickasaw Roll
3	No. 1			Lucy Colley nee. Burris	"	Pontotoc
4	No. 1			No. 2		
5	No. 1			No. 2		
6	No. 1			No. 2		
7	No. 1			No. 2		

(NOTES)

No. 1 on Chickasaw Roll as William Colley   *(No. 1 Dawes' Roll No. 248)*

(Entry illegible)

No. 5 Died July 3rd 1899

No. 7 Enrolled May 6, 1901.

No. 6 Enrolled Dec. 3/99.

No. 3 has been placed on card No. 1544 with husband, A.E. Hawley.

P.O. Pontotoc I.T. 11/20/02.   Sept. 3/98.

RESIDENCE: Pontotoc   **COUNTY**   **CARD NO.**

POST OFFICE: Stonewall, Ind. Ter.   **FIELD NO.**

	NAME	RELATION-SHIP TO PERSON FIRST NAMED	AGE	SEX	BLOOD	TRIBAL ENROLLMENT		
						YEAR	COUNTY	PAGE
1	Smith, Charles S.	FIRST NAMED	33	M	I.W.	1897	Pontotoc	80
2	" Martha C.	Wife	31	F	7/8	1897	"	40
3	" Mable M	Dau	11	"	7/16	1897	"	40

Chickasaw Enrollment Cards 1898-1914
Chickasaw by Blood   Volume II

4	" Morris B.		Son	7	M	7/16	1897		"		40

TRIBAL ENROLLMENT OF PARENTS

	NAME OF FATHER	YEAR	COUNTY	NAME OF MOTHER	YEAR	COUNTY
1	Wm. J. Smith		Non Citizen	Maria Smith		Non Citizen
2	Humphrey Colbert	1897	Pontotoc	Elmira Colbert	Dead	Pontotoc
3	No. 1			No. 2		
4	No. 1			No. 2		

(NOTES)

No. 2 on roll as Martha.　　*(No. 1 Dawes Roll No. 79)*
No. 4 " " " M.B.

P.O. Newcastle, I.T.　　　　　　　　　　　　Sept. 3/98.

RESIDENCE: Choctaw Nation COUNTY　　CARD NO.
POST OFFICE: Lehigh, Ind. Ter.　　FIELD NO.

NAME	RELATIONSHIP TO PERSON FIRST NAMED	AGE	SEX	BLOOD	TRIBAL ENROLLMENT		
					YEAR	COUNTY	PAGE
1 Foster, Sallie	NAMED	39	F	1/2			

TRIBAL ENROLLMENT OF PARENTS

	NAME OF FATHER	YEAR	COUNTY	NAME OF MOTHER	YEAR	COUNTY
1	Aleck Folsom	Dead	Choctaw Roll	Jane	Dead	Chickasaw Roll

(NOTES)

on Choctaw Census Roll No. 2 Page 403 as Sallie Primer
" " " " 1896 Atoka County No. 10552 as Sallie Primer

　　　　　　　　　　　　　　　　　　　　Sept. 3/98.
CANCELLED Stamped across card.
Transferred to Choctaw Card No. 5372.

RESIDENCE: Pontotoc COUNTY　　CARD NO.
POST OFFICE: Conway, Ind. Ter.　　FIELD NO.

NAME	RELATIONSHIP TO PERSON FIRST NAMED	AGE	SEX	BLOOD	TRIBAL ENROLLMENT		
					YEAR	COUNTY	PAGE
1 Russell, Sissy	NAMED	52	F	Full	1897	Pontotoc	45
2 Wolfe, Agnes	Ward	11	"	"	1897	"	46

TRIBAL ENROLLMENT OF PARENTS

	NAME OF FATHER	YEAR	COUNTY	NAME OF MOTHER	YEAR	COUNTY
1	Sa-to-chi-key	Dead	Chickasaw Roll	Fo-lo-ti-qe	Dead	Chickasaw Roll
2	John Wolfe	"	" "	Mulcey	"	Pontotoc

118

(NOTES)

Sept. 3/98.

RESIDENCE: Pontotoc COUNTY					CARD NO.			
POST OFFICE: Stonewall, Ind. Ter.					FIELD NO.			
NAME	RELATION-SHIP TO PERSON FIRST NAMED	AGE	SEX	BLOOD	TRIBAL ENROLLMENT			
					YEAR	COUNTY	PAGE	
1 Lillard, Benjamin	NAMED	25	M	I.W.	1897	Pontotoc	80	
2 " Mary Louise	Wife	23	F	7/8	1897	"	44	
3 " Rossie O.	Son	2	M	7/16	1897	"	44	

TRIBAL ENROLLMENT OF PARENTS

NAME OF FATHER	YEAR	COUNTY	NAME OF MOTHER	YEAR	COUNTY
1 Wm. R. Lillard	Dead	Non Citizen	Tobithe Lillard		Non Citz
2 Humphrey Colbert	1897	Pontotoc	Emina Colbert		Pontotoc
3 No. 1			No. 2		

(NOTES)

Rossie O. on roll as Rosie.
No. 1 Admitted by Dawes Commission in 1896 as an intermarried citizen Chickasaw Case #247.
No appeal.   *(No. 1 Dawes 'Roll No. 247)*
No. 2 on 1897 Chickasaw Roll as N.L. Lillard.

P.O. Story, I.T. 10/24/02   Sept. 3/98.

RESIDENCE: Pontotoc COUNTY					CARD NO.			
POST OFFICE: Ada, Ind. Ter.					FIELD NO.			
NAME	RELATION-SHIP TO PERSON FIRST NAMED	AGE	SEX	BLOOD	TRIBAL ENROLLMENT			
					YEAR	COUNTY	PAGE	
1 Hays, Amos H.	NAMED	39	M	Full	1897	Pontotoc	39	
2 " Bettie	Wife	41	F	1/2	1897	"	39	
3 " Amanda	Dau	21	"	Full	1897	"	40	
4 " Ida	"	12	"	"	1897	"	40	
5 " Daniel	Nephew	18	M	1/2	1897	"	39	
6 " Sarah	Sister	44	F	Full	1897	"	40	
7 Burris, Elsie	StepDau	15	F	3/4	1897	"	40	
8 McGee, Billie Perry	G.Son	1	M	Full				

TRIBAL ENROLLMENT OF PARENTS

NAME OF FATHER	YEAR	COUNTY	NAME OF MOTHER	YEAR	COUNTY
1 Hays	Dead	Chickasaw roll	*(Name Illegible)*	Dead	Chickasaw Roll

2	Joshua McKinney	"	Choctaw "	Sukey		"	"	"
3	No. 1			Betsey		"	"	"
4	No. 1			"		"	"	"
5	St. John		Non Citizen	Sarah Hays -No. 6-		1897	Pontotoc	
6	Hays	Dead	Chickasaw Roll	*(Name Illegible)*		Dead	Chickasaw Roll	
7	Sampson Burris	"	" "	No. 2				
8	Reuben McGee	1897	Pontotoc	No. 3				

(NOTES)

Evidence of birth of No. 8 received and filed June 3, 1902
No. 1 on 1897 Chickasaw Roll as A.H. Hays

Sept. 3/98.

RESIDENCE: Pontotoc COUNTY						CARD NO.		
POST OFFICE: Conway, Ind. Ter.						FIELD NO.		

NAME		RELATION- SHIP TO PERSON FIRST NAMED	AGE	SEX	BLOOD	TRIBAL ENROLLMENT		
						YEAR	COUNTY	PAGE
1	Johnson, Chisolm	NAMED	32	M	Full	1897	Pontotoc	46
2	" Millie	Wife	32	F	"	1897	"	46

TRIBAL ENROLLMENT OF PARENTS

	NAME OF FATHER	YEAR	COUNTY	NAME OF MOTHER	YEAR	COUNTY
1	Ma-ah-mun-tub-by	Dead	Chickasaw Roll	Fo-lo-ti-ke	Dead	Chickasaw roll
2	Ashome	1897	Chick residing in Choctaw N. 1st Dist	Sim-a-ka-ke	"	" "

(NOTES)

No. 2 Died Jan 31, 1902. Evidence of death filed July 2nd 1902.

Sept. 2/98.

RESIDENCE: Pontotoc COUNTY						CARD NO.		
POST OFFICE: Ada, Ind. Ter.						FIELD NO.		

NAME		RELATION- SHIP TO PERSON FIRST NAMED	AGE	SEX	BLOOD	TRIBAL ENROLLMENT		
						YEAR	COUNTY	PAGE
1	Leader, John	NAMED	43	M	Full	1897	Pontotoc	42
2	" Luina	Wife	37	F	"	1897	"	42
3	" Susan	Dau	26	"	"	1897	"	42
4	" Cassie	"	16	"	"	1897	"	42
5	Collins, Edmund	Ward	4	M	"	1897	"	60
6	Futishcha, Jewell	"	1	M	"			
7	Leader, Rena	G.Dau	4mo	F	"			

120

TRIBAL ENROLLMENT OF PARENTS

	NAME OF FATHER	YEAR	COUNTY	NAME OF MOTHER	YEAR	COUNTY
1	Cager Leader	Dead	Chickasaw Roll	Art-we-ta	Dead	Chickasaw Roll
2	Futishcha	"	" "	Sho-ni-ka	"	" "
3	No. 1			Elsey	"	" "
4	No. 1			"	"	" "
5	Eastman Collins	Dead	Chickasaw Roll	Serena Collins	"	Pontotoc
6	(Illegitemate)[sic]			" "	"	"
7	(Illegitemate)[sic]			No. 4		

(NOTES)

No. 5 on Chickasaw roll as Eastman Collins Jr.
No. 7 enrolled Feby 26ᵗʰ 1900
No. 6 is dead. Died Sept 10, 1901, proof of death filed Feby 13, 1902.

Sept. 3/98.

RESIDENCE: Choctaw Nation   COUNTY   CARD NO.
POST OFFICE: FIELD NO.

	NAME	RELATION-SHIP TO PERSON FIRST NAMED	AGE	SEX	BLOOD	TRIBAL ENROLLMENT		
						YEAR	COUNTY	PAGE
1	Perry, Charles J.	FIRST NAMED	42	M	Full	1897	Chick residing in Choctaw N. 1ˢᵗ Dist.	67
2	" Mattie	Wife	27	F	"	1897	" " " "	67
3	" Beckie	Dau	17	"	"	1897	" " " "	67
4	Perry, Martha	"	14	F	1/2	1897	" " " "	67
5	" Albert	Son	12	M	1/2	1897	" " " "	67
6	" Eli	Nephew	24	"	Full	1897	" " " "	67

TRIBAL ENROLLMENT OF PARENTS

	NAME OF FATHER	YEAR	COUNTY	NAME OF MOTHER	YEAR	COUNTY
1	Johnson Perry	Dead	Chickasaw roll	Lizzie Perry	Dead	Chickasaw Roll
2	Ashoma Durant	1897	Chick residing in Choctaw N. 1ˢᵗ Dist.	Jiney	Dead	" "
3	No. 1			Narcissa	Dead	
4	No. 1			"	"	
5	No. 1			"	"	
6	Fillman Perry	Dead	Chickasaw roll	Chulway	"	Chickasaw Roll

(NOTES)

No. 2 Died January 20, 1902. Proof of death filed May 5, 1904.
No. 3 Died November, 1901. Proof of death filed May 5, 1904.

P.O. McAlester, I.T.   Sept. 3/98.

RESIDENCE: Pontotoc COUNTY						CARD NO.		
POST OFFICE: Ada, Ind. Ter.						FIELD NO.		
NAME	RELATION-SHIP TO PERSON FIRST NAMED	AGE	SEX	BLOOD	**TRIBAL ENROLLMENT**			
					YEAR	COUNTY		PAGE
1 Brown, Houston	NAMED	40	M	Full	1897	Pontotoc		59

TRIBAL ENROLLMENT OF PARENTS							
NAME OF FATHER	YEAR	COUNTY	NAME OF MOTHER	YEAR	COUNTY		
1 Par-na-cha	Dead	Chickasaw Roll	Char-lo-ke	Dead	Chickasaw Roll		

(NOTES)

Sept. 3/98.

RESIDENCE: COUNTY						CARD NO.		
POST OFFICE: Davis, Ind. Ter.						FIELD NO.		
NAME	RELATION-SHIP TO PERSON FIRST NAMED	AGE	SEX	BLOOD	**TRIBAL ENROLLMENT**			
					YEAR	COUNTY		PAGE
1 Ashton, Bird I.	NAMED	30	M	I.W.				
2 " Julia V.	Wife	19	F	1/8	1897	Pontotoc		56
3 Greenwood, Bessie E.	Step-Dau	4	"	5/8	1897	"		56
4 " Julius T.	" Son	3	M	5/8	1897	"		56
5 Ashton, Annie Lucy	Dau	5mo	F	1/16				
6 " Alfred Jackson	Son	6mo	M	1/16				

TRIBAL ENROLLMENT OF PARENTS							
NAME OF FATHER	YEAR	COUNTY	NAME OF MOTHER	YEAR	COUNTY		
1 Ayn Ashton		non citizen	Annie Ashton	Dead	non citizen		
2 Alfred Victo		Choctaw roll	Lucy Victor	"	Pontotoc		
3 Wilson Greenwood	1897	Pontotoc	No. 2				
4 " "	1897	"	No. 2				
5 No. I			No. 2				
6 No. I			No. 2				

(NOTES)

No. 2 on Chickasaw roll as Julia V. Greenwood
No. 4 "   "   " " Julias T.   "
No. 5 enrolled May 24, 1900
No. 6 Born Aug. 16, 1901. enrolled Feby 21, 1902
No. I enrolled Mar 20/99. All others enrolled Sept. 3/98.

RESIDENCE: Pontotoc COUNTY					CARD NO.			
POST OFFICE: Roff, Ind. Ter.					FIELD NO.			
NAME	RELATION-SHIP TO PERSON FIRST NAMED	AGE	SEX	BLOOD	TRIBAL ENROLLMENT			
					YEAR	COUNTY	PAGE	
1 Kennedy, John W.	NAMED	47	M	I.W.	1897	Pontotoc	81	
2 " Mary C. I.	Wife	17	F	1/8	1897	"	57	
3 " Tandy Alfred	Son	3	M	1/16	1897	"	57	
4 " Daisy Ellen	Dau	9mo	F	1/16				
5 " Julia Elizabeth	Dau	3mo	F	1/16				
6 " William D.	Son	1mo	M	1/16				

TRIBAL ENROLLMENT OF PARENTS

	NAME OF FATHER	YEAR	COUNTY	NAME OF MOTHER	YEAR	COUNTY
1	T.J. Kennedy		Non Citizen	Elizabeth Kennedy		Non Citizen
2	Alfred Victor		Choctaw Roll	Lucy Victor	Dead	Pontotoc
3	No. 1			No. 2		
4	No. 1			No. 2		
5	No. 1			No. 2		
6	No. 1			No. 2		

(NOTES)

No. 3 on Chickasaw Roll as Fannie A. Kennedy
No. 5 enrolled May 24, 1900
No. 6 Born Sept. 11, 1901, enrolled Nov. 1st 1901.
Evidence of birth of No. 4 received and filed Feby 10, 1902.

Sept. 3/98.

RESIDENCE: Choctaw Nation COUNTY					CARD NO.			
POST OFFICE: South McAlester, Ind. Ter.					FIELD NO.			
NAME	RELATION-SHIP TO PERSON FIRST NAMED	AGE	SEX	BLOOD	TRIBAL ENROLLMENT			
					YEAR	COUNTY	PAGE	
1 Orphan, Levi	NAMED	29	M	Full	1897	Chick residing in Choctaw N. 1st Dist.	67	
2 " Rena	Wife	28	F	1/2	1897	" " " "	67	
3 " Suckey	Dau	10	"	3/4	1897	" " " "	67	
4 " Elmer S.	Son	6	M	3/4	1897	" " " "	67	
5 " Eugene F.	"	4	"	3/4	1897	" " " "	67	
6 " Myrtle	Dau	1	F	3/4				
7 " Sina	Dau	2	F	3/4				

Chickasaw Enrollment Cards 1898-1914
Chickasaw by Blood   Volume II

TRIBAL ENROLLMENT OF PARENTS

	NAME OF FATHER	YEAR	COUNTY	NAME OF MOTHER	YEAR	COUNTY
1	Stephen Arphan	Dead	Chickasaw Roll	Silbey Arpealer	1897	Chick residing in Choctaw N 1st Dist
2	Joe Folsom	"	Choctaw "	Hettie	Dead	Chickasaw Roll
3	No. 1			No. 2		
4	No. 1			No. 2		
5	No. 1			No. 2		
6	No. 1			No. 2		
7	No. 1			No. 2		

(NOTES)

All of above names appear on Chickasaw Roll as Arplear

No. 6 born March 22, 1897. proof of birth filed July 3, 1903.

No. 7 Born Aug 31, 1901, application first made March 19, 1902, final proof of birth received and filed July 2, 1903.

Stuart, I.T.   Sept. 3/98.

RESIDENCE: Choctaw Nation	COUNTY				CARD NO.		
POST OFFICE: Tandy, Ind. Ter.					FIELD NO.		

NAME	RELATION-SHIP TO PERSON FIRST NAMED	AGE	SEX	BLOOD	TRIBAL ENROLLMENT		
					YEAR	COUNTY	PAGE
1 Johnston, B.F.	FIRST NAMED	43	M	1/4	1897	Chick residing in Choctaw N. 1st Dist.	70

TRIBAL ENROLLMENT OF PARENTS

	NAME OF FATHER	YEAR	COUNTY	NAME OF MOTHER	YEAR	COUNTY
1	Jack Johnston	Dead	Non Citizen	Mary Johnston nee Cheetle	Dead	Chickasaw Roll

(NOTES)

B.F. Johnston on Chickasaw Roll as Frank Johnson

" "   "   husband of Jane Johnston, Choctaw Roll Card No. 19.

Sept. 3/98.

RESIDENCE: Pontotoc COUNTY					CARD NO.		
POST OFFICE: Center, Ind. Ter.					FIELD NO.		

NAME	RELATION-SHIP TO PERSON FIRST NAMED	AGE	SEX	BLOOD	TRIBAL ENROLLMENT		
					YEAR	COUNTY	PAGE
1 Lewis, William Martin	NAMED	16	M	3/8	1897	Pontotoc	48
2 " Docia	Sister	15	F	3/8	"	"	48
3 " Mintie	"	18	"	3/8	"	"	48

4	"	Bertha Maybell	Dau	1	F	3/16			

TRIBAL ENROLLMENT OF PARENTS

	NAME OF FATHER	YEAR	COUNTY	NAME OF MOTHER	YEAR	COUNTY
1	Jack Lewis	Dead	Chickasaw roll	Sarah Ralston		
2	" "	"	" "	" "		
3	" "	"	" "	" "		
4	No. 1			Nora Lewis		Non Citizen

(NOTES)

No. 4 Born June 11, 1901, enrolled Nov. 28, 1902.
No. 1 is now husband of Nora Lewis, non citizen. Evidence of marriage filed Nov. 28, 1902
Sarah Ralston was married to Jack Lewis under the Chickasaw laws and the above named children were born in lawful wedlock. After the death of Jack Lewis, Sarah married one Ralston a non citizen.
She appears on Chickasaw Card #18
No. 1 on Chickasaw roll as William Lewis
No. 3 "   "   "   " Amelia   "
No. 2 Died Jan. 17, 1901. proof of death filed Nov. 14, 1902.

Sept. 3/98.

RESIDENCE: Pontotoc   COUNTY   CARD NO.
POST OFFICE: Ada, Ind. Ter.   FIELD NO.

NAME	RELATION-SHIP TO PERSON FIRST NAMED	AGE	SEX	BLOOD	TRIBAL ENROLLMENT		
					YEAR	COUNTY	PAGE
1 Leader, Melton	NAMED	29	M	Full	1897	Pontotoc	43
2 " Leah	Wife	30	F	"	"	"	43
3 Killcrease, Isum	StepSon	14	M	"	"	"	43
4 Collins, Norah	StepDau	11	F	"	"	"	43
5 Leader, Sallie	Dau	10	"	"	"	"	46
6 " Caroline	"	9	"	"	1897	"	95

TRIBAL ENROLLMENT OF PARENTS

	NAME OF FATHER	YEAR	COUNTY	NAME OF MOTHER	YEAR	COUNTY
1	John Leader	1897	Pontotoc	Ilsey	Dead	Pontotoc
2	Hicks	Dead	Chickasaw Roll	Sha-ka-a	"	Chickasaw Roll
3	Eastman Killcrease	1897	Pontotoc	No. 2		
4	Robinson Collins	Dead	Chickasaw Roll	No. 2		
5	No. 1			Ipsey Leader	Dead	Pontotoc
6	No. 1			" "	"	"

(NOTES)

No. 3 on Chickasaw Roll as Eastman Killcrease   *(No. 1 Dawes' Roll No. 301)   (No. 2 Dawes' Roll No. 302)*
No. 6 on 1893 Pay Roll page 141.   *(No. 3 Dawes' Roll No. 303)   (No. 4 Dawes' Roll No. 304)*
                    (No. 5 Dawes' Roll No. 305)   (No. 6 Dawes' Roll No. 306)   Sept. 3/98.

RESIDENCE: Pontotoc COUNTY CARD NO.

POST OFFICE: Waupanucka, Ind. Ter. FIELD NO.

NAME	RELATION-SHIP TO PERSON FIRST NAMED	AGE	SEX	BLOOD	TRIBAL ENROLLMENT		
					YEAR	COUNTY	PAGE
1 Worcester, Lyman D.	NAMED	38	M	Full	1897	Pontotoc	50
2 " Overton	Son	15	"	"	1897	"	50
3 " Mattie	Dau	14	F	"	1897	"	50
4 Colbert, Gipson	StepSon	20	M	"	1897	"	50
5 Worcester, Simeon	Cousin	14	"	3/4	1897	Choctaw N. 1st Dist.	71
6 " Laban	"	10	"	3/4	1897	" " " "	71
7 Perry, Stephen	Ward	14	"	3/4	1897	" " " "	69

TRIBAL ENROLLMENT OF PARENTS

	NAME OF FATHER	YEAR	COUNTY	NAME OF MOTHER	YEAR	COUNTY
1	Nicholas Worcester	Dead	Pontotoc	Talonickee	Dead	Pontotoc
2	No. 1			Katie Worcester	"	"
3	No. 1			" "	"	"
4	Allen Colbert	Dead	Pontotoc	" "	"	"
5	Abel Worcester	"	Chickasaw Roll	Elizabeth "	"	
6	" "	"	" "	" "	"	
7	Jackson Perry	"	" "	Subom Perry	"	Chickasaw Roll

(NOTES)

Simeon Worcester on Chickasaw Roll as Simon Worcester
No. 3 now the wife of Tecumseh Dye, Chick 365.
" 4 "   in jail at Atoka, I.T. 11/21/02.

Sept. 2/98.

RESIDENCE: Pontotoc COUNTY CARD NO.

POST OFFICE: Waupanucka, Ind. Ter. FIELD NO.

NAME	RELATION-SHIP TO PERSON FIRST NAMED	AGE	SEX	BLOOD	TRIBAL ENROLLMENT		
					YEAR	COUNTY	PAGE
1 Wesley, Rebecca	NAMED	70	F	Full	1897	Pontotoc	50
2 Durant, Mollie	G.Dau	24	F	"	1897	"	"
3 Hawkins, Winnie	Dau of No. 2	1	F	"			

TRIBAL ENROLLMENT OF PARENTS

	NAME OF FATHER	YEAR	COUNTY	NAME OF MOTHER	YEAR	COUNTY
1	(Name Illegible)	Dead	Chickasaw Roll	(Name Illegible)	Dead	Chickasaw Roll
2	Ashome Durant	1897	Choctaw N. 1st Dist	Amy Durant	"	" "

126

Chickasaw Enrollment Cards 1898-1914
Chickasaw by Blood   Volume II

3	Kingsberry Hawkins	1896	Pontotoc	No. 2		

(NOTES)

No. 1 Died Nov. 15, 1899. proof of death filed Nov. 7, 1902.

No. 3 Born Oct. 25, 1902. enrolled Nov. 7, 1902.   *(No. 3 Dawes' Roll No. 4015)*

No. 2 is now the wife of Kingsberry Hawkins, Choctaw #304 11/3/02,

No. 2 is not marries. See testimony of May 22, 1903.

Sept. 2/98.

RESIDENCE: Choctaw Nation   **COUNTY**   **CARD NO.**

POST OFFICE: McAlester, Ind. Ter.   **FIELD NO.**

NAME	RELATION-SHIP TO PERSON FIRST NAMED	AGE	SEX	BLOOD	TRIBAL ENROLLMENT		
					YEAR	COUNTY	PAGE
1 Alberson, Ben F.	NAMED	40	M	Full	1897	Choctaw N. 1st Dist.	67
2 " Louina	Wife	21	F	Full	"	" " " "	69
3 " Solomon	Son	2mo	M	"			
4 Hays, Samuel	GrSon	1	"	3/4			

TRIBAL ENROLLMENT OF PARENTS

	NAME OF FATHER	YEAR	COUNTY	NAME OF MOTHER	YEAR	COUNTY
1	Logan Alberson	Dead	Chickasaw Roll	*(Name Illegible)*	Dead	Chickasaw Roll
2	Dave Owens	1897	Pontotoc	Peggy Owens	"	" " "
3	No. 1			No. 2		
4	Daniel Hays			No. ?		

(NOTES)

Louina Owens on Roll as Louina Owen

No. 3 Enrolled Nov. 3/99.

No. 4 born Jan. 21, 1902. Application received May 10, 1905   *(No. 4 Dawes' Roll No. 4959)*

under Act of Congress approved March *(illegible)*

No. 4's father Daniel Hays on Chick card No. 111

final roll *(remainder illegible)*

Sept. 2, 1898.

RESIDENCE: Pontotoc   **COUNTY**   **CARD NO.**

POST OFFICE: Owl, Ind. Ter.   **FIELD NO.**

NAME	RELATION-SHIP TO PERSON FIRST NAMED	AGE	SEX	BLOOD	TRIBAL ENROLLMENT		
					YEAR	COUNTY	PAGE
1 Benton, Wesley	NAMED	23	M	Full	1897	Pontotoc	42

127

TRIBAL ENROLLMENT OF PARENTS							
NAME OF FATHER	YEAR	COUNTY	NAME OF MOTHER		YEAR	COUNTY	
1 Davis Benton	Dead	Chickasaw roll	Louisa Benton		1897	Pontotoc	

(NOTES)

Enrolled in Pontotoc Co, but now living near Owl, Choctaw Nation.

Sept. 2, 1898.

RESIDENCE: Choctaw Nation	COUNTY				CARD NO.		
POST OFFICE: Legal, Ind. Ter.					FIELD NO.		

NAME	RELATION-SHIP TO PERSON FIRST NAMED	AGE	SEX	BLOOD	TRIBAL ENROLLMENT		
					YEAR	COUNTY	PAGE
1 Leedy, James T.	NAMED	52	M	I.W.	1897	Choctaw N. 1st Dist.	82
2 " ~~Mary~~	~~Wife~~	~~53~~	F	~~1/2~~	"	" " " "	~~73~~
3 " James, Jr.	Son	13	M	1/4	"	" " " "	73

TRIBAL ENROLLMENT OF PARENTS							
NAME OF FATHER	YEAR	COUNTY	NAME OF MOTHER		YEAR	COUNTY	
1 Josiah Leedy	Dead	Non citizen	Margaret Leedy			non citizen	
2 ~~Doran Watkins~~	"	~~Chickasaw Roll~~	~~Dissy Watkins~~		~~Dead~~	~~Chickasaw Roll~~	
3 No. 1			No. 2				

(NOTES)

No. 2 Died July 18, 1902. proof of death filed Nov. 25, 1902.
Affidavit of F.M. Hare as to marriage of Nos. 1 and 2 filed Nov. 28, 1902.
No. 1 Mar. 19, 1904 Decision prepared. See decision of June 13/04.   *(No. 1 Dawes' Roll No. 380)*

P.O. Coalgate, I.T. 12/20/02   Sept. 2, 1898.

RESIDENCE: Pontotoc	COUNTY				CARD NO.		
POST OFFICE: Stonewall, Ind. Ter.					FIELD NO.		

NAME	RELATION-SHIP TO PERSON FIRST NAMED	AGE	SEX	BLOOD	TRIBAL ENROLLMENT		
					YEAR	COUNTY	PAGE
1 Stout, Jeff	NAMED	28	M	1/2	1897	Pontotoc	49
2 " Tena Thomas	Wife	23	F	Full	1897	Tishomingo	29
3 " Alice	Dau	11mo	"	3/4			
4 Thomas, Minnie	Step-Dau	8	"	Full	1897	Tishomingo	29
5 Stout, Liza	Dau	2mo	"	3/4			
6 " Lonzo	Son	5mo	M	3/4			

TRIBAL ENROLLMENT OF PARENTS							
NAME OF FATHER	YEAR	COUNTY	NAME OF MOTHER		YEAR	COUNTY	
1 Boren Stout	Dead	Chickasaw roll	Louisa Stout		Dead	Chickasaw Roll	

2	Butice	"	"	"	Susey Butice		"	"
3	No. 1				No. 2			
4	Ben Thomas	Dead	Tishomingo		No. 2			
5	No. 1				No. 2			
6	No. 1				No. 2			

(NOTES)

No. 2 on Chickasaw roll as Tena Thomas

No. 2 is mother of Isaac Thomas on Chickasaw card #68

No. 6 Born March 15, 1902. Enrolled Aug. 9, 1902.

No. 3 Died Nov. 10, 1898. Proof of death filed Nov. 12, 1902.

No. 5 Enrolled Nov. 3/99.

P.O. Franks, I.T. 8/9/02.

RESIDENCE: Pontotoc COUNTY						CARD NO.		
POST OFFICE: Roff, Ind. Ter.						FIELD NO.		
NAME	RELATION-SHIP TO PERSON FIRST NAMED	AGE	SEX	BLOOD	TRIBAL ENROLLMENT			
					YEAR	COUNTY	PAGE	
1 Rodke, Lawrence	NAMED	45	M	I.W.	1897	Pontotoc	80	
2 " Lizzie	Wife	26	F	3/4	1897	"	48	
3 " Leo	Son	8	M	3/8	1897	"	48	
4 " Loreno	Dau	5	F	3/8	1897	"	48	
5 " David L.	Son	2	M	3/8	1897	"	48	

TRIBAL ENROLLMENT OF PARENTS

	NAME OF FATHER	YEAR	COUNTY	NAME OF MOTHER	YEAR	COUNTY
1	John Rodke	Dead	non citizen	Apalonia	Dead	non citizen
2	Frank Perry	"	Pontotoc	Margaret Perry	1897	Pontotoc
3	No. 1			No. 2		
4	No. 1			No. 2		
5	No. 1			No. 2		

(NOTES)

No. 1 on Chickasaw roll as Lawrence Rodky   *(No. 1 Dawes' Roll No. 2)*

No. 4 "   "   1897 roll as Lareno May Rodke.

Sept. 2/98.

RESIDENCE: Pontotc   COUNTY   CARD No.

POST OFFICE: Conway, Ind. Ter.   FIELD No.

	NAME	RELATIONSHIP TO PERSON FIRST	AGE	SEX	BLOOD	TRIBAL ENROLLMENT		
						YEAR	COUNTY	PAGE
1	Wright, William	NAMED	29	M	Full	1897	Pontotoc	44
2	" Serena Fulsom	Wife	19	F	"	1897	"	46

TRIBAL ENROLLMENT OF PARENTS

	NAME OF FATHER	YEAR	COUNTY	NAME OF MOTHER	YEAR	COUNTY
1	Hickatubby	Dead	Pontotoc	Martha	1897	Pontotoc
2	Lyman Fulsom	1897	"	Lena Fulsom	Dead	"

(NOTES)

No. 2 on Chickasaw roll as Serena Fulsome.

RESIDENCE: Choctaw Nation   COUNTY   CARD No.

POST OFFICE: Owl, Ind. Ter.   FIELD No.

	NAME	RELATIONSHIP TO PERSON FIRST	AGE	SEX	BLOOD	TRIBAL ENROLLMENT		
						YEAR	COUNTY	PAGE
1	Underwood, Caroline	NAMED	?	F	Full	1897	Choctaw N. 3rd Dist.	73
2	" Johnie	Son	18	M	"	1897	" " " "	73
3	Burris, Logan	"	13	"	"	1897	" " " "	73
4	Jones, Susan	Dau	30	F	"	1897	" " " "	73
5	Roberts, Elias	Grand Son	6	M	1/2			
6	Benton, Agnes	Grand Dau	1	F	Full			
7	~~Jones, Nettie~~	~~Grand Dau~~	~~8mo~~	~~F~~	~~1/2~~			

TRIBAL ENROLLMENT OF PARENTS

	NAME OF FATHER	YEAR	COUNTY	NAME OF MOTHER	YEAR	COUNTY
1	I-ho-ka-tub-by	Dead	Chickasaw roll	Nikey	Dead	Chickasaw Roll
2	la-pe-sa	"	" " "	No. 1		
3	Aleck Burris	"	" " "	No. 1		
4	Bond Underwood	"	Pontotoc	No. 1		
5	Ramsey Roberts		Choctaw Roll	No. 4		
6	Louie Benton	1897	Choctaw N. 3rd Dist	No. 4		
7	~~W.E. Jones~~			~~No. 4~~		

(NOTES)

No. 7 Died Dec. 7, 1901. Enrollment cancelled By Dept. July 2, 1904.
       Elias Roberts is on Choctaw Census Roll No. 2, Page 414 as Elias Ramsey.
       he lives with his mother.
No. 3 Died March 15, 1902; Evidence of death filed July 14, 1902.

Chickasaw Enrollment Cards 1898-1914
Chickasaw by Blood   Volume II

Elias Roberts on Choctaw Roll 1896, Atoka County No. 10964 as Elias Ramsey.
Evidence of birth of No. 5 received and filed July 23, 1902.
    Jany 19/00 No. 4 is now Susan Jones
No. 7 Enrolled January 15, 1901.
No. 1 Died June 20, 1901. Proof of death filed Nov. 22, 1902.
No. 6 Died Aug 11, 1901. Proof of death filed Nov. 22, 1902.
No. 7 Died Dec. 7, 1901. Proof of death filed Nov. 22, 1902.
No. 5 transferred to Choctaw card #4226 with father Ramsey Roberts Dec. 19, 02.

Sept. 2/98.

RESIDENCE: Pontotoc COUNTY					CARD NO.		
POST OFFICE: Conner, Ind. Ter.					FIELD NO.		
NAME	RELATION-SHIP TO PERSON FIRST NAMED	AGE	SEX	BLOOD	TRIBAL ENROLLMENT		
					YEAR	COUNTY	PAGE
1 Loman, Eli	NAMED	26	M	Full	1897	Pontotoc	55

TRIBAL ENROLLMENT OF PARENTS

NAME OF FATHER	YEAR	COUNTY	NAME OF MOTHER	YEAR	COUNTY
1 Hawkins Loman	Dead	Chickasaw Roll	Bicey Loman	Dead	Chickasaw roll

(NOTES)
No. 1 was the husband of Nannie *(Illegible)* Chickaaw Card #855 at the time of her
    death June 27, 1902. Sept. 4, 1902.
No. 1 Died Oct. 25, 1902. Proof of death filed Nov. 7, 1902.

Sept. 2/98.

RESIDENCE: Choctaw Nation COUNTY					CARD NO.		
POST OFFICE: Sitre, Ind. Ter.					FIELD NO.		
NAME	RELATION-SHIP TO PERSON FIRST NAMED	AGE	SEX	BLOOD	TRIBAL ENROLLMENT		
					YEAR	COUNTY	PAGE
4 ~~Killercase, Charlotte~~	NAMED	~~35~~	~~F~~	~~Full~~	~~1897~~	~~Pontotoc~~	~~44~~
2 Porter, Franklin	Son	5	M	"	1897	"	44

TRIBAL ENROLLMENT OF PARENTS

NAME OF FATHER	YEAR	COUNTY	NAME OF MOTHER	YEAR	COUNTY
4 ~~Ellis~~	~~Dead~~	~~Chickasaw Roll~~	~~(Name Illegible)~~	~~Dead~~	~~Chickasaw Roll~~
2 *(Name Illegible)*	1897	Pontotoc	No. 1		

(NOTES)
(Entry illegible)
No. 1 died in February 1900; Enrollment cancelled *(remainder illegible)*

Sept. 2/98.

131

Chickasaw Enrollment Cards 1898-1914
Chickasaw by Blood   Volume II

RESIDENCE: Pontotoc COUNTY   CARD NO.

POST OFFICE: Stonewall, Ind. Ter.   FIELD NO.

	NAME	RELATION-SHIP TO PERSON FIRST NAMED	AGE	SEX	BLOOD	TRIBAL ENROLLMENT		
						YEAR	COUNTY	PAGE
1	Easter	NAMED	40	F	Full	1897	Pontotoc	40
2	Colbert, Wilburn	Son	4	M	"	1897	"	40
3	Darin, Markham	"	12	"	"	1897	"	40
4	Stephen, Gano	"	7	"	"	1897	"	40
5	Stephen, Liney	Dau	8	F	"	1897	"	97
6	Wright, Frank	Son	5mo	M	"			

TRIBAL ENROLLMENT OF PARENTS

	NAME OF FATHER	YEAR	COUNTY	NAME OF MOTHER	YEAR	COUNTY
1	Amos-pa-stubby	Dead	Chickasaw Roll	Lucy	1897	Pontotoc
2	Davis Colbert	"	Pontotoc	No. 1		
3	Richard Darin	1897	"	No. 1		
4	Albert Stephen	Dead	"	No. 1		
5	" "	"	"	No. 1		
6	William Wright		"	No. 1		

(NOTES)

Markham Darin on Chickasaw roll as Marker Darin

No. 5 enrolled Aug./99.

No. 5 on 1893 Roll page 204 as Linsy Stephen

" 5 " 1896 " " 97 " Linsey Stephens.

Sept. 2/98.

RESIDENCE: Choctaw Nation COUNTY   CARD NO.

POST OFFICE: Susanna, Ind. Ter.   FIELD NO.

	NAME	RELATION-SHIP TO PERSON FIRST NAMED	AGE	SEX	BLOOD	TRIBAL ENROLLMENT		
						YEAR	COUNTY	PAGE
1	Brown, Robert	NAMED	56	M	Full	1897	Choctaw N. 1st Dist.	69

TRIBAL ENROLLMENT OF PARENTS

	NAME OF FATHER	YEAR	COUNTY	NAME OF MOTHER	YEAR	COUNTY
1	Te-to-he	Dead	Chickasaw Roll	So-??-cha	Dead	Chickasaw Roll

(NOTES)

Sept. 2/98.

Chickasaw Enrollment Cards 1898-1914
Chickasaw by Blood   Volume II

	RESIDENCE: Choctaw Nation COUNTY	CARD NO.						
	POST OFFICE: McAlester, Ind. Ter.		FIELD NO.					

	NAME	RELATION-PSHIP TO PERSON FIRST NAMED	AGE	SEX	BLOOD	TRIBAL ENROLLMENT		
						YEAR	COUNTY	PAGE
1	Pusley, Irena	NAMED	30	F	3/4	1897	Choctaw N. 1st Dist	67
2	" Harriet	Dau	1	"	3/4			
3	Davis, Julius	Son	9	M	3/8	1897	Choctaw N. 1st Dist.	69
4	Arpealer, Melvina	Dau	?	F	3/8			

	TRIBAL ENROLLMENT OF PARENTS						
	NAME OF FATHER	YEAR	COUNTY	NAME OF MOTHER	YEAR	COUNTY
1	Forbus	Dead	Chickasaw Roll	Harriet	Dead	Chickasaw Roll
2	Allington Pusley		Choctaw Citz	No. 1		
3	Audie Davis			No. 1		
4	William *(Illegible)*			No. 1		

(NOTES)

Irena Pusley wife of Allington Pusley Tobuckey Co Roll Choctaw Nation
" " on Chickasaw Roll as Irena McGee.
Julius Davis on Chickasaw Roll as Julia Davis
Ellen Cole is guardian of No. 2 and appeared before the Commission at South McAlester, Dec. 23, *(illegible)*
No. 2 Born March 29, 1896, proof of birth filed March 6, 1903.
No. 4 born July 3, 1901. Application received Apl. 21, 1905 under Act of Congress, approved
    March 3, 1905.   *(No. 4 Dawes' Roll No. 4958)*

Sept. 2/98.

	RESIDENCE: Choctaw Nation COUNTY	CARD NO.						
	POST OFFICE: South McAlester, Ind. Ter.		FIELD NO.					

	NAME	RELATION-SHIP TO PERSON FIRST NAMED	AGE	SEX	BLOOD	TRIBAL ENROLLMENT		
						YEAR	COUNTY	PAGE
1	Arpealer, William	NAMED	45	M	Full	1897	Choctaw N. 1st Dist.	68
2	" Sippy	Wife	38	F	1/2	1897	" " " "	68
3	" Sophia	Dau	18	"	3/4	1897	" " " "	68
4	" Lyntch	Son	15	M	3/4	1897	" " " "	68
5	" Nellie	Dau	9	F	3/4	1897	" " " "	69
6	" Katie	"	4	"	3/4	1897	" " " "	69
7	" Noley	"	1	"	3/4		" " " "	
8	Taylor, Green	Ward	4	M	1/2	1897	" " " "	69

Chickasaw Enrollment Cards 1898-1914
Chickasaw by Blood   Volume II

TRIBAL ENROLLMENT OF PARENTS

	NAME OF FATHER	YEAR	COUNTY	NAME OF MOTHER	YEAR	COUNTY
1	Arpaler Tubby	Dead	Chickasaw Roll	Charlotte	Dead	Chickasaw Roll
2	Abel Worcester	"	" "	Nawsey	"	Choctaw "
3	No. 1			No. 2		
4	No. 1			No. 2		
5	No. 1			No. 2		
6	No. 1			No. 2		
7	No. 1			No. 2		
8	Ben Nail		Choctaw Roll	I-sa-ben-ta	Dead	Chickasaw Roll

(NOTES)

No. 7 correct name is Noley. See testimony taken Jan. 16, 1905.   *(No. 7 Dawes' Roll No. 4930)*

No. 7 born July 13, 1897; proof of birth filed *(illegible)*

Sept. 2/98.

RESIDENCE: Choctaw Nation   COUNTY   CARD NO.

POST OFFICE: Citra, Ind. Ter.   FIELD NO.

	NAME	RELATION-SHIP TO PERSON FIRST NAMED	AGE	SEX	BLOOD	TRIBAL ENROLLMENT		
						YEAR	COUNTY	PAGE
1	Shield, Mandy	NAMED	22	F	Full	1897	Pontotoc	46
2	" Jacob	Son	3	M	"	1897	"	46
3	" Esau	"	1	"	"			

TRIBAL ENROLLMENT OF PARENTS

	NAME OF FATHER	YEAR	COUNTY	NAME OF MOTHER	YEAR	COUNTY
1	Nicholas Jones	Dead	Chickasaw Roll	Louisa	1897	Pontotoc
2	Simeon	1897	Pontotoc	No. 1		
3	"			No. 1		

(NOTES)

No. 3 born September 25, 1902. Application received April 29, 1905   *(No. 3 Dawes' Roll No. 4957)*
under Act of Congress approved March 5, 1905.

Sept. 2/98.

RESIDENCE: Choctaw Nation   COUNTY   CARD NO.

POST OFFICE: South McAlester, Ind. Ter.   FIELD NO.

	NAME	RELATION-SHIP TO PERSON FIRST NAMED	AGE	SEX	BLOOD	TRIBAL ENROLLMENT		
						YEAR	COUNTY	PAGE
1	Folsom, Phoebie	NAMED	32	F	Full	1897	Choctaw N. 1st Dist.	69
2	Nail, George	Son	16	M	"	1897	" " " "	69

TRIBAL ENROLLMENT OF PARENTS

	NAME OF FATHER	YEAR	COUNTY	NAME OF MOTHER	YEAR	COUNTY
1	Mahenneh	Dead	Chickasaw Roll	Charlehneh	Dead	Chickasaw roll
2	Nail	"	" "	No. 1		

(NOTES)

Phoebie Folsom is the wife of Lyman Folsom Choctaw Card No. 17,

Sept. 2/98.

RESIDENCE: Pontotoc   COUNTY   CARD NO.

POST OFFICE: Stonewall, Ind. Ter.   FIELD NO.

	NAME	RELATION-SHIP TO PERSON FIRST NAMED	AGE	SEX	BLOOD	TRIBAL ENROLLMENT		
						YEAR	COUNTY	PAGE
1	Reed, Frank	NAMED	37	M	Full	1897	Pontotoc	51
2	" Icy	Wife	33	F	"	1897	"	51
3	" Jincy	Dau	11	"	"	1897	"	51
4	" ~~Wilson~~	~~Son~~	~~7~~	~~M~~	~~"~~	~~1897~~	~~"~~	~~51~~
5	Blunt, Benson	Step Son	15	"	"	1897	"	51
6	Reed, Dina	Dau	13	F	"	1897	"	51
7	" Edmon	Son	9	M	"	1897	"	51
8	" Ivan	Son	5	M	"			

TRIBAL ENROLLMENT OF PARENTS

	NAME OF FATHER	YEAR	COUNTY	NAME OF MOTHER	YEAR	COUNTY
1	E-mo-nubby	Dead	Chickasaw Roll	Mi-e-cha	1897	Pontotoc
2	Wilson Alexander	"	" "	Ro-E-ho-ke	1897	"
3	No. 1			Si-sey	Dead	Chickasaw roll
4	~~No. 1~~			~~No. 2~~		
5	Simon Blunt	Dead	Chickasaw Roll	No. 2		
6	Jackson Reed	"	" "	No. 2		
7	" "	"	" "	No. 2		
8	No. 1			No. 2		

(NOTES)

No. 4 Died July 25, 1899, Proof filed June 28, 1901.
No. 5 Died Feby 7, 1902. Proof of death filed April 19, 1902.
Evidence of birth of No. 8 received and filed April 19, 1902.
From Card No. D.2 Aug. 28/99.

P.O. Pontotoc, Ind. Ter.   Sept. 2/98.

	RESIDENCE: Pontotoc COUNTY					CARD NO.			
	POST OFFICE: Waupanuka, Ind. Ter.					FIELD NO.			
04	Cope, I.T. 9/9- NAME	RELATION- SHIP TO PERSON FIRST NAMED	AGE	SEX	BLOOD	TRIBAL ENROLLMENT			
						YEAR	COUNTY	PAGE	
1	Wells, Willard W.	NAMED	29	M	1/16	1897	Pontotoc	49	
2	" W.W. Jr.	Son	9	"	1/32	1897	"	49	
3	" James F.	"	7	"	1/32	1897	"	49	
4	" Claude W.	"	5	"	1/32	1897	"	49	
5	" Ida L.	Dau	3	F	1/32	1897	"	49	
6	" Charles M	Son	1	M	1/32	~~1897~~	"	~~90~~	
7	" Norman	"	2mo	"	1/32				
8	" Robert L.	"	2mo	"	1/32				

TRIBAL ENROLLMENT OF PARENTS

	NAME OF FATHER	YEAR	COUNTY	NAME OF MOTHER	YEAR	COUNTY	
1	Frank K. Wells	Dead	Non Citizen	Malissa Nesbit	Dead	Chickasaw roll	
2	No. 1			Lula C. Wells		Non Citizen	
3	No. 1			" " "		" "	
4	No. 1			" " "		" "	
5	No. 1			" " "		" "	
6	No. 1			" " "		" "	
7	No. 1			" " "		" "	
8	No. 1			" " "		" "	

(NOTES)

Decendants of John McLish.
No. 3 on Chickasaw roll as J.F. Wells, Jr.
No. 4 "   "   "   " C.W. Wells.
No. 5 "   "   "   " I.L. Wells.
No. 6 "   "   "   " C.M. Wells.   *(No. 6 Dawes'Roll No. 4043)*
No. 6 proof of birth received and filed Sept. 13, 1902.
Nos. 7 and 8 enrolled Nov. 3/99.

P.O. Seems to be Darthie, I.T. 9/19/02
P.O. Cope I.T. 8/10-04.   Sept. 2/98.

	RESIDENCE: Choctaw Nation COUNTY					CARD NO.			
	POST OFFICE: Sitre, Ind. Ter.					FIELD NO.			
	NAME	RELATION- SHIP TO PERSON FIRST NAMED	AGE	SEX	BLOOD	TRIBAL ENROLLMENT			
						YEAR	COUNTY	PAGE	
1	Brown, Melisia	NAMED	28	F	1/2	1897	Pontotoc	44	

2	Wolfe, Mary	Dau	4	F	3/4	1897	"	44
3	Shields, Ennet	"	1	"	1/2			

TRIBAL ENROLLMENT OF PARENTS

	NAME OF FATHER	YEAR	COUNTY	NAME OF MOTHER	YEAR	COUNTY
1	Hudson	Dead	Creek Citz	Ja-ho-ye	Dead	Chickasaw roll
2	Jesse Wolfe		Pontotoc	No. 1		
3	Henry Shields		"	"		

(NOTES)

No. 3 born June 8, 1902. Application received May 1, 1905. under Act of Congress approved March 3, 1905. Father of No. 3 is on Chick card No. 789, final roll No. 2343.

(No. 3 Dawes' Roll No. 4967)

Sept. 2/98.

RESIDENCE: Pontotoc	***COUNTY***				***CARD NO.***			
POST OFFICE: Waupanucka, Ind. Ter.					***FIELD NO.***			

	NAME	RELATION-SHIP TO PERSON FIRST NAMED	AGE	SEX	BLOOD	TRIBAL ENROLLMENT		
						YEAR	COUNTY	PAGE
~~1~~	~~Emuhimtubby, Mina~~		~~40~~	~~F~~	~~Full~~	~~1897~~	~~Pontotoc~~	~~51~~

TRIBAL ENROLLMENT OF PARENTS

	NAME OF FATHER	YEAR	COUNTY	NAME OF MOTHER	YEAR	COUNTY
~~1~~	~~*(Name Illegible)*~~			~~*(Name Illegible)*~~	~~Dead~~	~~Chickasaw roll~~

(NOTES)

No. 1 died in August 1897, proof of death filed *(illegible)*

Sept. 2/98.

RESIDENCE: Pontotoc	***COUNTY***				***CARD NO.***			
POST OFFICE: Waupanuka, Ind. Ter.					***FIELD NO.***			

	NAME	RELATION-SHIP TO PERSON FIRST NAMED	AGE	SEX	BLOOD	TRIBAL ENROLLMENT		
						YEAR	COUNTY	PAGE
1	Greenwood, Sarah		58	F	1/2	1897	Pontotoc	51
2	" Thos. W.	Son	28	M	3/4	1897	"	56
3	" Mattie	Dau	26	F	3/4	1897	"	51

TRIBAL ENROLLMENT OF PARENTS

	NAME OF FATHER	YEAR	COUNTY	NAME OF MOTHER	YEAR	COUNTY
1	*(Name Illegible)*	Dead	Choctaw Citz	*(Name Illegible)*	Dead	Chickasaw Roll
2	Harris Greenwood	"	Chickasaw Roll	No. 1		
3	" "	"	" "	No. 1		

(NOTES)

No. 2 on Chickasaw roll as T.W. Greenwood.

Sept. 2/98.

RESIDENCE: Choctaw Nation	COUNTY				CARD NO.			
POST OFFICE: McAlester, Ind. Ter.					FIELD NO.			
NAME	RELATION-SHIP TO PERSON FIRST NAMED	AGE	SEX	BLOOD	TRIBAL ENROLLMENT			
					YEAR	COUNTY		PAGE
1 Dana, Peter	NAMED	34	M	1/2	1897	Choctaw N. 1st Dist.		68
2 " Agnes	Dau	6	F	3/4	1897	" " " "		68
3 Alberson, Johnie	Ward	9	M	Full	1897	" " " "		69

	TRIBAL ENROLLMENT OF PARENTS						
NAME OF FATHER	YEAR	COUNTY	NAME OF MOTHER	YEAR	COUNTY		
1 Tonney	Dead	Chickasaw Freed.	Mintehoya	Dead	Chickasaw Roll		
2 No. 1			Sena	"	" "		
3 Ben Alberson	1897	Choctaw N. 1st Dist.	Peggy	"	" "		

(NOTES)

Johnie Alberson on roll as Johnie Brown.

Sept. 2/98.

RESIDENCE: Pontotoc	COUNTY				CARD NO.			
POST OFFICE: Conway, Ind. Ter.					FIELD NO.			
NAME	RELATION-SHIP TO PERSON FIRST NAMED	AGE	SEX	BLOOD	TRIBAL ENROLLMENT			
					YEAR	COUNTY		PAGE
1 Crosbey, Annie	NAMED	18	F	1/2	1897	Pontotoc		44

	TRIBAL ENROLLMENT OF PARENTS						
NAME OF FATHER	YEAR	COUNTY	NAME OF MOTHER	YEAR	COUNTY		
1 Walter Burns (I.W.)	1897	Pickens	Elizabeth Fulsom	Dead	Chickasaw roll		

(NOTES)

No. 1 on Chickasaw roll as Annie Burnes
No. 1 is now wife of William E. Nutt on Chickasaw Card #1542
No. 1 was wife of Charles Crosby on Chickasaw Card #D134.
No. 1 is now wife of William E. Nutt, on Chickasaw Card #1542.
For evidence of marriage of No. 1 and W.E. Nutt see Jacket #1542.

Sept. 2/98.

Chickasaw Enrollment Cards 1898-1914
Chickasaw by Blood   Volume II

	RESIDENCE: Pontotoc COUNTY					CARD NO.		
	POST OFFICE: Stonewall, Ind. Ter.					FIELD NO.		

	NAME	RELATION-SHIP TO PERSON FIRST NAMED	AGE	SEX	BLOOD	TRIBAL ENROLLMENT		
						YEAR	COUNTY	PAGE
1	Porter, Joe	NAMED	29	M	Full	1897	Pontotoc	58
2	" Elsie	Wife	28	F	1/2	1897	"	58
3	" Mary	Dau	5	"	1/2	1897	"	58
4	" Herbert	Son	10	M	1/2	1897	"	89
5	" Hamp.	"	8	"	1/2	1897	"	89
6	" Mollie	Mother	64	F	Full	1897	"	58

TRIBAL ENROLLMENT OF PARENTS

	NAME OF FATHER	YEAR	COUNTY	NAME OF MOTHER	YEAR	COUNTY
1	Henderson Porter	Dead	Chickasaw roll	Molly Porter	1897	Pontotoc
2	Jackson		Cherokee Citz	Liza	Dead	Chickasaw roll
3	No. 1			Katie	"	Non Citizen
4	No. 1			"	"	" "
5	No. 1			"	"	" "
6	Oklahabey	Dead	Chickasaw Roll	Panhahoya	"	Chickasaw Roll

(NOTES)

No. 4 Also on 1897 roll Page 96 as Hobart Porter.
No. 5 "   " 1897 "   " 96 " Hamp.   "
No. 6 "   " 1897 "   " 96 " Millie   "
No. 4 is identified on page 183 of 1893 pay roll as Hobbert Porter.
No. 5 is identified on page 183 of 1893 pay roll as Hamp Porter.

Sept. 2/98.

	RESIDENCE: Pontotoc COUNTY					CARD NO.		
	POST OFFICE: Conway Ind. Ter.					FIELD NO.		

	NAME	RELATION-SHIP TO PERSON FIRST NAMED	AGE	SEX	BLOOD	TRIBAL ENROLLMENT		
						YEAR	COUNTY	PAGE
1	Lewis, Benton	NAMED	28	M	Full	1897	Pontotoc	47
2	" Polly	Wife	24	F	"	1897	"	47
3	" Edmon	Son	6	M	"	1897	"	47
4	" Susan	Dau	4	F	"	1897	"	47
5	" Maggie	"	2	F	"	1897	II	47

TRIBAL ENROLLMENT OF PARENTS

	NAME OF FATHER	YEAR	COUNTY	NAME OF MOTHER	YEAR	COUNTY
1	Wilson Lewis	Dead	Chickasaw Roll	Dina Lewis	Dead	Chickasaw roll

Chickasaw Enrollment Cards 1898-1914
Chickasaw by Blood Volume II

2	Pesomkatubby	"	"	"	Melinda	1897	Pontotoc
3	No. 1				No. 2		
4	No. 1				No. 2		
5	No. 1				No. 2		

(NOTES)

Maggie (No. 5) on roll as *(Name Illegible)*
No. 1 died in February 1901. Proof of death filed January 23, 1905.
No. 2 died in October, 1899. Proof of death filed January 23, 1905.

Sept. 2/98.

RESIDENCE: Pontotoc COUNTY
POST OFFICE: Ada, Ind. Ter.

CARD NO.
FIELD NO.

NAME	RELATION-SHIP TO PERSON FIRST NAMED	AGE	SEX	BLOOD	TRIBAL ENROLLMENT		
					YEAR	COUNTY	PAGE
1 Hayes, Agnes	NAMED	19	F	Full	1897	Pontotoc	43
2 " Clara	Dau	2	"	1/2	1897	"	43
3 " Nora	"	1mo	"	1/2			
4 " Jseph William	Son	2mo	M	1/2			

	NAME OF FATHER	YEAR	COUNTY	NAME OF MOTHER	YEAR	COUNTY
1	Martin Melville	1897	Chickasaw Roll	Jane Melville	1897	Chickasaw Roll
2	Willie Hayes		Seminole Roll	No. 1		
3	" "		" "	No. 1		
4	" "		" "	No. 1		

(NOTES)

Agnes Hayes is the wife of Willie Hays, a Seminole on Wm Connor band roll
Clara " on Chickasaw roll as Clarence Hays.
Husband of No. 1 on Chick D.322 (6/5/1900).
No. 4 Born Sept 15, 1902. enrolled Nov. 13, 1902.   *(No. 4 Dawes'Roll No. 4942)*

RESIDENCE: Choctaw Nation COUNTY
POST OFFICE: Legal, Ind. Ter.

CARD NO.
FIELD NO.

NAME	RELATION-SHIP TO PERSON FIRST NAMED	AGE	SEX	BLOOD	TRIBAL ENROLLMENT		
					YEAR	COUNTY	PAGE
1 Juzan, Pierre	NAMED	29	M	1/4	1897	Choctaw N. 3rd Dist.	73
2 " Eliza	Sister	21	F	1/4	1897	" " " "	73

TRIBAL ENROLLMENT OF PARENTS

	NAME OF FATHER	YEAR	COUNTY	NAME OF MOTHER	YEAR	COUNTY
1	Chas. Juzan	Dead	Choctaw Citz.	Mary Leedy	1897	Choctaw N. 3rd Dist

140

Chickasaw Enrollment Cards 1898-1914
Chickasaw by Blood   Volume II

2	Chas. Juzan	"	" "	" "	1897	" " " "

(NOTES)

Pierre Juzan on Chickasaw Roll as *(Name Illegible)*
No. 2 is now the wife of Hugh A. Bradley a noncitizen 11/19/02,

P.O. Paoli, I.T. 2/26-04   Sept. 2/98.

RESIDENCE: Pontotoc   **COUNTY**   **CARD NO.**
POST OFFICE: Stonewall, Ind. Ter.   **FIELD NO.**

	NAME	RELATIONSHIP TO PERSON FIRST NAMED	AGE	SEX	BLOOD	TRIBAL ENROLLMENT		
						YEAR	COUNTY	PAGE
1	Atkins, John	NAMED	59	M	Full	1897	Pontotoc	54
2	" Hattie	Wife	55	F	"	1897	"	54
3	" Abner	Son	26	M	"	1897	"	54
4	" Susie	Dau	23	F	"	1897	"	54
5	" Abel	Son	15	M	"	1897	"	54

TRIBAL ENROLLMENT OF PARENTS

	NAME OF FATHER	YEAR	COUNTY	NAME OF MOTHER	YEAR	COUNTY
1	Tu-wah-ye	Dead	Chickasaw Roll	Sally	Dead	Chickasaw roll
2	Ya-ha-ko-che	"	" "	Thar-to	"	" "
3	No. 1			No. 2		
4	No. 1			No. 2		
5	No. 1			No. 2		

(NOTES)

John Atkins on Chickasaw Roll as John Atkin
Abel " " " " Able "
Surname of all " " *(remainder illegible)*

                                                         Sept. 2/98.

RESIDENCE: Pickens   **COUNTY**   **CARD NO.**
POST OFFICE: Alma, Ind. Ter.   **FIELD NO.**

	NAME	RELATIONSHIP TO PERSON FIRST NAMED	AGE	SEX	BLOOD	TRIBAL ENROLLMENT		
						YEAR	COUNTY	PAGE
1	Jones, D.H	NAMED	50	M	1/16	1893	Pickens	P.R.#2 120
2	Spivey, Cora M.	Wife	25	F	I.W.			

141

TRIBAL ENROLLMENT OF PARENTS						
NAME OF FATHER	YEAR	COUNTY	NAME OF MOTHER	YEAR	COUNTY
1	Aldrich Jones	Dead	Non Citizen	Elvira Love Jones	Dead	Chickasaw roll
2	S.T. McBride		Non Citizen	Martha McBride	Dead	Non Citizen

(NOTES)

On Chickasaw roll as Dave H. Jones

"   "   "   "   "   "   " Page 94.

See also Chickasaw Card D.288.

No. 2 transferred from Chickasaw D.288. June 1st 1900.

No. 2 married to Tom Spivey, a white man, in May, 1901.

See supplemental testimony taken Jan 30th 1904 and May 3, 1904.

P.O. McMillan, I.T. 2/26/03   Sept. 2/98.

RESIDENCE: Choctaw Nation   COUNTY   CARD NO.

POST OFFICE: Sitre, Ind. Ter.   FIELD NO.

NAME	RELATION-SHIP TO PERSON FIRST NAMED	AGE	SEX	BLOOD	TRIBAL ENROLLMENT		
					YEAR	COUNTY	PAGE
1 Brown, Louisa	NAMED	40	F	Full	1897	Pontotoc	44

TRIBAL ENROLLMENT OF PARENTS						
NAME OF FATHER	YEAR	COUNTY	NAME OF MOTHER	YEAR	COUNTY
1 No-yeh	Dead	Chickasaw roll	Shak-weh-keh	Dead	Chickasaw roll

(NOTES)

RESIDENCE: Pontotoc   COUNTY   CARD NO.

POST OFFICE: Pontotoc, Ind. Ter.   FIELD NO.

NAME	RELATION-SHIP TO PERSON FIRST NAMED	AGE	SEX	BLOOD	TRIBAL ENROLLMENT		
					YEAR	COUNTY	PAGE
1 Seeley, Joe	NAMED	30	M	Full	1897	Pontotoc	50
2 " Parley	Wife	26	F	"	1897	"	50
3 " Walter	Son	9	M	"	1897	"	50
4 " Alonzo	"	2	"	"	1897	"	50

TRIBAL ENROLLMENT OF PARENTS						
NAME OF FATHER	YEAR	COUNTY	NAME OF MOTHER	YEAR	COUNTY
1 Joseph Seeley	Dead	Chickasaw roll	Mary Seeley	1897	Pontotoc
2 Alonzo Green	"	" "	Louisa	1897	"
3 No. 1			No. 2		
4 No. 1			No. 2		

Chickasaw Enrollment Cards 1898-1914
Chickasaw by Blood   Volume II

(NOTES)

Sir Name on Chickasaw roll Sealy.

Sept. 2/98.

RESIDENCE: Pontotoc   **COUNTY**   **CARD NO.**
POST OFFICE: Stonewall, Ind. Ter.   **FIELD NO.**

	NAME	RELATION-SHIP TO PERSON FIRST NAMED	AGE	SEX	BLOOD	TRIBAL ENROLLMENT		
						YEAR	COUNTY	PAGE
1	Underwood, Rena	NAMED	40	F	Full	1897	Pontotoc	39
2	Thomas, Isaac	Ward	5	M	"	1897	Tishomingo	29

TRIBAL ENROLLMENT OF PARENTS

	NAME OF FATHER	YEAR	COUNTY	NAME OF MOTHER	YEAR	COUNTY
1	Parker	Dead	Chickasaw roll	Lattie	Dead	Chickasaw roll
2	Ben Thomas	"	" "	Tena Stout	1897	Tishomingo

(NOTES)

No. 2 is Son of Tena Thomas Stout on Chickasaw Card #95

Sept. 2/98.

RESIDENCE: Pontotoc   **COUNTY**   **CARD NO.**
POST OFFICE: Stonewall, Ind. Ter.   **FIELD NO.**

	NAME	RELATION-SHIP TO PERSON FIRST NAMED	AGE	SEX	BLOOD	TRIBAL ENROLLMENT		
						YEAR	COUNTY	PAGE
1	Byrd, J.W.	NAMED	30	M	Full	1897	Tishomingo	38
2	" Emma M.	Wife	18	F	"	1897	"	38
3	" Johnson	Son	2	M	"	1897	"	38
4	" Stella V	Dau	7mo	F	"			
5	" Palmer W.	Son	3mo	M	"			

TRIBAL ENROLLMENT OF PARENTS

	NAME OF FATHER	YEAR	COUNTY	NAME OF MOTHER	YEAR	COUNTY
1	Nicholas Tiashtubby	Dead	Chickasaw Roll	Sally	Dead	Chickasaw Roll
2	Wallace Underwood	"	" "	Rena Underwood	1897	Pontotoc
3	No. 1			No. 2		
4	No. 1			No. 2		
5	No. 1			No. 2		

(NOTES)

No. 2 on Chickasaw Roll as E.M. Byrd
No. 4 Enrolled Nov. 3/99.
No. 5 Born August 15, 1902; Enrolled Dec. *(illegible)*   *(No. 5 Dawes' Roll No. 4614)*

P.O. Jesse, I.T. 12/5/02

143

RESIDENCE:	Pontotoc	COUNTY					CARD NO.			
POST OFFICE:	Allen, Ind. Ter.						FIELD NO.			

	NAME	RELATION-SHIP TO PERSON FIRST NAMED	AGE	SEX	BLOOD	TRIBAL ENROLLMENT			
						YEAR	COUNTY		PAGE
1	Wolfe, Simon	NAMED	68	M	Full	1897	Pontotoc		46
2	" Charlotte	Wife	49	F	"	1897	"		46
3	" Sale	Dau	43	"	"	1897	"		46
4	Brown, Wiken	G.Son	14	M	"	1897	"		46

	TRIBAL ENROLLMENT OF PARENTS							
	NAME OF FATHER	YEAR	COUNTY	NAME OF MOTHER		YEAR	COUNTY	
1	Sani-tub-by	Dead	Chickasaw roll	Mollea		Dead	Chickasaw Roll	
2	Thompson	"	" "	Oh-te-ma-ho-ke		"	" "	
3	No. 1			Ma-ho-te		"	" "	
4	Houston Brown	1897	Chickasaw roll	No. 3				

(NOTES)

No. 1 Evidence of death filed June 30, 1902. Died Jan 11th 1902.

Sept. 2/98.

RESIDENCE:	Pontotoc	COUNTY					CARD NO.			
POST OFFICE:	Ada, Ind. Ter.						FIELD NO.			

	NAME	RELATION-SHIP TO PERSON FIRST NAMED	AGE	SEX	BLOOD	TRIBAL ENROLLMENT			
						YEAR	COUNTY		PAGE
1	Fulsome, Liza Ann	NAMED	27	F	Full	1897	Pontotoc		45

	TRIBAL ENROLLMENT OF PARENTS							
	NAME OF FATHER	YEAR	COUNTY	NAME OF MOTHER		YEAR	COUNTY	
1	Wyley Sealey	Dead	Chickasaw Roll	Ah-ka-ya-ho-ke		Dead	Chickasaw roll	

(NOTES)

No. 1 is now the wife of Albert Perry on Chickasaw Card (illegible)

Sept. 2/98.

RESIDENCE:	Pontotoc	COUNTY					CARD NO.			
POST OFFICE:	Conway, Ind. Ter.						FIELD NO.			

	NAME	RELATION-SHIP TO PERSON FIRST NAMED	AGE	SEX	BLOOD	TRIBAL ENROLLMENT			
						YEAR	COUNTY		PAGE
1	Wright, Martha	NAMED	70	F	Full	1897	Pontotoc		45

Chickasaw Enrollment Cards 1898-1914
Chickasaw by Blood   Volume II

TRIBAL ENROLLMENT OF PARENTS							
NAME OF FATHER	YEAR	COUNTY	NAME OF MOTHER		YEAR	COUNTY	
1 Thos. Frazier	Dead	Chickasaw roll	*(Name Illegible)*		Dead	Chickasaw Roll	

(NOTES)

Sept. 2/98.

RESIDENCE: Choctaw Nation   *COUNTY*   CARD NO.
POST OFFICE: Stewart, Ind. Ter.   FIELD NO.

NAME	RELATIONSHIP TO PERSON FIRST NAMED	AGE	SEX	BLOOD	TRIBAL ENROLLMENT		
					YEAR	COUNTY	PAGE
1 McLish, Leondus	NAMED	38	M	Full	1897	Choctaw N. 1st Dist.	69
2 " Sallie	Wife	30	F	"	1897	" " " "	69

TRIBAL ENROLLMENT OF PARENTS						
NAME OF FATHER	YEAR	COUNTY	NAME OF MOTHER	YEAR	COUNTY	
1 I-yar-nin-tubby	Dead	Chickasaw roll	Tos-se-yo-ke	Dead	Chickasaw Roll	
2 Chow-wis	"	" "	Ta-ma-ho-ye	"	" "	

(NOTES)

Sept. 2/98.

RESIDENCE: Choctaw Nation   *COUNTY*   CARD NO.
POST OFFICE: McAlester, Ind. Ter.   FIELD NO.

NAME	RELATIONSHIP TO PERSON FIRST NAMED	AGE	SEX	BLOOD	TRIBAL ENROLLMENT		
					YEAR	COUNTY	PAGE
1 Durant, Judias	NAMED	28	M	Full	1897	Choctaw N. 1st Dist.	67
2 " Preman J.	Son	6	"	"	1897	" " " "	67
3 " Mary	Wife	34	F	I.W.			

TRIBAL ENROLLMENT OF PARENTS						
NAME OF FATHER	YEAR	COUNTY	NAME OF MOTHER	YEAR	COUNTY	
1 Ashome Durant	1897	Choctaw N. 1st Dist	Jinsey	Dead	Chickasaw roll	
2 No. 1			Eliza	"	" "	
3 Edward Hairs	Dead	Non Citizen	Mary Jane Huff	"	Non Citizen	

(NOTES)

Preman J. Durant on Chickasaw Roll as Beman J. Durant
No. 2 transferred from Chickasaw D.449 Apr. 10, 1902
See decision of *(remainder illegible)*

P.O. Scipio, I.T. Jan 10, 1902.   Sept. 2/98.

RESIDENCE: Choctaw Nation   *COUNTY*   *CARD NO.*

POST OFFICE: McAlester, Ind. Ter.   *FIELD NO.*

NAME	RELATION-SHIP TO PERSON FIRST NAMED	AGE	SEX	BLOOD	TRIBAL ENROLLMENT		
					YEAR	COUNTY	PAGE
1 Durant, Ashome	NAMED	60	M	Full	1897	Choctaw N. 1st Dist.	67
2 " Jacob	Son	21	"	"	1897	" " " "	67
3 " Burney	"	19	"	"	1897	" " " "	67

	NAME OF FATHER	YEAR	COUNTY	NAME OF MOTHER	YEAR	COUNTY
1	An-no-kus-na	Dead	Chickasaw roll	Ko-na-ho-ye	Dead	Chickasaw roll
2	No. I			Jinsey	"	" "
3	No. I			"	"	" "

(NOTES)

No. 3 also known as Bond Durant *(remainder illegible)*

Sept. 2/98.

RESIDENCE: Choctaw Nation   *COUNTY*   *CARD NO.*

POST OFFICE: Stewart. Ind. Ter.   *FIELD NO.*

NAME	RELATION-SHIP TO PERSON FIRST NAMED	AGE	SEX	BLOOD	TRIBAL ENROLLMENT		
					YEAR	COUNTY	PAGE
1 Sealey, Adam	NAMED	23	M	Full	1897	Choctaw N. 1st Dist.	69

TRIBAL ENROLLMENT OF PARENTS

	NAME OF FATHER	YEAR	COUNTY	NAME OF MOTHER	YEAR	COUNTY
1	Abel Sealey	Dead	Chickasaw roll	Te-ma	Dead	Chickasaw roll

(NOTES)

(Notation illegible)

Sept. 2/98.

RESIDENCE: Choctaw Nation   *COUNTY*   *CARD NO.*

POST OFFICE: Stewart, Ind. Ter.   *FIELD NO.*

NAME	RELATION-SHIP TO PERSON FIRST NAMED	AGE	SEX	BLOOD	TRIBAL ENROLLMENT		
					YEAR	COUNTY	PAGE
1 Arpealer, Semaney	NAMED	27	F	Full	1897	Choctaw N. 1st Dist.	68
2 " Juliann	Dau	9	"	"	1897	" " " "	68
3 Nelson, Joseph	Son	11/2	M	"			

TRIBAL ENROLLMENT OF PARENTS

	NAME OF FATHER	YEAR	COUNTY	NAME OF MOTHER	YEAR	COUNTY
1	Stephen Orfen	Dead	Chickasaw roll	Silbey Arpealer	1897	Choctaw N. 1st Dist.

2	Jonas Arpealer	1897	Choctaw N. 1st Dist	No. 1		
3	Philip Nelson		" " " "	No. 1		

(NOTES)

No. 1 Semaney Arpealer on Chickasaw roll as Senora Arpealer *(No. 1 Dawes' Roll No. 4040)*
No. 2 Juliann " " " " " Julian "
Is not No. 3 son of Phillip Nelson on Chickasaw card #939?
No. 3 died in April 1902. Proof of death filed *(illegible)*

Sept. 2/98.

RESIDENCE: Choctaw Nation **COUNTY** **CARD NO.**
POST OFFICE: Stewart, Ind. Ter. **FIELD NO.**

	NAME	RELATION-SHIP TO PERSON FIRST NAMED	AGE	SEX	BLOOD	TRIBAL ENROLLMENT		
						YEAR	COUNTY	PAGE
1	Arpealer, Aaron		47	M	Full	1897	Choctaw N. 1st Dist.	68
2	" Silbey	Wife	52	F	"	1897	" " " "	68
3	" Gilbert H.	Son	22	M	"	1897	" " " "	68
4	Alberson, Mollie	Ward	16	F	"	1897	" " " "	69
5	" Isaac	"	14	M	"	1897	" " " "	69

TRIBAL ENROLLMENT OF PARENTS

	NAME OF FATHER	YEAR	COUNTY	NAME OF MOTHER	YEAR	COUNTY
1	Arpealer tubby	Dead	Chickasaw roll	Charlotte	Dead	Chickasaw roll
2	Ah-nos-ka-na-tubby	"	" "	O-na-ho-ye	"	" "
3	No. 1			No. 2		
4	Ben Alberson	1897	Choctaw N. 1st Dist	Peggy	Dead	Chickasaw roll
5	Peter "	Dead	Chickasaw roll	Annie	"	" "

(NOTES)

Nos. 4 and 5 are orphans living with aaron Arpealer
Mollie Alberson on Chickasaw Roll as Mollie Brown
Isaac " " " " " Isaac Nelson.

Sept. 2/98.

RESIDENCE: Pontotoc **COUNTY** **CARD NO.**
POST OFFICE: Waupanuka, Ind. Ter. **FIELD NO.**

	NAME	RELATION-SHIP TO PERSON FIRST NAMED	AGE	SEX	BLOOD	TRIBAL ENROLLMENT		
						YEAR	COUNTY	PAGE
1	Dyer, Adeline		21	F	1/2	1897	Pontotoc	51
2	Owens, Frances	Dau	4	"	1/2	1897	"	51
3	Colbert, Agnes	"	10mos	"	1/2			

Chickasaw Enrollment Cards 1898-1914
Chickasaw by Blood   Volume II

TRIBAL ENROLLMENT OF PARENTS

	NAME OF FATHER	YEAR	COUNTY	NAME OF MOTHER	YEAR	COUNTY
1	Daniel Dyer	Dead	Chickasaw roll	Louisa Miller	1897	Pontotoc
2	Solomon Owens	1897	Pontotoc	No. 1		
3	Jim Colbert	1897	"	No. 1		

(NOTES)

No. 1 on Chickasaw roll as Adaline Dyer
No. 2 "   "   " " Francis Owens
No. 2 died November 10, 1899. Proof of death filed Aug. 3, 1901.
No. 3 Died Feby 27, 1900. Proof of death filed Nov. 7, 1902.

P.O. Bynum, I.T. 11/4/02.   Sept. 2/98.

RESIDENCE: Pontotoc COUNTY   CARD NO.

POST OFFICE: Waupanuka, Ind. Ter.   FIELD NO.

	NAME	RELATION-SHIP TO PERSON FIRST	AGE	SEX	BLOOD	TRIBAL ENROLLMENT		
						YEAR	COUNTY	PAGE
1	Miller, Robert C.	NAMED	33	M	1/2	1897	Pontotoc	51
2	" Louisa	Wife	39	F	1/2	1897	"	51
3	" William	Bro	10	M	1/2	1897	Pickens	18
4	" Colbert	"	14	"	1/2	"	"	18
5	" Eula	Dau	6mo	F	1/2			

TRIBAL ENROLLMENT OF PARENTS

	NAME OF FATHER	YEAR	COUNTY	NAME OF MOTHER	YEAR	COUNTY
1	Thos Miller	Dead	Chickasaw Roll	Maria Miller	Dead	Chickasaw Roll
2	Jackson Colbert	"	" "	Sallie Colbert	"	" "
3	Thos Miller	"	" "	Maria Miller	"	" "
4	" "	"	" "	" "	"	" "
5	No. 1			No. 2		

(NOTES)

No. 2 Died November 15, 1899. Proof of death filed Aug. 3, 1901.
No. 1 Died in September 1898. Proof of death filed Aug. 5, 1901.
No. 5 Died in Dec, 1899. Proof of death filed Nov. 3, 1902.
    Enrolled No. 5 Sept. 5/99.

                                              Sept. 2/98.

Chickasaw Enrollment Cards 1898-1914
Chickasaw by Blood   Volume II

RESIDENCE: Pontotoc   COUNTY   CARD NO.
POST OFFICE: Conway, Ind. Ter.   FIELD NO.

	NAME	RELATION-SHIP TO PERSON FIRST NAMED	AGE	SEX	BLOOD	TRIBAL ENROLLMENT		
						YEAR	COUNTY	PAGE
1	Fussell, James E.	NAMED	28	M	I.W.	1897	Pontotoc	80
2	" Alice	Wife	22	F	1/2	1897	"	44
3	" Charley	Son	3	M	1/4	1897	"	44
4	" Monie	Dau	6mo	F	1/4			
5	" Lola Francis	Dau	4mo	F	1/4			

TRIBAL ENROLLMENT OF PARENTS

	NAME OF FATHER	YEAR	COUNTY	NAME OF MOTHER	YEAR	COUNTY
1	Chas Fussell		Non Citz	Fannie Fussell	Dead	Non Citz
2	Walter Burns		" "	Elizabeth Burns	"	Chickasaw Roll
3	No. 1			No. 2		
4	No. 1			No. 2		
5	No. 1			No. 2		

(NOTES)

No. 1 On Chickasaw roll as J.D. Fussell   (No. 1 Dawes' Roll No. 76)
No. 3 "   "   " " Charles "
No. 5 born Dec. 4, 1901. Enrolled April 23, 1902.
No. 4 Enrolled (illegible)

RESIDENCE: Pontotoc   COUNTY   CARD NO.
POST OFFICE: Waupanucka, Ind. Ter.   FIELD NO.

	NAME	RELATION-SHIP TO PERSON FIRST NAMED	AGE	SEX	BLOOD	TRIBAL ENROLLMENT		
						YEAR	COUNTY	PAGE
1	Cass, Lewis	NAMED	25	M	1/2	1897	Pontotoc	51
2	" Rhoda Nail	Wife	18	F	Full	1897	"	51
3	" William	Son	3mo	M	3/4			
4	" William M	Son	1mo	M	3/4			

TRIBAL ENROLLMENT OF PARENTS

	NAME OF FATHER	YEAR	COUNTY	NAME OF MOTHER	YEAR	COUNTY
1	Noel Cass	Dead	Choctaw Citz	Elsie Cass	Dead	Chickasaw roll
2	Thompson Nail	"	Chickasaw roll	Louisa Nail	1897	Pontotoc
3	No. 1			No. 2		
4	No. 1			No. 2		

(NOTES)

No. 2 on Chickasaw roll as Rhoda Nail.

No. 4 Enrolled December 26, 1900
No. 3 Died April 9, 1899. Evidence of death filed July 2nd 1902.

RESIDENCE: Pontotoc COUNTY					CARD No.		
POST OFFICE: Stonewall, Ind. Ter.					FIELD No.		

NAME	RELATION-SHIP TO PERSON FIRST NAMED	AGE	SEX	BLOOD	TRIBAL ENROLLMENT		
					YEAR	COUNTY	PAGE
1 Brown, Lillie	NAMED	22	F	Full	1897	Pontotoc	53
2 " Aaron	Son	2	M	"	1897	"	53

TRIBAL ENROLLMENT OF PARENTS							
NAME OF FATHER	YEAR	COUNTY	NAME OF MOTHER		YEAR	COUNTY	
1 Abel Brown	Dead	Chickasaw roll	Tarkarwa		Dead	Chickasaw roll	
2 Levi Brown	1897	Pontotoc	No. 1				

(NOTES)

P.O. Jesse I.T. 5/27/04

RESIDENCE: Pontotoc COUNTY					CARD No.		
POST OFFICE: Stonewall, Ind. Ter.					FIELD No.		

NAME	RELATION-SHIP TO PERSON FIRST NAMED	AGE	SEX	BLOOD	TRIBAL ENROLLMENT		
					YEAR	COUNTY	PAGE
1 Bolen, Wicey	NAMED	25	F	Full	1897	Pontotoc	52
2 " Morgan	Son	8	M	"	1897	"	52
3 " James E	"	5	"	"	1897	"	52
4 " Joseph	"	2	"	"	1897	"	52

TRIBAL ENROLLMENT OF PARENTS							
NAME OF FATHER	YEAR	COUNTY	NAME OF MOTHER		YEAR	COUNTY	
1 Ishtikona	Dead	Chickasaw roll	Shekonneha		Dead	Chickasaw roll	
2 Jenkin Bolen	"	Pontotoc	No. 1				
3 " "	"	"	No. 1				
4 " "	"	"	No. 1				

(NOTES)

Chickasaw Enrollment Cards 1898-1914
Chickasaw by Blood   Volume II

RESIDENCE: Pontotoc   COUNTY   CARD NO.

POST OFFICE: Stonewall, Ind. Ter.   FIELD NO.

NAME	RELATION-SHIP TO PERSON FIRST NAMED	AGE	SEX	BLOOD	TRIBAL ENROLLMENT		
					YEAR	COUNTY	PAGE
1 Brown, Alfred	NAMED	35	M	Full	1897	Pontotoc	53
2 " Louvina	Wife	20	F	"	1897	"	53
3 " ~~Byington~~	~~Son~~	~~20~~	~~M~~	~~"~~	~~1897~~	~~"~~	~~53~~

	TRIBAL ENROLLMENT OF PARENTS						
	NAME OF FATHER	YEAR	COUNTY	NAME OF MOTHER	YEAR	COUNTY	
1	Ishtickono	Dead	Chickasaw roll	Shekonhaha	Dead	Chickasaw roll	
2	Frank Frazier	"		Ishtarharwa	"	" "	
3	~~No.1~~			~~(Name Illegible)~~	"	" "	

(NOTES)

No. 1 Died Jany 8, 1902. Proof of death filed March 18, 1902.
No. 3 Died in July, 1901. Proof of Death filed Nov. 11, 1902.

RESIDENCE: Pontotoc   COUNTY   CARD NO.

POST OFFICE: Stonewall, Ind. Ter.   FIELD NO.

NAME	RELATION-SHIP TO PERSON FIRST NAMED	AGE	SEX	BLOOD	TRIBAL ENROLLMENT		
					YEAR	COUNTY	PAGE
1 ~~Walton, Joe~~	NAMED	~~50~~	~~M~~	~~Full~~	~~1897~~	~~Pontotoc~~	~~39~~
2 " Salina	Wife	48	F	3/4	1897	"	39

	NAME OF FATHER	YEAR	COUNTY	NAME OF MOTHER	YEAR	COUNTY	
1	~~Tashkeyoha Walton~~	~~Dead~~	~~Chickasaw roll~~	~~Chickahta Walton~~	~~Dead~~	~~Chickasaw roll~~	
2	Alfred Caldwell	"	" "	Hetty Caldwell	"	" "	

(NOTES)

No. 1 Died February 3, 1900, Evidence of death filed May 25, 1901.

RESIDENCE: Pontotoc   COUNTY   CARD NO.

POST OFFICE: Ada, Ind. Ter.   FIELD NO.

NAME	RELATION-SHIP TO PERSON FIRST NAMED	AGE	SEX	BLOOD	TRIBAL ENROLLMENT		
					YEAR	COUNTY	PAGE
1 Filmore, William	NAMED	38	M	Full	1897	Pontotoc	43
2 " Linna	Wife	38	F	I.W.			

Chickasaw Enrollment Cards 1898-1914
Chickasaw by Blood   Volume II

TRIBAL ENROLLMENT OF PARENTS

	NAME OF FATHER	YEAR	COUNTY	NAME OF MOTHER	YEAR	COUNTY
1	Nittak *(remainder illegible)*	Dead	Chickasaw roll	Louisa	1897	Pontotoc
2	Aleck Nance	"	Non Citizen	Malinda Nance	Dead	Non Citizen

(NOTES)

No. 2 is not on Chickasaw roll.   *(No. 2 Dawes' Roll No. 1)*

P.O. Maxwell, I.T.

RESIDENCE: Pontotoc COUNTY				CARD NO.			
POST OFFICE: Ada. Ind. Ter.				FIELD NO.			

	NAME	RELATION-SHIP TO PERSON FIRST NAMED	AGE	SEX	BLOOD	TRIBAL ENROLLMENT		
						YEAR	COUNTY	PAGE
1	Wesley, Stone	NAMED	27	M	Full	1897	Pontotoc	43
2	" Selina	Wife	24	F	"	1897	"	43
3	Brown, Linton	Ward	6	M	"	1897	"	53

	NAME OF FATHER	YEAR	COUNTY	NAME OF MOTHER	YEAR	COUNTY
1	Wesley Cononelstubby	Dead	Chickasaw roll	*(Name Illegible)*	Dead	Chickasaw roll
2	*(Name Illegible)*	"	" "	Annie Ishtincheyon	1897	Pontotoc
3	Harris Brown	1897	Pontotoc	Fannie Brown	1897	Pontotoc

(NOTES)

(All notations illegible)

RESIDENCE: Pontotoc COUNTY				CARD NO.			
POST OFFICE: Ada. Ind. Ter.				FIELD NO.			

	NAME	RELATION-SHIP TO PERSON FIRST NAMED	AGE	SEX	BLOOD	TRIBAL ENROLLMENT		
						YEAR	COUNTY	PAGE
1	Melville, Martin C.	NAMED	63	M	I.W.	1897	Pontotoc	80
2	" Jane Perry	Wife	61	F	Full	1897	"	43
3	" Samuel C.	Son	16	M	1/2	1897	"	43

TRIBAL ENROLLMENT OF PARENTS

	NAME OF FATHER	YEAR	COUNTY	NAME OF MOTHER	YEAR	COUNTY
1	James Melville	Dead	Non Citz	Jane Melville	Dead	Non citizen
2	Portak	"	Chickasaw roll	Phinomah	"	Chickasaw roll
3	No. 1			No. 2		

(NOTES)

No. 1 on Chickasaw roll as M.C. Melvin   *(No. 1 Dawes' Roll No. 300)*
No. 2 "   "   "   " Jane   "

152

Chickasaw Enrollment Cards 1898-1914
Chickasaw by Blood   Volume II

No. 3 "   "   "   " S.C.   "

No. 3 is now the husband of Frances Johnson on Chick, Card #142 Mch 12, 1902.

RESIDENCE: Pontotoc **COUNTY**   **CARD NO.**

POST OFFICE: Stonewall, Ind. Ter.   **FIELD NO.**

NAME	RELATION-SHIP TO PERSON FIRST NAMED	AGE	SEX	BLOOD	TRIBAL ENROLLMENT		
					YEAR	COUNTY	PAGE
1 Futishoha, Johnnie	NAMED	25	M	1/2	1897	Pontotoc	53

TRIBAL ENROLLMENT OF PARENTS

NAME OF FATHER	YEAR	COUNTY	NAME OF MOTHER	YEAR	COUNTY
1 *(Name Illegible)*		Choctaw Freedman	Shonikaka	Dead	Chickasaw roll

(NOTES)

No. 1 is now the husband of Wincy Edwards on Chickasaw Card *(illegible)* Sept. 15, *(illegible)*

P.O. Ada, I.T.

RESIDENCE: Pontotoc **COUNTY**   **CARD NO.**

POST OFFICE: Connersville, Ind. Ter.   **FIELD NO.**

NAME	RELATION-SHIP TO PERSON FIRST NAMED	AGE	SEX	BLOOD	TRIBAL ENROLLMENT		
					YEAR	COUNTY	PAGE
1 Owens, David	NAMED	50	M	Full	1897	Pontotoc	56
2 " Seely	Wife	48	F	"	1897	"	56
3 " Frank	Son	21	M	"	1897	"	56

TRIBAL ENROLLMENT OF PARENTS

NAME OF FATHER	YEAR	COUNTY	NAME OF MOTHER	YEAR	COUNTY
1 *(Name Illegible)*	Dead	Chickasaw roll	Sukey	Dead	Chickasaw roll
2 *(Name Illegible)*	"	"	"	*(Name Illegible)*	"	"	"
3 No. 1			No. 2		

(NOTES)

Sir name on Chickaaw roll is Owen.

RESIDENCE: Pontotoc **COUNTY**   **CARD NO.**

POST OFFICE: Stonewall, Ind. Ter.   **FIELD NO.**

NAME	RELATION-SHIP TO PERSON FIRST NAMED	AGE	SEX	BLOOD	TRIBAL ENROLLMENT		
					YEAR	COUNTY	PAGE
1 Burris, Colbert A.	NAMED	71	M	Full	1897	Pontotoc	40

Chickasaw Enrollment Cards 1898-1914
Chickasaw by Blood   Volume II

2	" Laura A	Wife	62	F	I.W.	1897	"		40
3	" *(Illegible)* J.	Son	19	M	1/2	1897	"		40
4	Rennie, Lula D.	Dau	17	F	1/2	1897	"		41
5	Burris, Daisy	"	13	"	1/2	1897	"		41
6	" Cecelia	"	10	"	1/2	1897	"		41
7	" Lillie B	"	8	"	1/2	1897	"		41
8	Rennie, Louise Ella	Grand Dau	3mo	F	1/4				

TRIBAL ENROLLMENT OF PARENTS

	NAME OF FATHER	YEAR	COUNTY	NAME OF MOTHER	YEAR	COUNTY
1	John Burris	Dead	Chickasaw roll	Checatah Burris	Dead	Chickasaw roll
2	*(Illegible)* Bradley	"	non Citz	*(Name Illegible)*	"	Non Citz.
3	No. 1			No. 2		
4	No. 1			No. 2		
5	No. 1			No. 2		
6	No. 1			No. 2		
7	No. 1			No. 2		
8	*(Illegible)* Rennie, Jr.		Pickens	No. 4		

(NOTES)
(All notations illegible)   *(No. 2 Dawes' Roll No. 246)*

RESIDENCE: Pontotoc **COUNTY**   **CARD NO.**
POST OFFICE: Oakman, Ind. Ter.   **FIELD NO.**

	NAME	RELATIONSHIP TO PERSON FIRST NAMED	AGE	SEX	BLOOD	TRIBAL ENROLLMENT		
						YEAR	COUNTY	PAGE
1	Alberson, Alias	NAMED	14	M	Full	1897	Pontotoc	46

TRIBAL ENROLLMENT OF PARENTS

	NAME OF FATHER	YEAR	COUNTY	NAME OF MOTHER	YEAR	COUNTY
1	*(Illegible)* Alberson	Dead	Cickasw roll	Lizzie Edwards	Dead	Chickasaw roll

(NOTES)
(All notations illegible)

RESIDENCE: Pontotoc **COUNTY**   **CARD NO.**
POST OFFICE: Oakman, Ind. Ter.   **FIELD NO.**

	NAME	RELATIONSHIP TO PERSON FIRST NAMED	AGE	SEX	BLOOD	TRIBAL ENROLLMENT		
						YEAR	COUNTY	PAGE
1	Brown, Harley	NAMED	25	M	Full	1897	Pontotoc	46

2	" Louisa	Wife	22	F	"	1897	"	46
3	" Abel	Son	6	M	"	1897	"	46
4	" Edmund	"	4	"	"	1897	"	46
5	" John	"	2	"	"	1897	"	46

TRIBAL ENROLLMENT OF PARENTS

	NAME OF FATHER	YEAR	COUNTY	NAME OF MOTHER	YEAR	COUNTY
1	William White	Dead	Chickasaw roll	Lizzie Edwards	Dead	Chickasaw roll
2	*(Name Illegible*			Suhu	"	" "
3	No. 1			No. 2		
4	No. 1			No. 2		
5	No. 1			No. 2		

(NOTES)

(All notations illegible)

RESIDENCE: Pontotoc ***COUNTY*** ***CARD NO.***
POST OFFICE: Connersville, Ind. Ter. ***FIELD NO.***

	NAME	RELATION-SHIP TO PERSON FIRST NAMED	AGE	SEX	BLOOD	TRIBAL ENROLLMENT		
						YEAR	COUNTY	PAGE
1	Grayson, Gibson		55	M	Full	1897	Pontotoc	55
2	" Ema	Dau	23	F	"	1897	"	55
3	" Felix	Son	21	M	"	1897	"	55
4	" James	"	17	"	"	1897	"	55
5	" Anna	Dau	15	F	"	1897	"	55
~~6~~	~~" George~~	~~Son~~	~~12~~	~~M~~	~~"~~	~~1897~~	~~"~~	~~55~~

TRIBAL ENROLLMENT OF PARENTS

	NAME OF FATHER	YEAR	COUNTY	NAME OF MOTHER	YEAR	COUNTY
1	Tony Grayson	Dead	Chickasaw Roll	Martha Grayson	Dead	Chickasaw roll
2	No. 1			Mary "	"	" "
3	No. 1			" "	"	" "
4	No. 1			" "	"	" "
5	No. 1			Jennie Grayson	"	" "
~~6~~	~~No. 1~~			~~" "~~	~~"~~	~~" "~~

(NOTES)

No. 1 on Chickasaw roll *(illegible)*
No. 4 " " " as *(illegible)*
No. 1 is now the husband of Lizzie Petigrew on Chickasaw Card #749, May 10, 1902.
No. 6 Died Apr 3. 1901. Proof of death filed Nov. 12, 1902.

Chickasaw Enrollment Cards 1898-1914
Chickasaw by Blood   Volume II

RESIDENCE: Pontotoc   COUNTY   CARD NO.

POST OFFICE: Ada, Ind. Ter.   FIELD NO.

NAME	RELATION-SHIP TO PERSON FIRST NAMED	AGE	SEX	BLOOD	TRIBAL ENROLLMENT		
					YEAR	COUNTY	PAGE
1 King, Wall	NAMED	28	M	Full	1897	Pontotoc	39
2 " Celian	Wife	24	F	Full	1897	"	43
3 " Patsey	Dau	6	"	Full	1897	"	43
4 " Andrew	Son	1	M	"	~~1897~~	"	~~90~~
5 " Anderson	Son	15mo	M	"			

TRIBAL ENROLLMENT OF PARENTS

NAME OF FATHER	YEAR	COUNTY	NAME OF MOTHER	YEAR	COUNTY
1 (Illegible) King	Dead	Chickasaw roll	Gracia King	Dead	Choctaw
2 (Name Illegible)	Dead	" "	(Name Illegible)	"	Chickasaw roll
3 No. 1			No. 2		
4 No. 1			No. 2		
5 No. 1			No. 2		

(NOTES)

Evidence of birth of No. 4 received and filed Sept. 19, 1902.   (No. 4 Dawes' Roll No. 4098)

No. 5 Born May 27, 1901. Enrolled (illegible)   (No. 5 Dawes' Roll No. 4099)

RESIDENCE: Pontotoc   COUNTY   CARD NO.

POST OFFICE: Ada, Ind. Ter.   FIELD NO.

NAME	RELATION-SHIP TO PERSON FIRST NAMED	AGE	SEX	BLOOD	TRIBAL ENROLLMENT		
					YEAR	COUNTY	PAGE
1 Underwood, Gabriel	NAMED	43	M	Full	1897	Pontotoc	45
2 " Nancy	Wife	41	F	"	1897	"	45
3 " Wesley	Son	15	M	"	1897	"	45
4 " Alice	Dau	14	F	"	1897	"	45
5 " Bina	"	12	"	"	1897	"	45
6 " Hagen	Son	10	M	"	1897	"	45
7 " Louis	"	8	"	"	1897	"	45
8 Gully, Jim		10	"	1/2	1897	"	45
9 Sealy, Sallie		16	F	Full	1897	"	45
10 Dyer, Dawes		1mo	M	"			
11 Sealy, Joel **DEAD**		20	"	"			
12 Underwood, Phoebe	Dau	5	F	Full			
13 Lewis, Joseph[sic]	Son of No. 9	2	M	Full			

156

	NAME OF FATHER	YEAR	COUNTY	NAME OF MOTHER	YEAR	COUNTY
1	Ish-to-?i-nah-he	Dead	Chickasaw Roll	Shinnontiche	Dead	Chickasaw Roll
2	Wiley Sealy	"	" "	Akoyohoke	"	" "
3	No. 1			No. 2		
4	No. 1			No. 2		
5	No. 1			No. 2		
6	No. 1			No. 2		
7	No. 1			No. 2		
8	Eugene Gully		non-citizen	Lizzie Ann Gully	1897	Pontotoc
9	Martin Sealy	Dead	Chickasaw Roll	Chewika Sealy	Dead	Chickasaw roll
10	Joe Dyer			No. 9		
11	Wiley Sealy	Dead	Chickasaw roll	*(Name Illegible)*	Dead	Chickasaw roll
12	*(Name Illegible)*			*(Name Illegible)*		
13	Benton Lewis		Pontotoc	No. 9		

(NOTES)

No. 3 born Aug. 1901; application *(remainder illegible)*
No. 5 on Chickasaw Roll as Bennie Underwood
No. 7 " " " " Loui "
No. 8 " " " " Jim Sealy
Evidence of birth of No. 10 received and filed April 8, 1902.
No. 11 Died Dec. 23, 1901; proof of death filed 9/18/02
" 12 on 1897 Chickasaw roll as Julia Underwood.
" 12 was first placed on Chickasaw card #D10 but no identification from tribal rolls placed on this card May 26, 1902. See letter of Gabriel Underwood.

RESIDENCE: Pontotoc ***COUNTY*** ***CARD NO.***
POST OFFICE: Stonewall, Ind. Ter. ***FIELD NO.***

	NAME	RELATIONSHIP TO PERSON FIRST NAMED	AGE	SEX	BLOOD	TRIBAL ENROLLMENT		
						YEAR	COUNTY	PAGE
1	Truax, Geo. Henry		41	M	I.W.	1897	Pontotoc	80
2	" Mary	Wife	34	F	1/2	1897	"	41
3	" Pearl	Dau	9	"	1/4	1897	"	41
4	" Ruby	"	3	"	1/4	1897	"	41
5	" William B	Son	1	M	1/4	1897	"	41
6	" *(Illegible)*	Dau	1mo	F	1/4			

TRIBAL ENROLLMENT OF PARENTS

	NAME OF FATHER	YEAR	COUNTY	NAME OF MOTHER	YEAR	COUNTY
1	John B. Truax	Dead	Non Citizen	Emily Truax	Dead	Non Citizen
2	Geo. W. Calbert		Choctaw Citz	Lizzie Calbert	"	Pontotoc

3	No. 1			No. 2		
4	No. 1			No. 2		
5	No. 1			No. 2		
6	No. 1			No. 2		

(NOTES)

(All notations illegible)   *(No. 1 Dawes' Roll No. 75)*

RESIDENCE: Pontotoc   **COUNTY**   **CARD NO.**

POST OFFICE: Stonewall, Ind. Ter.   **FIELD NO.**

NAME	RELATION-SHIP TO PERSON FIRST NAMED	AGE	SEX	BLOOD	TRIBAL ENROLLMENT		
					YEAR	COUNTY	PAGE
1 Johnson, Napoleon B.	NAMED	40	M	1/2	1897	Pontotoc	44
2 " Drucilla	Wife	30	F	I.W.	1897	"	80
3 " Leewellyn	Son	5	M	1/4	1897	"	44
4 " Gertrude	Dau	4mo	F	1/4			

	NAME OF FATHER	YEAR	COUNTY	NAME OF MOTHER	YEAR	COUNTY
1	John Johnstone (I.W.)	Dead	Chickasaw roll	Mary Johnstone	Dead	Chickasaw roll
2	John Barrett		Non citizen	Nancy Barrett	"	Non citz.
3	No. 1			No. 2		
4	No. 1			No. 2		

(NOTES)

(All notations illegible)   *(No. 2 Dawes' Roll No. 74)*

RESIDENCE: Choctaw Nation   **COUNTY**   **CARD NO.**

POST OFFICE: Savanna, Ind. Ter.   **FIELD NO.**

NAME	RELATION-SHIP TO PERSON FIRST NAMED	AGE	SEX	BLOOD	TRIBAL ENROLLMENT		
					YEAR	COUNTY	PAGE
1 ~~Alberson, Nicholas~~	NAMED	44	M	~~Full~~	~~1897~~	~~Choctaw N. 1st Dist.~~	~~64~~
2 ~~" Fannie~~	~~Sister~~	50	F	~~"~~	~~1897~~	~~" " " "~~	~~68~~

TRIBAL ENROLLMENT OF PARENTS

	NAME OF FATHER	YEAR	COUNTY	NAME OF MOTHER	YEAR	COUNTY
1	~~Logan Alberson~~	~~Dead~~	~~Chickasaw roll~~	~~Iohtenahoya~~	~~Dead~~	~~Chickasaw roll~~
2	~~" "~~	~~"~~	~~" "~~	~~"~~	~~"~~	~~" "~~

(NOTES)

No. 1 died prior to September 25, 1902
not entitled to land or money
No. 2 died prior to September 25, 1902
not entitled to land or money

Chickasaw Enrollment Cards 1898-1914
Chickasaw by Blood   Volume II

RESIDENCE: Choctaw Nation COUNTY					CARD NO.			
POST OFFICE: Savannah, Ind. Ter.					FIELD NO.			
NAME	RELATION-SHIP TO PERSON FIRST NAMED	AGE	SEX	BLOOD	TRIBAL ENROLLMENT			
					YEAR	COUNTY	PAGE	
1 Nelson, Ward	NAMED	22	M	1/2	1897	Choctaw N. 1st Dist	67	

TRIBAL ENROLLMENT OF PARENTS

NAME OF FATHER	YEAR	COUNTY	NAME OF MOTHER	YEAR	COUNTY
1 Bill Nelson	Dead	Choctaw Citz	Annie Nelson	Dead	Chickasaw roll

(NOTES)

Ward Nelson on Chickasaw roll as Wade Nelson.

RESIDENCE: Choctaw Nation COUNTY					CARD NO.			
POST OFFICE: Savannah, Ind. Ter.					FIELD NO.			
NAME	RELATION-SHIP TO PERSON FIRST NAMED	AGE	SEX	BLOOD	TRIBAL ENROLLMENT			
					YEAR	COUNTY	PAGE	
1 Sealy, Levi	NAMED	75	M	Full	1897	Choctaw N. 1st Dist	71	

TRIBAL ENROLLMENT OF PARENTS

NAME OF FATHER	YEAR	COUNTY	NAME OF MOTHER	YEAR	COUNTY
1 Harkin Sealy	Dead	Chickasaw roll	Ishte Yahoya	Dead	Chickasaw roll

(NOTES)

Take no action relative to
allotment to No. 105
See Letter File No. 8654

RESIDENCE: Pontotoc COUNTY					CARD NO.			
POST OFFICE: Stonewall, Ind. Ter.					FIELD NO.			
NAME	RELATION-SHIP TO PERSON FIRST NAMED	AGE	SEX	BLOOD	TRIBAL ENROLLMENT			
					YEAR	COUNTY	PAGE	
1 Collins, George R.	NAMED	42	M	I.W.	1897	Pontotoc	81	
2 " Wm B.	Son	9	M	1/8	1897	"	64	
3 " S.C.	"	7	"	1/8	1897	"	64	
4 " George R. Jr.	"	5	"	1/8	1897	"	64	

TRIBAL ENROLLMENT OF PARENTS

NAME OF FATHER	YEAR	COUNTY	NAME OF MOTHER	YEAR	COUNTY
1 Lafayette Collins	Dead	Non Citizen	Elizabeth Collins	Dead	Non Citizen
2 No. 1			Julia B. Collins	"	Chickasaw roll
3 No. 1			" " "	"	" "

| 4 | | No. 1 | | | Adaline Collins | | " | Pontotoc |

(NOTES)

No. 1 on Chickasaw roll as George Callins   *(No. 1 Dawes' Roll No. 245)*

    Evidence of marriage between No. 1 and mother of No. 4 received and filed Nov. 13, 1902.

P.O. Roff, I.T.

RESIDENCE:	Choctaw Nation	COUNTY			CARD NO.			
POST OFFICE:	Allen, Ind. Ter.				FIELD NO.			

NAME	RELATION-SHIP TO PERSON FIRST NAMED	AGE	SEX	BLOOD	TRIBAL ENROLLMENT		
					YEAR	COUNTY	PAGE
1 Williams, Robert		18	M	1/2	1897	Pontotoc	97

TRIBAL ENROLLMENT OF PARENTS

	NAME OF FATHER	YEAR	COUNTY	NAME OF MOTHER	YEAR	COUNTY
1	Edward Williams	Dead	Chickasaw roll	Julia Haynes	1897	Chick residing in Choctaw N. 1st Dist.

(NOTES)

On Choctaw Census Record No. 2, page 434 transferred to Chickasaw roll by Dawes Com. -

On Choctaw Roll 1896, Atoka County

    Cancelled not transferred to Choctaw Card No. 5681 Aug. 15, 1903

RESIDENCE:	Pontotoc	COUNTY			CARD NO.			
POST OFFICE:	Allen, Ind. Ter.				FIELD NO.			

NAME	RELATION-SHIP TO PERSON FIRST NAMED	AGE	SEX	BLOOD	TRIBAL ENROLLMENT		
					YEAR	COUNTY	PAGE
1 Billie, John		22	M	1/2	1897	Pontotoc	93

TRIBAL ENROLLMENT OF PARENTS

	NAME OF FATHER	YEAR	COUNTY	NAME OF MOTHER	YEAR	COUNTY
1	John Billie	Dead	Choctaw Roll	Julia Haynes	1897	Chick residing in Choctaw N. 1st Dist.

(NOTES)

Also on 1896 Choctaw Roll Tobucksy Co, Page 23, No. 905, as Jno. M. Bailey

No. 1 Died Dec. 31, 1901, proof of death filed July 30, 1902.

Sept. 2/98.

Chickasaw Enrollment Cards 1898-1914
Chickasaw by Blood   Volume II

	RESIDENCE: Pontotoc COUNTY					CARD No.			

	POST OFFICE: Stonewall, Ind. Ter.					FIELD No.			

	NAME	RELATION-SHIP TO PERSON FIRST NAMED	AGE	SEX	BLOOD	TRIBAL ENROLLMENT		
						YEAR	COUNTY	PAGE
1	Collins, Odus Lynn	NAMED	22	M	Full	1897	Pontotoc	54
2	" Cecil Cline	Son	1	"	1/2	1897	"	80

	TRIBAL ENROLLMENT OF PARENTS						
	NAME OF FATHER	YEAR	COUNTY	NAME OF MOTHER	YEAR	COUNTY
1	Judson Colline	1897	Pontotoc	Salina E. Collins	1897	Pontotoc
2	No. 1			Mamie C. Collins	Dead	Non Citizen

(NOTES)

No. 1 on Chickasaw roll as Odus L. Collins
No. 2 "   "   "   " Cecil C.   "   *(No. 2 Dawes' Roll No. 4097)*
Odus Lynn Collins was married to Mamie C. Collins under U.S. law.
  Evidence of marriage filed Sept. 24, 1902.
No. 2 Affidavit of No. 1 as to birth received and filed Sept. 24, 1902.
Affidavit of Lucy Hays, Martha Brown and Jackson Hart as to the birth of No. 2 filed Oct. 24, 02

	RESIDENCE: Pontotoc COUNTY					CARD No.			

	POST OFFICE: Stonewall, Ind. Ter.					FIELD No.			

	NAME	RELATION-SHIP TO PERSON FIRST NAMED	AGE	SEX	BLOOD	TRIBAL ENROLLMENT		
						YEAR	COUNTY	PAGE
4	Cravatt, Susan	NAMED	18	F	Full	1897	Pontotoc	58

	TRIBAL ENROLLMENT OF PARENTS						
	NAME OF FATHER	YEAR	COUNTY	NAME OF MOTHER	YEAR	COUNTY
4	Anderson Cravatt	Dead	Chickasaw roll	Louisey	Dead	Chickasaw roll

(NOTES)

On Chickasaw roll as Susan *(Illegible)*
No. 1 died in October, 1897, proof of death filed Dec. 1st *(illegible)*

	RESIDENCE: Pontotoc COUNTY					CARD No.			

	POST OFFICE: Stonewall, Ind. Ter.					FIELD No.			

	NAME	RELATION-SHIP TO PERSON FIRST NAMED	AGE	SEX	BLOOD	TRIBAL ENROLLMENT		
						YEAR	COUNTY	PAGE
4	Colbert, Wash	NAMED	45	M	Full	1897	Pontotoc	58
2	Brown, Margaret	Ward	5	F	"	1897	"	59

TRIBAL ENROLLMENT OF PARENTS						
NAME OF FATHER	YEAR	COUNTY	NAME OF MOTHER	YEAR	COUNTY
1 ~~(Illegible) Colbert~~	~~Dead~~	~~Chickasaw Roll~~	~~Il-la-ke~~	~~Dead~~	~~Chickasaw roll~~
2 George Brown	1897	Pontotoc	Elsey	1897	Pontotoc

(NOTES)

No. 1 died December 11, 1900. Evidence of death filed April 15, 1901.
Mother of No. 2 is Elsie Roberts on Chickasaw card #192. See letter G. O F #8537 1902

RESIDENCE: Pontotoc	COUNTY				CARD NO.		
POST OFFICE: Purcell, Ind. Ter.					FIELD NO.		

NAME	RELATION-SHIP TO PERSON FIRST NAMED	AGE	SEX	BLOOD	TRIBAL ENROLLMENT		
					YEAR	COUNTY	PAGE
1 Walker, David		19	M	1/16	1897	Pontotoc	63

TRIBAL ENROLLMENT OF PARENTS						
NAME OF FATHER	YEAR	COUNTY	NAME OF MOTHER	YEAR	COUNTY
1 Wm. W. Walker (I.W.)	Dead	Chickasaw roll	Sallie Walker Phillips	1897	Pontotoc

(NOTES)

RESIDENCE: Pontotoc	COUNTY				CARD NO.		
POST OFFICE: Purcell, Ind. Ter.					FIELD NO.		

NAME	RELATION-SHIP TO PERSON FIRST NAMED	AGE	SEX	BLOOD	TRIBAL ENROLLMENT		
					YEAR	COUNTY	PAGE
1 Phillips, Hill	NAMED	47	M	I.W.	1897	Pontotoc	81
2 " Sallie Walker	Wife	37	F	1/8	1897	"	63
3 " Ada	Dau	13	"	1/16	1897	"	63
4 " Louisa	"	11	"	1/16	1897	"	63
5 " Lucy	"	10	"	1/16	1897	"	63
6 " Hill, Jr.	Son	7	M	1/16	1897	"	63
7 " Elmes	"	4	"	1/16	1897	"	63
8 " Robert B.	"	2	"	1/16	1897	"	63
9 " Winona	Dau	6mo	F	1/16			

TRIBAL ENROLLMENT OF PARENTS						
NAME OF FATHER	YEAR	COUNTY	NAME OF MOTHER	YEAR	COUNTY
1 John M. Phillips	Dead	Non Citizen	Louisa Phillips	Dead	non citz
2 John Thompson	"	Cherokee Citz.	Julia Thompson	"	Chickasaw roll
3 No. 1			No. 2		
4 No. 1			No. 2		

Chickasaw Enrollment Cards 1898-1914
Chickasaw by Blood   Volume II

5	No. 1			No. 2		
6	No. 1			No. 2		
7	No. 1			No. 2		
8	No. 1			No. 2		
9	No. 1			No. 2		

(NOTES)

No. 2 on Chickasaw roll as Sallie Philips.   *(No. 1 Dawes' Roll No. 73)*
No. 8 "   "   " " Robert   "
No. 9 enrolled Aug. 3, *(illegible)*

RESIDENCE: Pontotoc   COUNTY   CARD NO.
POST OFFICE: Center, Ind. Ter.   FIELD NO.

NAME	RELATION- SHIP TO PERSON FIRST NAMED	AGE	SEX	BLOOD	TRIBAL ENROLLMENT		
					YEAR	COUNTY	PAGE
1 Hawkins, Morris H.		28	M	Full	1897	Pontotoc	47
2 " Charlie	Son	1mo	M	1/2			

TRIBAL ENROLLMENT OF PARENTS

	NAME OF FATHER	YEAR	COUNTY	NAME OF MOTHER	YEAR	COUNTY
1	Walis Hawkins	Dead	Pontotoc	Betsey Hawkins	Dead	Pontotoc
2	No. 1			Mary Hawkins		Non Citizen

(NOTES)

On Chickasaw roll as M.H. Hawkins
No. 1 is the husband of Mary Hawkins a non citizen
Evidence of marriage filed Aug. 21, 1902.
No. 2 born July 12, 1902. Enrolled Aug. 21, 1902.

P.O. Maxwell, I.T. 8/21/02.

RESIDENCE: Pontotoc   COUNTY   CARD NO.
POST OFFICE: Stonewall, Ind. Ter.   FIELD NO.

NAME	RELATION- SHIP TO PERSON FIRST NAMED	AGE	SEX	BLOOD	TRIBAL ENROLLMENT		
					YEAR	COUNTY	PAGE
1 Sealy, Eli		30	M	Full	1897	Pontotoc	52
2 " Annie	Wife	26	F	"	1897	"	52
3 " Josephine	Dau	5	"	"	1897	"	52
4 " Lora	"	4	"	"	1897	"	52
5 " Sampson	Son	5wks	M	"			

Chickasaw Enrollment Cards 1898-1914
Chickasaw by Blood   Volume II

TRIBAL ENROLLMENT OF PARENTS						
NAME OF FATHER	YEAR	COUNTY	NAME OF MOTHER	YEAR	COUNTY
1 E-yo-ke	Dead	Chickasaw roll	Liney	Dead	Chickasaw roll
2 *(Name Illegible)*	"	" "	Mi-yitch-a	1897	Pontotoc
3 No. 1			No. 2		
4 No. 1			No. 2		
5 No. 1			No. 2		

(NOTES)

Sampson Sealy born Dec 9/99 on Card No. 0. *(illegible)*
No. 5 born December 9, 1899 transferred to this card February 1, 1902.
No. 4 Died Jany 14, 1901, proof of death filed Oct. *(illegible)*

RESIDENCE: Pontotoc COUNTY						CARD NO.		
POST OFFICE: Ada, Ind. Ter.						FIELD NO.		
NAME	RELATION-SHIP TO PERSON FIRST NAMED	AGE	SEX	BLOOD	TRIBAL ENROLLMENT			
					YEAR	COUNTY	PAGE	
1 Perry, Billie	NAMED	51	M	3/4	1897	Pontotoc	47	
2 " Eliza	Wife	46	F	1/2	1897	"	47	
3 " James	Son	14	M	5/8	1897	"	47	
4 " Lee	"	11	"	5/8	1897	"	47	
5 " Tena	Dau	8	F	5/8	1897	"	47	
6 " Wilson	Son	5	M	5/8	1897	"	47	

TRIBAL ENROLLMENT OF PARENTS						
NAME OF FATHER	YEAR	COUNTY	NAME OF MOTHER	YEAR	COUNTY
1 James Perry	Dead	Chickasaw roll	Easter Perry	Dead	Chickasaw roll
2 Winchester Colbert	"	" "	Amma Leu	"	" "
3 No. 1			No. 2		
4 No. 1			No. 2		
5 No. 1			No. 2		
6 No. 1			No. 2		

(NOTES)

Eliza Perry on Chickasaw Roll as Lizzie Perry
Tena   "   "   "   " " Tena *(Illegible)*

Chickasaw Enrollment Cards 1898-1914
Chickasaw by Blood   Volume II

RESIDENCE: Pontotoc COUNTY   CARD NO.
POST OFFICE: Ada, Ind. Ter.   FIELD NO.

	NAME	RELATION-SHIP TO PERSON FIRST NAMED	AGE	SEX	BLOOD	TRIBAL ENROLLMENT		
						YEAR	COUNTY	PAGE
1	Perry, Albert	NAMED	27	M	1/2	1897	Pontotoc	47
2	" Charles Guy	Son	7	M	3/4	1897	"	47
3	" Ella	Dau	2	F	3/4	1897	"	47

TRIBAL ENROLLMENT OF PARENTS

	NAME OF FATHER	YEAR	COUNTY	NAME OF MOTHER	YEAR	COUNTY
1	Billy Perry	1897	Pontotoc	Eliza Perry	1897	Pontotoc
2	No. 1			Ellen Perry	Dead	Pontotoc
3	No. 1			" "	"	"

(NOTES)
No. 2 on Chickasaw roll as C.G. Perry
No. 1 is now the husband of Liza Ann Sealy on Chick #65.

RESIDENCE: Pontotoc COUNTY   CARD NO.
POST OFFICE: Franks, Ind. Ter.   FIELD NO.

	NAME	RELATION-SHIP TO PERSON FIRST NAMED	AGE	SEX	BLOOD	TRIBAL ENROLLMENT		
						YEAR	COUNTY	PAGE
1	Colbert, Walton	NAMED	35	M	3/4	1897	Pontotoc	50
2	" Louisa	Wife	30	F	Full	1897	"	50
3	" Amanda	Dau	11	"	7/8	1897	"	50
4	" Minnie	"	9	"	7/8	1897	"	50
5	" Frank	Son	8	M	7/8	1897	"	50
6	" Serena	Dau	6	F	7/8	1897	"	50
7	" Nora	"	4	"	7/8	1897	"	50
8	" Salina	"	2	"	7/8		"	
9	" Mack	Son	11mo	M	7/8			
10	" Zeno	"	7mo	M	7/8			
11	" Guy	"	?mo	M	7/8			

TRIBAL ENROLLMENT OF PARENTS

	NAME OF FATHER	YEAR	COUNTY	NAME OF MOTHER	YEAR	COUNTY
1	Humphrey Colbert	1897	Pontotoc	Elmica Colbert	Dead	Chickasaw roll
2	Jesse Brown	Dead	Chickasaw roll	Lucy Brown	1897	Pontotoc
3	No. 1			No. 2		
4	No. 1			No. 2		
5	No. 1			No. 2		

6	No. 1			No. 2		
7	No. 1			No. 2		
8	No. 1			No. 2		
9	No. 1			No. 2		
10	No. 1			No. 2		
11	No. 1			No. 2		

(NOTES)

No. 10 Died Oct. 8, 1900. Proof of death filed Nov. 12, 1902.
Walton Colbert on Chickasaw Roll as Wallie Colbert.
No. 3 proof of birth received and filed Nov. 15, 1902.
No. 10 Enrolled Febry 24th 1900.
Evidence of birth of No. 8 received and filed June 10, 1902; returned for further information June 11, 1902.
Evidence of birth of No. 9 received and filed June 10, 1902.
No. 11 Born July 17, 1902. Enrolled Nov. 13, 1902.   *(No. 11 Dawes' Roll No. 4096)*

RESIDENCE: Choctaw Nation   COUNTY   CARD NO.
POST OFFICE: Coalgate, Ind. Ter.   FIELD NO.

NAME	RELATION-SHIP TO PERSON FIRST NAMED	AGE	SEX	BLOOD	TRIBAL ENROLLMENT		
					YEAR	COUNTY	PAGE
1 Trentham, Henderson	NAMED	27	M	1/16	1897	Choctaw N. 1st Dist.	71
2 " Belle Smith	Wife	23	F	I.W.		Dawes Com Case #89	
3 " Lena	Dau	2	"	1/32	1897	Choctaw N. 1st Dist.	71
4 " Mary	"	5mo	"	1/32			

TRIBAL ENROLLMENT OF PARENTS

	NAME OF FATHER	YEAR	COUNTY	NAME OF MOTHER	YEAR	COUNTY
1	Joe Trentham		White man	Mary Lewis Trentham	Dead	Chickasaw roll
2	George W. Smith		Non Citizen	Eliza Smith		Non Citizen
3	No. 1			No. 2		
4	No. 1			No. 2		

(NOTES)

Henderson Trentham on Chickasaw roll as Henderson Trenton
Lena   "   "   "   "   "   Lena   "   *(No. 2 Dawes' Roll No. 299)*
No. 2 admitted to Chickasaw Citizenship by Dawes Commission in 1896 = Case #89 = No appeal.
                                                      No. 4 enrolled Nov. 3rd/99.

Chickasaw Enrollment Cards 1898-1914
Chickasaw by Blood   Volume II

RESIDENCE: Pontotoc   COUNTY   CARD NO.

POST OFFICE: Stonewall, Ind. Ter.   FIELD NO.

	NAME	RELATION-SHIP TO PERSON FIRST NAMED	AGE	SEX	BLOOD	TRIBAL ENROLLMENT		
						YEAR	COUNTY	PAGE
1	Lewis, Galloway	NAMED	25	M	Full	1897	Pontotoc	42
2	" Jackson	Son	8	"	"	1897	"	42
3	" Mary	Dau	2mo	F	"			
4	" Wilson	Son	4mo	M	"			
5	" Nancy	Wife	32	F	"	1897	"	42

TRIBAL ENROLLMENT OF PARENTS

	NAME OF FATHER	YEAR	COUNTY	NAME OF MOTHER	YEAR	COUNTY
1	Wilson Lewis	Dead	Pontotoc	Se-ma-ka-key	Dead	Pontotoc
2	No. 1			Jinsey Lewis	"	Pontotoc
3	No. 1			Nancy Lewis		Chickasaw
4	No. 1			" "		"
5	Jesse Brown	Dead	Chickasaw	Lucy Brown	1897	Pontotoc

(NOTES)

No. 3 died October 7, 1900; proof of death filed July 16, 1901.

No. 4 Enrolled July 20, 1901.

Nancy Lewis Wife of No. 1 was listed for enrollment as Nancy Brown on Chickasaw card #175. See
  letter of ODus L. Collins filed herein Aug. 1, 1901.

Nos. 3 and 4 are the children of Nancy Brown. No. 3 on Chickasaw card #175 ~~and trans-~~
  ~~ferred to this card Nov. 11th 1901.~~

No. 5 on 1896 Chickasaw roll as Nancy Brown.

No. 5 also on 1897 roll page 93, Pontotoc County

No. 5 was enrolled Sept 5, 1899 on Chickasaw card #175 and transferred to this card Nov. 11th 1901.

P.O. Franks, I.T.

RESIDENCE: Pontotoc   COUNTY   CARD NO.

POST OFFICE: Center, Ind. Ter.   FIELD NO.

	NAME	RELATION-SHIP TO PERSON FIRST NAMED	AGE	SEX	BLOOD	TRIBAL ENROLLMENT		
						YEAR	COUNTY	PAGE
1	Chapman, Harriet E.G.	NAMED	37	F	1/8	1897	Pontotoc	49
2	" Charles L.	Son	17	M	1/16	1897	"	49
3	" ~~Laura T.~~	~~Dau~~	~~15~~	~~F~~	~~1/16~~	~~1897~~	"	~~49~~
4	" James W.	Son	13	M	1/16	1897	"	49
5	" Virginia C.	Dau	12	F	1/16	1897	"	49

| 6 | " | Claud C. | Son | 8 | M | 1/16 | 1897 | " | 49 |
| 7 | " | Richard F. | " | 5 | " | 1/16 | 1897 | " | 50 |

TRIBAL ENROLLMENT OF PARENTS

	NAME OF FATHER	YEAR	COUNTY	NAME OF MOTHER		YEAR	COUNTY
1	George Moore	Dead	Chickasaw roll	Mary Moore	(I.W.)	1897	Pontotoc
2	Jas. W. Chapman	"	Adopted Chickasaw	No. 1			
3	" " "	"	" "	No. 1			
4	" " "	"	" "	No. 1			
5	" " "	"	" "	No. 1			
6	" " "	"	" "	No. 1			
7	" " "	"	" "	No. 1			

(NOTES)

No. 1 on Chickasaw roll as H.E.G. Chapman
No. 2 "   "   "   " L.C.   "
No. 4 "   "   "   " James W. "   Jr.
No. 5 "   "   "   " Virginia "
No. 6 "   "   "   " Claude C. "

RESIDENCE: Choctaw Nation   COUNTY   CARD NO.
POST OFFICE: Savana, Ind. Ter.   FIELD NO.

	NAME	RELATIONSHIP TO PERSON FIRST NAMED	AGE	SEX	BLOOD	TRIBAL ENROLLMENT		
						YEAR	COUNTY	PAGE
1	Holloway, Kitsie	NAMED	67	F	1/2	1897	Choctaw N. 1st Dist.	67
2	Alborson, Cornelia	Dau	20	"	3/4	1897	" " " "	67
3	James, Perline	G.Dau	3mo	F	7/8			

TRIBAL ENROLLMENT OF PARENTS

	NAME OF FATHER	YEAR	COUNTY	NAME OF MOTHER	YEAR	COUNTY
1	Ka-nul-la-tub-by	Dead	Choctaw Citz	Ste-ho-ye	Dead	Chickasaw roll
2	Peter Alberson	Dead	Chickasaw roll	No. 1		
3	Go;bert James	1896	Chickasaw residing in Choctaw Nation	No. 2		

(NOTES)

Kitsie Holloway on Chickasaw Roll as Kitsie Alberson
No. 3 Born May 20, 1902. Enrolled Sept. 9, 1902.   *(No. 3 Dawes' Roll No. 4095)*

Chickasaw Enrollment Cards 1898-1914
Chickasaw by Blood   Volume II

RESIDENCE: Pontotoc   COUNTY

POST OFFICE: Stonewall, Ind. Ter.

CARD NO.

FIELD NO.

	NAME	RELATION-SHIP TO PERSON FIRST NAMED	AGE	SEX	BLOOD	TRIBAL ENROLLMENT		
						YEAR	COUNTY	PAGE
1	Brown, Levi	NAMED	20	M	Full	1897	Pontotoc	50
2	" Elizabeth	Wife	22	F	Full	1897	Pontotoc	39
3	Beans, Rosa	StepDau	4	"	"	1897	"	39
4	Brown, Scott	Son	1	M	"	New Born		
5	" Andy	Son	1mo	M	"	New Born		

TRIBAL ENROLLMENT OF PARENTS

	NAME OF FATHER	YEAR	COUNTY	NAME OF MOTHER	YEAR	COUNTY
1	Jesse Brown	Dead	Chickasaw Roll	Lucy Brown	1897	Pontotoc
2	Sias	Dead	" "	Maria Underwood	1897	Pontotoc
3	Phelan Beans			No. 2		
4	No. 1			No. 2		
5	No. 1			No. 2		

(NOTES)

No. 2 on Chickasaw roll as Elizabeth Johnson
No. 4 Born March 30, 1897. Evidence of birth filed June 20th 1902.
No. 5 Enrolled June 8, 1902.

RESIDENCE: Pontotoc   COUNTY

POST OFFICE: Ada, Ind. Ter.

CARD NO.

FIELD NO.

	NAME	RELATION-SHIP TO PERSON FIRST NAMED	AGE	SEX	BLOOD	TRIBAL ENROLLMENT		
						YEAR	COUNTY	PAGE
1	Underwood, George	NAMED	45	M	Full	1897	Pontotoc	39
2	" Maria	Wife	46	F	1/2	1897	"	39
3	Fulsom, Charlie	Ward	15	M	Full	1897	"	39
4	Harris, Walton	"	7	M	1/2	1897	"	39

TRIBAL ENROLLMENT OF PARENTS

	NAME OF FATHER	YEAR	COUNTY	NAME OF MOTHER	YEAR	COUNTY
1	Ish-to-ka-nok-ke	Dead	Chickasaw roll	Sim-mon-ti-e-che	Dead	Chickasaw Roll
2	To-ah-sha	Dead	Choctaw Citz	No-ke-sha	Dead	" "
3	Sampon[sic] Folsom	Dead	Chickasaw Roll	Mary Folsom	Dead	" "
4	William ?ore		Choctaw Citz	Carrie Harris	Dead	" "

(NOTES)

No. 3 on Chickasaw roll as Charles Fulsom
No. 2 died in February 1899 *(remainder illegible)*

	NAME	RELATION-SHIP TO PERSON FIRST	AGE	SEX	BLOOD	TRIBAL ENROLLMENT		
						YEAR	COUNTY	PAGE
1	Apala, Jonas	NAMED	27	M	Full	1897	Choct. N. 1st Dist.	67
2	" Kizzie	Wife	25	F	"	1897	" " " "	67
3	" Henrietta	Dau	6	F	"	1897	" " " "	67
4	" Ophelia	Dau	4	F	"	1897	" " " "	67
5	" Myrtle Paul	Dau	1	F	"			
6	" Lemull	Son	4mo	M	"			
7	" Mulbert	Son	5mo	M	"			

RESIDENCE: Choctaw Nation *COUNTY*   *CARD No.*
POST OFFICE: Savannah, I.T.   *FIELD No.*

TRIBAL ENROLLMENT OF PARENTS

	NAME OF FATHER	YEAR	COUNTY	NAME OF MOTHER	YEAR	COUNTY
1	Istey Kona	Dead	Chickasaw roll	Charity	dead	Chickasaw roll
2	Pete Alberson	Dead	" "	Kitsey Alberson	1897	Choc. N. 1st Dist.
3	No. 1			No. 2		
4	No. 1			No. 2		
5	No. 1			No. 2		
6	No. 1			No. 2		
7	No. 1			No. 2		

(NOTES)

No. 2 Kizzie Apala on Chickasaw roll as Kizzy Alberson
No. 4 Ophelia " " " " " Abellia Apala.
No. 5 Born March 14, 1897.
No. 7 Born Dec. 25, 1901. Enrolled May 7, 1902.
No. 1 Died May 3, 1901. Proof of death filed Sept. 3, 1902.
No. 5 Proof of birth received and filed Sept. 11, 1902.

No. 6 enrolled Mar. 22/99.

	NAME	RELATION-SHIP TO PERSON FIRST	AGE	SEX	BLOOD	TRIBAL ENROLLMENT		
						YEAR	COUNTY	PAGE
1	Yancey, James I.	NAMED	42	M	I.W.	1897	Choctaw N. 1st Dist.	82
2	" Minnie	Wife	21	F	1/16	1897	" " " "	79

RESIDENCE: Choctaw Nation 3rd Dist. *COUNTY*   *CARD No.*
POST OFFICE: Coalgate, Ind. Ter.   *FIELD No.*

Chickasaw Enrollment Cards 1898-1914
Chickasaw by Blood   Volume II

3	"	Lillian	Dau	3	"	1/32	1897	"	"	"	"	79
4	"	Mattie Ella	"	2	"	1/32	1897	"	"	"	"	79
5	"	Clara	"	4	"	1/32	1897	"	"	"	"	79
6	"	William C.	Son	2mo	M	1/32						
7	"	Emri Ancher	Son	2mo	M	1/32						

TRIBAL ENROLLMENT OF PARENTS

	NAME OF FATHER	YEAR	COUNTY	NAME OF MOTHER	YEAR	COUNTY
1	W.C. Yancey	Dead	Non Citizen	Rebecca Yancey	Dead	Non Citizen
2	John Trentam (I.W.)		White Man	Mary Trentam	"	Chickasaw roll
3	No. 1			No. 2		
4	No. 1			No. 2		
5	No. 1			No. 2		
6	No. 1			No. 2		
7	No. 1			No. 2		

(NOTES)

No. 1 on Chickasaw roll as James J. Yancy   *(No. 1 Dawes' Roll No. 244)*
James I. Yancey was admitted by Dawes Commission Case No. 130.
No. 7 Born Dec. 27, 1901. enrolled March 1, 1902.
No. 4 Evidence of birth received and filed Sept. 4, 1902.   *(No. 4 Dawes' Roll No. 4093)*
No. 6 Died April 18, 1902. Proof of death filed Nov. 25, 1902.
No. 6 Enrolled Nov. 3/99.

RESIDENCE: Cherokee Nation   COUNTY   CARD NO.
POST OFFICE: Braggs, Ind. Ter.   FIELD NO.

NAME	RELATION-SHIP TO PERSON FIRST NAMED	AGE	SEX	BLOOD	TRIBAL ENROLLMENT		
					YEAR	COUNTY	PAGE
1 McLish, Ollie M.	NAMED	13	F	1/2	1897	Choctaw N. 1st Dist.	70

TRIBAL ENROLLMENT OF PARENTS

	NAME OF FATHER	YEAR	COUNTY	NAME OF MOTHER	YEAR	COUNTY
1	Brad McLish		Choctaw Citz	Lena Fallen	Dead	Chickasaw roll

(NOTES)

No. 1 duplicate enrollment of Ollie Fallen
on Chickasaw Card #1551.

171

Chickasaw Enrollment Cards 1898-1914
Chickasaw by Blood   Volume II

RESIDENCE:	Choctaw Nation	COUNTY				CARD NO.		
POST OFFICE:	Alderson, Ind. Ter.					FIELD NO.		

	NAME	RELATION-SHIP TO PERSON FIRST NAMED	AGE	SEX	BLOOD	TRIBAL ENROLLMENT		
						YEAR	COUNTY	PAGE
1	Benton, Peter	FIRST NAMED	54	M	Full	1897	Chick residing in Choctaw N. 1st Dist.	69
2	" ~~Sarah~~	~~Wife~~	~~65~~	~~F~~	~~"~~	~~1897~~	~~" " " "~~	~~69~~
3	" Ellen	Dau	18	"	"	1897	" " " "	69

TRIBAL ENROLLMENT OF PARENTS

	NAME OF FATHER	YEAR	COUNTY	NAME OF MOTHER	YEAR	COUNTY
1	(Name Illegible)	Dead	Chickasaw roll	Nah-ho-kee	Dead	Chickasaw roll
2	~~Ta-t?-he~~	"	" " "	~~Ma-ka-ho-ya~~	"	" " "
3	No. 1			No. 2		

(NOTES)
No. 2 Died May 4-1899. Evidence of death filed May 6, 1901.
No. 3 Now the Wife of No. 9 on Chickasaw Card No. 147
Evidence of marriage requested 11/10/02.

No. I enrolled Sept. 30/95

RESIDENCE:	Choctaw Nation 1st Dist	COUNTY				CARD NO.		
POST OFFICE:	McAlester, Ind. Ter.					FIELD NO.		

	NAME	RELATION-SHIP TO PERSON FIRST NAMED	AGE	SEX	BLOOD	TRIBAL ENROLLMENT		
						YEAR	COUNTY	PAGE
1	Davis, Adam A **DEAD**	NAMED	69	M	I.W.	1897	Choctaw N. 1st Dist.	82
2	" Martha	Wife	27	F	1/2	1897	" " " "	69
3	" Maggie	Dau	6	"	1/4	1897	" " " "	69

TRIBAL ENROLLMENT OF PARENTS

	NAME OF FATHER	YEAR	COUNTY	NAME OF MOTHER	YEAR	COUNTY
1	Jesse Davis	Dead	Non-Citizen	Betsey Davis	Dead	Non Citizen
2	Sampson (Illegible)	"	Chickasaw roll	Sarah Barton	1897	Choctaw N. 1st Dist.
3	No. 1			No. 2		

(NOTES)
No. I died April 14, 1900; Proof of death filed Dec. 23, 1902.

RESIDENCE: Pontotoc **COUNTY**					**CARD NO.**			
POST OFFICE: Stonewall, Ind. Ter.					**FIELD NO.**			

	NAME	RELATION-SHIP TO PERSON FIRST NAMED	AGE	SEX	BLOOD	TRIBAL ENROLLMENT		
						YEAR	COUNTY	PAGE
1	Agakatubby, Thompson	NAMED	44	M	Full	1897	Pontotoc	53
2	" Mina	Wife	4?	F	Full	1897	"	53
3	" Austin	Son	2?	M	"	1897	"	53
4	" Agnes	Dau	18	F	"	1897	"	53
5	" Willie	Son	16	M	"	1897	"	53
6	" Mary	Dau	?	F	"	1897	"	53
7	" Dixon	Son	4	M	"	1897	"	53
8	" Dorena	Dau	3	F	"	1897	"	53
9	" (Illegible)	Son	1	M	"	1897	"	53
10	" (Illegible)	?	14	F	"	1897	"	53

TRIBAL ENROLLMENT OF PARENTS

	NAME OF FATHER	YEAR	COUNTY	NAME OF MOTHER	YEAR	COUNTY
1	Agakatubby	Dead	Chickasaw roll	Inohe	Dead	Chickasaw roll
2	Billy (Illegible)	1897	Pontotoc	(Name Illegible)	Dead	" "
3	No. 1			No. 2		
4	No. 1			No. 2		
5	No. 1			No. 2		
6	No. 1			No. 2		
7	No. 1			No. 2		
8	No. 1			No. 2		
9	No. 1			No. 2		
10	(Name Illegible)	?	Pontotoc	(Name Illegible)	Dead	?

(NOTES)

No. 1 Died Sept. ?, 1902. proof of death filed Nov. 21, 1902.
No. 10 on page 41 (remainder illegible)
(Entry illegible)
No. 5 died March 29, 1901. Proof of death filed June 5, 1901.
No. 9 Died Oct. 1st 1899. proof of death filed Sept. 3rd 1902.
No. 3 Died Aug 20, 1901. proof of death filed Sept. 8-1902.
No. 10 enrolled Oct. 5/98,
Others   "   Sept 1/98.

No. 4 P.O. Hogan, I.T. 11/22/02.
P.O. Jesse I.T. 7/19-04

RESIDENCE: Pontotoc	COUNTY				CARD NO.			
POST OFFICE: Stonewall, Ind. Ter.					FIELD NO.			

NAME	RELATION-SHIP TO PERSON FIRST NAMED	AGE	SEX	BLOOD	TRIBAL ENROLLMENT		
					YEAR	COUNTY	PAGE
1 Loving, Wesley D.	NAMED	41	M	I.W.	1897	Pontotoc	81
2 " Isabell	Wife	50	F	3/4	1897	"	44

TRIBAL ENROLLMENT OF PARENTS

	NAME OF FATHER	YEAR	COUNTY	NAME OF MOTHER	YEAR	COUNTY
1	Noah Loving	Dead	non-citizen	Ellen Loving	Dead	Non citizen
2	(Name Illegible)	"	Chickasaw roll	Aneckey	"	Chickasaw roll

(NOTES)

No. I on Chickasaw roll as W.B. Loving   (No. I Dawes' Roll No. 72)
No. I See affidavits of Wm D. Byrd and (Name Illegible)
Marriage filed Sept. 22, 1902.

RESIDENCE: Choctaw Nation	COUNTY				CARD NO.			
POST OFFICE: Waupanucka, Ind. Ter.					FIELD NO.			

NAME	RELATION-SHIP TO PERSON FIRST NAMED	AGE	SEX	BLOOD	TRIBAL ENROLLMENT		
					YEAR	COUNTY	PAGE
1 Colbert, Jackson R.	NAMED	36	M	Full	1897	Choctaw N. 1st Dist.	67
2 " Mary Woy	Wife	28	F	"	1897	Pontotoc	55
3 " David	StSon	2	M	"	1897	"	?
4 " Isabel	Dau	3mo	F	"			
5 Cuberry, Davis	Bro in law	18	M	"	1897	Pickens	?
6 Colbert, Lucy	Dau	7mo	F	"			
7 " Amanda	Dau	10mo	F	"			

TRIBAL ENROLLMENT OF PARENTS

	NAME OF FATHER	YEAR	COUNTY	NAME OF MOTHER	YEAR	COUNTY
1	Jackson Colbert	Dead	Chickasaw roll	Sally Colbert	Dead	Chickasaw roll
2	(Name Illegible)	"	" "	Rhoda Cuberry	"	" "
3	(Name Illegible)		" "	No. 2		
4	No. I			No. 2		
5	Cole Cuberry	Dead	Chickasaw Roll	(Name Illegible)	Dead	Chickasaw roll
6	No. I			No. 2		
7	No. I			No. 2		

(NOTES)

(Four entries illegible)

No. 7 Born Sept ?, 1901. enrolled July 23, 1902.
No. 4 Born May 16th 1898 proof of birth filed Aug. 5th 1903.
No. 3 died Oct. 16, 1898; proof of death filed Oct. 21, 1904.

P.O. Stuart I.T. 7/29/02,

NAME	RELATION-SHIP TO PERSON FIRST NAMED	AGE	SEX	BLOOD	TRIBAL ENROLLMENT		
					YEAR	COUNTY	PAGE
1 Benton, Elizabeth	NAMED	27	F	1/4		Pontotoc	57
2 " Isaac B.	Son	4	M	1/8		"	57
3 " Eliza M.	Dau	2	F	1/8		"	57
4 Neal, Isabell	Dau	9	"			"	57

RESIDENCE: Pontotoc   COUNTY   CARD NO.
POST OFFICE: Victor, Ind. Ter.   FIELD NO.

TRIBAL ENROLLMENT OF PARENTS

	NAME OF FATHER	YEAR	COUNTY	NAME OF MOTHER	YEAR	COUNTY
1	Chas. Strickland	Dead		Martha Strickland	Dead	Non Citizen
2	*(Name Illegible)*			No. 1		
3	" "			No. 1		
4	Bill Neal			No. 1		

(NOTES)

CANCELLED *Stamped across card.*
(An "X" marked across card)

RESIDENCE: Pontotoc   COUNTY   CARD NO.
POST OFFICE: Wayne, Ind. Ter.   FIELD NO.

NAME	RELATION-SHIP TO PERSON FIRST NAMED	AGE	SEX	BLOOD	TRIBAL ENROLLMENT		
					YEAR	COUNTY	PAGE
1 Seifried, Minnie	NAMED	23	F	3/8	1897	Pontotoc	62
2 " Henry	Bro	19	M	"	1897	"	62
3 " Charley	"	17	"	"	1897	"	62
4 " Mattie	Sister	14	F	"	1897	"	62
5 " Mary	"	12	"	"	1897	"	62
6 " Lucy	"	10	"	"	1897	"	62

TRIBAL ENROLLMENT OF PARENTS

	NAME OF FATHER	YEAR	COUNTY	NAME OF MOTHER	YEAR	COUNTY
1	Wm. ? Seifried	Dead	Non Citizen	Julia Seifried	Dead	Chickasaw roll

2	" " "	"	"	"	"	"		"	"	"
3	" " "	"	"	"	"	"		"	"	"
4	" " "	"	"	"	"	"		"	"	"
5	" " "	"	"	"	"	"		"	"	"
6	" " "	"	"	"	"	"		"	"	"

(NOTES)

(All notations illegible)

CANCELLED *Stamped across card.*
(An "X" marked across card)

RESIDENCE: Pontotoc COUNTY   CARD NO.
POST OFFICE: Stonewall, Ind. Ter.   FIELD NO.

NAME	RELATION-SHIP TO PERSON FIRST NAMED	AGE	SEX	BLOOD	TRIBAL ENROLLMENT		
					YEAR	COUNTY	PAGE
1 Walker, Robert T	NAMED	27	M	1/16	1897	Pontotoc	43
2 " Alice	Wife	23	F	1/4	1897	"	43
3 " William D.	Son	6mo	M	5/16	New born!		
4 " Robertha	Dau	2	F	5/16	1897	"	43
5 " Daisy *(Illegible)*	Dau	12	F	5/16			

TRIBAL ENROLLMENT OF PARENTS

	NAME OF FATHER	YEAR	COUNTY	NAME OF MOTHER	YEAR	COUNTY
1	*(Name Illegible)*		Pontotoc	*(Illegible)* I. Walker		
2	*(Name Illegible)*	Dead		Margaret Bishop		Pontotoc
3	No. 1			No. 2		
4	No. 1			No. 2		
5	No. 1			No. 2		

(NOTES)

No. 1 on Chickasaw roll as R.T. Walker   *(No. 2 Dawes' Roll No. 3998)*
(No. 3 Dawes' Roll No. 3999)   *(No. 4 Dawes' Roll No. 4090)*   *(No. 5 Dawes' Roll No. 4091)*
(Remainder illegible)

RESIDENCE: Pontotoc COUNTY   CARD NO.
POST OFFICE: Stonewall, Ind. Ter.   FIELD NO.

NAME	RELATION-SHIP TO PERSON FIRST NAMED	AGE	SEX	BLOOD	TRIBAL ENROLLMENT		
					YEAR	COUNTY	PAGE
1 Walker, Tandy C.	NAMED	58	M	1/8	1897	Pontotoc	43
2 " I.T.	Son	24	"	1/16	1897	"	43

Chickasaw Enrollment Cards 1898-1914
Chickasaw by Blood   Volume II

	NAME	REL	AGE	SEX	BLOOD	YEAR		PAGE
3	" J.C.	"	22	"	"	1897	"	43
4	Byrd, Ida	Dau	16	F	"	1897	"	43
5	Walker, G.C.	Son	13	M	"	1897	"	43
6	" Minnie	Dau	11	F	"	1897	"	43
7	Byrd, Eugean	Son	4mo	M	1/32			
8	" Chester Temple	Grand Son	2 1/2m	M	1/32			
9	Walker, Mary Amelia	Grand Dau	1mo	F	1/32			

TRIBAL ENROLLMENT OF PARENTS

	NAME OF FATHER	YEAR	COUNTY	NAME OF MOTHER	YEAR	COUNTY
1	Louis Walker	Dead	Choctaw Indian	Mary Walker	Dead	Chickasaw roll
2	No. 1			Mary I. Walker		
3	No. 1			" " "		
4	No. 1			" " "		
5	No. 1			" " "		
6	No. 1			" " "		
7	J.M. Byrd		Inter married	No. 4		
8	" " "		" "	No. 4		
9	No. 3			Lucy Walker		Non Citz

(NOTES)

No. 1 on Chickasaw roll as T.C. Walker
No. 3 "   "   " C.F. "
No. 5 "   "   " ? Cleveland "
Wife of No. 1 and mother of his children on Choctaw Card No. D.180
No. 7 enrolled May 25, 1902.
3/20/99 No. 4 married to J.M. Byrd. See card No. 1375
No. 8 Born Aug. 2, 1901 and enrolled Oct. 25, 1901.
No. 9 Born Oct. 30, 1901. Enrolled Dec. 4, 1901.
No. 2 is the husband of Lucy Walker a non citizen. Evidence of marriage filed Dec. 4, 1901.

RESIDENCE: Choctaw Nat'n. Kiamitia	COUNTY			CARD NO.			
POST OFFICE: Nelson, I.T.				FIELD NO.			

	NAME	RELATIONSHIP TO PERSON FIRST NAMED	AGE	SEX	BLOOD	YEAR	COUNTY	PAGE
1	Smith, Bird Q.	NAMED	48	M	I.W.			
2	" Deliah	Wife	28	F	1/4			
3	" Sim	Son	10	N	1/8			
4	" Fred	"	8	"	1/8			
5	" Ray	"	6	"	1/8			

6	" Eric	"	4	"	1/8				
7	" Pearl	Dau	2	F	1/8				
8	" Annie	"	3wks	"	1/8				
9	" Phoebe	Dau	3mo	F	1/8				

TRIBAL ENROLLMENT OF PARENTS

	NAME OF FATHER	YEAR	COUNTY	NAME OF MOTHER	YEAR	COUNTY
1	E.L. Smith	Dead	Non Citz	Rhoda R. Smith	Dead	Non Citz
2	Sim Harrison	1896	Choctaw Roll	Phoebe Harrison	"	Chick Roll
3	No. 1			No. 2		
4	No. 1			No. 2		
5	No. 1			No. 2		
6	No. 1			No. 2		
7	No. 1			No. 2		
8	No. 1			No. 2		
9	No. 1			No. 2		

(NOTES)

No. 2 died Dec. 4, 1901; Evidence of death filed Feby. 7, 1902.
No. 1 on 1896 Choctaw Roll, Page 400, No. 15052. Kiamitia Co. as Quincy Smith
No. 2 " 1896 " " " 298 " 11530, Kiamitia Co. as Lilie Smith
No. 3 " 1896 " " " 298 " 11531, " " (remainder illegible)
No. 4 " 1896 " " " 298 " 11532, " " as Fred Smith
No. 5 " 1896 " " " 298 " 11533, " " as Roy Smith
No. 6 " 1896 " " " 298 " 11534, " " as Erick Smith
All transferred to Chickasaw roll by Dawes Commission.
No. 9 born Nov. 18, 1901; Enrolled Feby. 7, 1902.

5/11/98.

RESIDENCE: Choctaw Nat'n. Towson	COUNTY				CARD NO.			
POST OFFICE: Doaksville, I.T.					FIELD NO.			

NAME	RELATIONSHIP TO PERSON FIRST NAMED	AGE	SEX	BLOOD	TRIBAL ENROLLMENT		
					YEAR	COUNTY	PAGE
1 Folsom, Pitman		47	M	1/4			

TRIBAL ENROLLMENT OF PARENTS

	NAME OF FATHER	YEAR	COUNTY	NAME OF MOTHER	YEAR	COUNTY
1	Henry Folsom	Dead	Choctaw Roll	Harriet Folsom	Dead	Chick Roll

(NOTES)

On 1896 Choctaw Roll, Page 100. No. 4134, Towson Co.
Transferred to Chickasaw Roll by Dawes Commission.
No. 1 Died Aug. 10, 1901; proof of death filed July 29, 1902.

5/11/99.

Chickasaw Enrollment Cards 1898-1914
Chickasaw by Blood   Volume II

RESIDENCE: Choctaqw Nat'n., Kiamitia COUNTY   CARD NO.

POST OFFICE: Goodland, I.T.   FIELD NO.

| | NAME | RELATION-SHIP TO PERSON FIRST | AGE | SEX | BLOOD | TRIBAL ENROLLMENT | | |
						YEAR	COUNTY	PAGE
1	Ward, Phoebe	NAMED	40	F	1/2			
2	" Ida	Dau	15	"	1/4			
3	" Eastman	Son	8	M	1/4			
4	" Sampson	"	6	"	1/4			
5	" Samuel	"	3	"	1/4			
6	" Harvey	"	6mo	"	1/4			

TRIBAL ENROLLMENT OF PARENTS

	NAME OF FATHER	YEAR	COUNTY	NAME OF MOTHER	YEAR	COUNTY
1	William Billis	Dead	Choctaw Roll	Winey Goforth	Dead	Chick Roll
2	Allington Ward	1896	" "	No. 1		
3	" "	1896	" "	No. 1		
4	" "	1896	" "	No. 1		
5	" "	1896	" "	No. 1		
6	" "	1896	" "	No. 1		

(NOTES)

No. 1 on 1896 Choctaw Roll, Page 360 No. 13744, Kiamitia County
No. 2 " 1896   "   "   " 360 " 13746   "   "
No. 3 " 1896   "   "   " 360 " 13747   "   "
No. 4 " 1896   "   "   " 360 " 13748   "   "
    All transferred to Chickasaw Roll by Dawes Commission.
    Husband of No. 1 on Choctaw Caard No. 1605
No. 1 Died April 22, 1901; Evidence of Death filed July 16, 1902.

                                        5/11/99.

RESIDENCE: Choctaw Nat'n. Kiamitia COUNTY   CARD NO.

POST OFFICE: Nelson, I.T.   FIELD NO.

| | NAME | RELATION-SHIP TO PERSON FIRST | AGE | SEX | BLOOD | TRIBAL ENROLLMENT | | |
						YEAR	COUNTY	PAGE
1	Harrison, Rutha	NAMED	25	F				
2	" Solomon	Bro	20	M				
3	" Sinie	Sister	15	F				

TRIBAL ENROLLMENT OF PARENTS

	NAME OF FATHER	YEAR	COUNTY	NAME OF MOTHER	YEAR	COUNTY
1	Sim Harrison	1896	Choctaw Roll	Phoebe Harrison	Dead	Chickasaw Roll

2	"	"	1896	"	"	"	"		"	"	"
3	"	"	1896	"	"	"	"		"	"	"

(NOTES)

No. 1 on 1896 Choctaw Roll Page 140 No. 5767. Kiamitia County
No. 2 " 1896   "   "   " 140 " 5768   "   "
No. 3 " 1896   "   "   " 140 " 5769   "   "

    All transferred to Chickasaw Roll by Dawes Commission

No. 3 on 1896 Choctaw Roll as Sinie Harrison, Jr.
    Father, Sim Harrison, on Choctaw Card No. 1589.

5/11/99.

RESIDENCE: Choctaw Nat'n. Kiamitia COUNTY	CARD NO.
POST OFFICE: Nelson, I.T.	FIELD NO.

	NAME	RELATION-SHIP TO PERSON FIRST NAMED	AGE	SEX	BLOOD	TRIBAL ENROLLMENT		
						YEAR	COUNTY	PAGE
1	Griggs, Willy	NAMED	27	M	1/4			
2	" Mary	Wife	25	F	1/4			
3	" Joel	Son	1	M	1/4			
4	" Wilson N.	Son	4mo	M	1/4			
5	" Pate J.	"	1mo	M	1/4			

TRIBAL ENROLLMENT OF PARENTS

	NAME OF FATHER	YEAR	COUNTY	NAME OF MOTHER	YEAR	COUNTY
1	Thos. Griggs	1896	Choctaw Roll	Mary Griggs	Dead	Chick. Roll
2	Wm LaFlore	1896	" "	Roseana LeFlore	1896	" "
3	No. 1			No. 2		
4	No. 1			No. 2		
5	No. 1			No. 2		

(NOTES)

No. 1 on 1896 Choctaw roll, Page 117 No. 4814 Kiamitia County
No. 2 " 1896   "   "   " 117 " 4833   "   "
    Both transferred to Chickasaw Roll by Dawes Commission.
No. 2 also on 1896 Choctaw Roll, Page 202, No. 8110, Jackson Co. as Mary LeFlore.
No. 3 Affidavit of birth to be supplied. Rec'd May 17/99.
No. 4 Enrolled June 23, 1900.
No. 5 Enrolled October 15, 1901.

5/10/99.

Chickasaw Enrollment Cards 1898-1914
Chickasaw by Blood   Volume II

RESIDENCE: Choctaw Nat'n, Kiamitia	COUNTY			CARD NO.			
POST OFFICE: Goodland, I.T.				FIELD NO.			

NAME	RELATION-SHIP TO PERSON FIRST NAMED	AGE	SEX	BLOOD	TRIBAL ENROLLMENT		
					YEAR	COUNTY	PAGE
1 Jefferson, Joe	NAMED	29	M	1/2			

TRIBAL ENROLLMENT OF PARENTS

NAME OF FATHER	YEAR	COUNTY	NAME OF MOTHER	YEAR	COUNTY
1 Kenos Jefferson	Dead	Choctaw Roll	Elsie Jefferson	Dead	Chick Roll

(NOTES)

On 1893 Pay roll, Choctaw Nation, Page 32, No. 310, Chickasaw District.
Transferred to Chickasaw Roll by Dawes Commission
Wife and family on Choctaw Card No. 1539.
No. 1 Died May 1901; Evidence of Death filed July 16, 1902.

5/10/98.

RESIDENCE: Choctaw Nation, Kiamitia	COUNTY			CARD NO.			
POST OFFICE: Goodland, I.T.				FIELD NO.			

NAME	RELATION-SHIP TO PERSON FIRST NAMED	AGE	SEX	BLOOD	TRIBAL ENROLLMENT		
					YEAR	COUNTY	PAGE
1 Locke, Benjamin F.	NAMED	45	M	I.W.			
2 Kelly, Mary	Ward	14	F	1/2			
3 " Dovey	"	10	"	1/2			
4 " Mahala	"	8	"	1/2			

TRIBAL ENROLLMENT OF PARENTS

NAME OF FATHER	YEAR	COUNTY	NAME OF MOTHER	YEAR	COUNTY
1 B.J. Locke	Dead	Non-Citz.	Mary Locke	Dead	Non Citz.
2 John Kelly	"	" "	Sarah Kelly	"	Chick Roll
3 " "	"	" "	" "	"	" "
4 " "	"	" "	" "	"	" "

(NOTES)

No. 1 was married to Hattie Wilson, Chick. Citz. under Choctaw Laws, in 1875. Lived with her until she died
   in 1887. Then married a Choctaw Citz. who has since died. He is now a widower. License lost or destroyed
   with records of Towson County which were destroyed by fire in 1897. See testimony of No. 1, Henry Williams
   and E.W. Tims, hereto attached.
No. 1 on Choctaw 1896 roll, Page 393 No. 14771 Kiamitia County as B.F. Locke
No. 2 "   "   1896 "   " 186 No. 7523 Cedar   "
No. 3 "   "   1896 PayRoll " 47 No. 389 Kiamitia   "
No. 4 "   "   1896 Roll " 186 No. 7524 Cedar   " as Mahale Kelly.
No. 3 also on 1896 Choctaw Roll, Page 190, No. 7663 as E. Kelly Nov. 15/99.   5/8/99.

181

RESIDENCE: Choctaw Nat'n, Towson COUNTY					CARD No.			
POST OFFICE: Doaksville, I.T.					FIELD No.			
NAME	RELATION-SHIP TO PERSON FIRST NAMED	AGE	SEX	BLOOD	TRIBAL ENROLLMENT			
					YEAR	COUNTY		PAGE
1 Wilson, John D.	NAMED	35	M	1/4				

TRIBAL ENROLLMENT OF PARENTS

NAME OF FATHER	YEAR	COUNTY	NAME OF MOTHER	YEAR	COUNTY
1 John Wilson	Dead	Choctaw Roll	Jane Wilson	1896	Chick residing in Choc Nation -

(NOTES)
On 1896 Choctaw roll, Page 346, No. 13179, Towson, County.
Wife and children on Choctaw Card No. 1426.

5/8/99.

RESIDENCE: Choctaw Nat'n, Kiamitia COUNTY					CARD No.			
POST OFFICE: Goodland, I.T.					FIELD No.			
NAME	RELATION-SHIP TO PERSON FIRST NAMED	AGE	SEX	BLOOD	TRIBAL ENROLLMENT			
					YEAR	COUNTY		PAGE
1 Miller, Sinie	NAMED	68	F	3/4				

TRIBAL ENROLLMENT OF PARENTS

NAME OF FATHER	YEAR	COUNTY	NAME OF MOTHER	YEAR	COUNTY
1 William Homma	Dead	Choc. Roll	Lisa Homma	Dead	Chick Roll

(NOTES)
On 1896 Choctaw roll, Kiamitia County, No. 8730, Page 218.
Transferred to Chickasaw roll by Dawes Commission.

5/8/99.

RESIDENCE: Choctaw Nation, Towson COUNTY					CARD No.			
POST OFFICE: Garvin, I.T.					FIELD No.			
NAME	RELATION-SHIP TO PERSON FIRST NAMED	AGE	SEX	BLOOD	TRIBAL ENROLLMENT			
					YEAR	COUNTY		PAGE
1 Austin, Lena	NAMED	18	F	1/2				

TRIBAL ENROLLMENT OF PARENTS

NAME OF FATHER	YEAR	COUNTY	NAME OF MOTHER	YEAR	COUNTY
1 Tobias Austin	Dead	Choctaw Roll	Becky Austin	Dead	Chick Roll

(NOTES)
On Choctaw roll, 1896, Towson County, Page 5, No. 186. Transferred to
Chickasaw roll by Dawes Commission.

5/8/99.

Chickasaw Enrollment Cards 1898-1914
Chickasaw by Blood   Volume II

RESIDENCE: Choctaw Nat'n, Red River   COUNTY   CARD NO.
POST OFFICE: Shawneetown, I.T.   FIELD NO.

	NAME	RELATION-SHIP TO PERSON FIRST NAMED	AGE	SEX	BLOOD	TRIBAL ENROLLMENT		
						YEAR	COUNTY	PAGE
1	Love, Robert M	NAMED	38	M	1/8			
2	" Kate D.	Wife	32	F	I.W.			
3	" Elma E.	Dau	10	"	1/16			
4	" Arthur	Son	7	M	1/16			
5	" Sidney	"	5	"	1/16			
6	" Harry	"	2	"	1/16			
7	" Robert M. Jr.	"	5mo	"	1/16			

TRIBAL ENROLLMENT OF PARENTS

	NAME OF FATHER	YEAR	COUNTY	NAME OF MOTHER	YEAR	COUNTY
1	Samuel Love	Dead	Non Citz	Frances Love	Dead	Chick Roll
2	Thomas DeVor	"	" "	Ellen DeVor	1897	Non Citz
3	No. 1			No. 2		
4	No. 1			No. 2		
5	No. 1			No. 2		
6	No. 1			No. 2		
7	No. 1			No. 2		

(NOTES)

No. 1 was admitted by the Dawes Commission as a Choctaw by blood, Case No. 1254. No appeal.

No. 2 was admitted by the Dawes Commission as an Intermarried Citizen Case No. 1255. No appeal.

No. 1 on Choctaw Roll, 1896, Page 200, No. 8057, Red River County ⎤
No. 2 "   "   "   1896, " 393, No. 14768, "   "   "   ⎬ All transferred to Chick Roll
No. 3 "   "   "   1896 " 200 No. 8058 "   "   "   ⎬ by the Dawes Commission
No. 4 "   "   "   1896 " 200 No. 8059 "   "   "   ⎬ May 2/99.
No. 5 "   "   "   1896 " 200 No. 8060 "   "   "   ⎦

No. 6 Affidavit of birth to be supplied. Rec'd May 12/99.

No. 7 Affidavit received but irregular and returned for correction Dec. 14/99. Rec'd & filed Jany 17, 1900.

CANCELLED *Stamped across card.*

RESIDENCE: Choctaw Nat'n, Towson   COUNTY   CARD NO.
POST OFFICE: Garvin, I.T.   FIELD NO.

	NAME	RELATION-SHIP TO PERSON FIRST NAMED	AGE	SEX	BLOOD	TRIBAL ENROLLMENT		
						YEAR	COUNTY	PAGE
1	Wilson, Edward H.	NAMED	30	M	1/4			

Chickasaw Enrollment Cards 1898-1914
Chickasaw by Blood   Volume II

TRIBAL ENROLLMENT OF PARENTS					
NAME OF FATHER	YEAR	COUNTY	NAME OF MOTHER	YEAR	COUNTY
1 John Wilson	Dead	Choctaw Roll	Jane Wilson	1896	Chick residing in Choc. Nation.

(NOTES)

On Choctaw Roll 1896, Page 347, No. 13183, Towson County.
Transferred to Chickasaw roll by Dawes Commission.
Wife and children on Choctaw Card No. 1287.

May 1/99.

CANCELLED *Stamped across card.*

RESIDENCE: Choctaw Nation, Towson COUNTY					CARD NO.		
POST OFFICE: Clear Creek, I.T.					FIELD NO.		

NAME	RELATION- SHIP TO PERSON FIRST NAMED	AGE	SEX	BLOOD	TRIBAL ENROLLMENT		
					YEAR	COUNTY	PAGE
1 Wilson, Raphael F.	NAMED	28	M	1/4			

TRIBAL ENROLLMENT OF PARENTS					
NAME OF FATHER	YEAR	COUNTY	NAME OF MOTHER	YEAR	COUNTY
1 John Wilson	Dead	Choctaw Roll	Jane Wilson	1896	Chick residing in Choc. Nation.

(NOTES)

On Choctaw Roll 1896, Page 347, No. 13219, Towson County.
Transferred to Chickasaw Roll by Dawes Commission.
On Choctaw Roll as Raphael Wilson.
Husband of Emma J. Wilson on Choctaw Card No. 992.

Apr. 27/99.

CANCELLED *Stamped across card.*

RESIDENCE: Towson COUNTY					CARD NO.		
POST OFFICE: Doaksville, I.T.					FIELD NO.		

NAME	RELATION- SHIP TO PERSON FIRST NAMED	AGE	SEX	BLOOD	TRIBAL ENROLLMENT		
					YEAR	COUNTY	PAGE
1 Wilson, Jane	NAMED	62	F	1/2			

TRIBAL ENROLLMENT OF PARENTS					
NAME OF FATHER	YEAR	COUNTY	NAME OF MOTHER	YEAR	COUNTY
1 *(Illegible)* James	Dead	Non Citz	Ruthis James	Dead	Chick descent.

(NOTES)

On Choctaw Roll, 1896, Towson County, Page 347,. No. 13187.
Transferred to Chickasaw roll by Dawes Commission.

April 20/99

CANCELLED *Stamped across card.*

Chickasaw Enrollment Cards 1898-1914
Chickasaw by Blood   Volume II

	RESIDENCE: Choctaw Nation, Towson	COUNTY	CARD NO.			

	POST OFFICE: Doaksville, Ind. Ter.	FIELD NO.				

NAME	RELATION-SHIP TO PERSON FIRST NAMED	AGE	SEX	BLOOD	TRIBAL ENROLLMENT		
					YEAR	COUNTY	PAGE
1 Wilson, W.W.		42	M	1/4			

TRIBAL ENROLLMENT OF PARENTS

	NAME OF FATHER	YEAR	COUNTY	NAME OF MOTHER	YEAR	COUNTY
1	John Wilson	Dead	Choc. descent	Jane Wilson	1896	Chick residing in Choctaw Nation

(NOTES)

W.W. Wilson is on the Choctaw Roll, 1896, Towson County, Page 347. No. 13204.
Transferred to Chickasaw roll by Dawes Commission.
Wife and family on Choctaw Card No. 587.

April 20/99.

CANCELLED *Stamped across card.*

	RESIDENCE: Panola	COUNTY	CARD NO.			

	POST OFFICE: Mead, Ind. Ter.	FIELD NO.				

NAME	RELATION-SHIP TO PERSON FIRST NAMED	AGE	SEX	BLOOD	TRIBAL ENROLLMENT		
					YEAR	COUNTY	PAGE
1 Davis, Mattie		24	F	Adopted White	1896	Panola No. 11	7
2 " Marian Jessie	Dau	1mo	F	"			

TRIBAL ENROLLMENT OF PARENTS

	NAME OF FATHER	YEAR	COUNTY	NAME OF MOTHER	YEAR	COUNTY
1	Wm. H. Bacon		Adopted White	Frances I. Bacon	Dead	Non Citz.
2	Marian G. Davis		non-citizen	No. 1		

(NOTES)

Nos. 1 & 2 See Decision of June 10/04 in Jacket 9-1408.
Note: These are white *(remainder illegible)*
    Daughter of William Henderson Bacon, Chickasaw Card No. D.169.
    On Chickasaw roll, marked "Adopted"
    "   "   " also "   "Rejected"
No. 2 Enrolled Sept. 11, 1901.
    Evidence of marriage of parents of No. 2 filed Sept. 26, 1901.
No. 1 1893 Payroll No. 2 Page 3

March 29/99.
From Card No. D.170, made Oct. 13/98.

RESIDENCE: Choctaw Nation   COUNTY   CARD NO.

POST OFFICE: Cole, Ind. Ter.   FIELD NO.

NAME	RELATION-SHIP TO PERSON	AGE	SEX	BLOOD	TRIBAL ENROLLMENT		
					YEAR	COUNTY	PAGE
1 Bacon, William Henderson	FIRST NAMED	54	M	Adopted White	1896	Panola No. II	12
2 " Will Hubbard	Son	5	"	"	1896	" "	12
3 " Anna	Dau	3	F	"	1896	" "	12
4 " Gertrude	"	21	"	"	1896	" "	12

TRIBAL ENROLLMENT OF PARENTS

	NAME OF FATHER	YEAR	COUNTY	NAME OF MOTHER	YEAR	COUNTY
1	Harvey Bacon	Dead	Non Citz	Mary Bacon	Dead	Non Citz
2	No. 1			Sammie E. Bacon		" "
3	No. 1			" " "		" "
4	No. 1			Isabella Bacon	Dead	" "

(NOTES)

Nos. 1, 2, 3 and 4 See decision of June 10'04.
   Note: these are all white *(remainder illegible)*
No. 1 on Chickasaw roll as W.H. Bacon   No. 1 on 1878 Annuity Roll Panola Co. No. 1
No. 2 "   "   " " W.H. "   No. 1 " 1898 Pay Roll No. 2 Page 3
   Adopted in Mississippi   No. 4 1893 Pay Roll No. 2 Page 3

               Mar. 29/99.
        From Card No. D.169 made Oct. 13/98.

RESIDENCE: Panola   COUNTY   CARD NO.

POST OFFICE: Colbert, Ind. Ter.   FIELD NO.

NAME	RELATION-SHIP TO PERSON	AGE	SEX	BLOOD	TRIBAL ENROLLMENT		
					YEAR	COUNTY	PAGE
1 Bacon, Henry Clinton	FIRST NAMED	3	M	Adopted White	Sept 22 1896	Panola No. IP	12

TRIBAL ENROLLMENT OF PARENTS

	NAME OF FATHER	YEAR	COUNTY	NAME OF MOTHER	YEAR	COUNTY
1	W.J. Bacon		Adopted white	Belle Bacon		Non citz.

(NOTES)

Note: No. 1 is a white *(remainder illegible)*
   On Chickasaw roll as Henry Bacon.
   Grandson of William H. Bacon, Chickasaw Card No. D.169 - 1408.
No. 1 The Son of William J. Bacon on Chickasaw Card #1559.

Chickasaw Enrollment Cards 1898-1914
Chickasaw by Blood   Volume II

CANCELLED *Stamped across card.*
transferred to Chickasaw Card 1559.

March 29/99.
From Card No. D174
Made Oct. 14/98.

NAME	RELATION-SHIP TO PERSON FIRST NAMED	AGE	SEX	BLOOD	TRIBAL ENROLLMENT		
					YEAR	COUNTY	PAGE
1 Bacon, Sam J.	FIRST NAMED	31	M	Adopted White	1893	Pickens	P.R. #1 137
2 " Bailey	Son	10mo	"	A.W.			
3 " Nellie	Dau	4	F	A.W.			
4 " Sammie	Son	5mo	M	A.W.			

RESIDENCE: Choctaw Nation   ~~COUNTY~~   CARD NO.
POST OFFICE: Utica, Ind. Ter.   FIELD NO.

TRIBAL ENROLLMENT OF PARENTS

	NAME OF FATHER	YEAR	COUNTY	NAME OF MOTHER	YEAR	COUNTY
1	Wm H. Bacon		Adopted White	Frances Bacon	Dead	Non-citz.
2	No. 1			Cora Belle Bacon		" "
3	No. 1			Becky Bacon		" "
4	No. 1			Cora Belle Bacon		

(NOTES)
Nos. 1, 2, 3 and 4 See decision of June 10-04 in Jacket 9-1408.
Note: These are all white people.
No. 3 Affidavit of attending physician to be supplied. Affidavit of Grandmother received Mar. 18/99,
No. 3 Enrolled Aug. 15/99
No. 4 Enrolled May 24/1900.

March 29/99.
From Card No. D.226, Made Nov. 26/98.

NAME	RELATION-SHIP TO PERSON FIRST NAMED	AGE	SEX	BLOOD	TRIBAL ENROLLMENT		
					YEAR	COUNTY	PAGE
1 Goldsby, Frank Walter	FIRST NAMED	35	M	1/16	1893	Pontotoc	No. 2 91
2 " Minnie	Wife	27	F	I.W.	1893	"	No. 2 91

RESIDENCE: Pontotoc   COUNTY   CARD NO.
POST OFFICE: Norman, Okl. Ter.   FIELD NO.

187

3	"	Frank Walter, Jr.	Son	6	M	1/32	1893	"	No. 2 91
4	"	Richard D.	"	4	"	1/32			
5	"	Bryan	"	2	"	1/32			
6	"	Nellie	Dau	3wks	F	1/32			
7	"	Clay	Son	2mo	M	1/32			

TRIBAL ENROLLMENT OF PARENTS

	NAME OF FATHER	YEAR	COUNTY	NAME OF MOTHER	YEAR	COUNTY
1	P.R. Goldsby	Dead	Non Citizen	Nancy A. Goldsby	Dead	Chickasaw roll
2	Josh Gunter	"	" "	Emma Gunter	"	Non Citizen
3	No. 1			No. 2		
4	No. 1			No. 2		
5	No. 1			No. 2		
6	No. 1			No. 2		
7	No. 1			No. 2		

(NOTES)

Approved by Commission Mar. 29/99.
No. 7 Enrolled Feby. 25, 1901.

(No. 2 Dawes' Roll No. 231)
(No. 4 Dawes' Roll No. 4214)

March 29/99.
From Card No. D.210 Made
Nov. 24/98.

RESIDENCE: Pickens COUNTY						CARD NO.		
POST OFFICE: Ardmore, Ind. Ter.						FIELD NO.		

NAME	RELATION-SHIP TO PERSON FIRST NAMED	AGE	SEX	BLOOD	TRIBAL ENROLLMENT		
					YEAR	COUNTY	PAGE
1 McCoy, Sallie Goldsby		44	F	1/32	1893	Panola	No. 2 6
2 Goldsby, Dettie	Sister	23	"	1/32	1893	"	No. 2 6

TRIBAL ENROLLMENT OF PARENTS

	NAME OF FATHER	YEAR	COUNTY	NAME OF MOTHER	YEAR	COUNTY
1	P.R. Goldsby	Dead	Non Citizen	Nancy Ann Goldsby	Dead	Chickasaw roll
2	" " "	"	" "	" " "	"	" "

(NOTES)

Approved by Commission Mar. 29/99.

No. 2 P.O. Lebanon, I.T. 12/4-03

Mar. 29/99.
From Card D.173.
Made Oct. 14/98.

Chickasaw Enrollment Cards 1898-1914
Chickasaw by Blood Volume II

RESIDENCE:	COUNTY					CARD NO.		
POST OFFICE: Marietta, Ind. Ter.						FIELD NO.		

NAME	RELATION- SHIP TO PERSON FIRST NAMED	AGE	SEX	BLOOD	TRIBAL ENROLLMENT		
					YEAR	COUNTY	PAGE
1 Love, Phoebe H.	NAMED	70	F	I.W.	1893	Chick Pay Roll No. 1	141

TRIBAL ENROLLMENT OF PARENTS

NAME OF FATHER	YEAR	COUNTY	NAME OF MOTHER	YEAR	COUNTY
1 Simon Waterman	Dead	Non Citizen	Anna Waterman	Dead	Non Citizen

(NOTES)

On 1893 Chickasaw Payroll, Page 141, No. 164.   *(No. 1 Dawes' Roll No. 489)*
Widow of Robert H. Love, married to him in 1862
Affidavits of R.S. Bell and Arvilla A. Bell as to the marriage between No. 1 and Robt. H. Love filed June 14, 1902.
See testimony of No. 1 and others taken Oct. 30, 1902.

Mar. 24/99.

RESIDENCE: Choctaw Nation ~~COUNTY~~						CARD NO.		
POST OFFICE: South Canadian, Ind. Ter.						FIELD NO.		

NAME	RELATION- SHIP TO PERSON FIRST NAMED	AGE	SEX	BLOOD	TRIBAL ENROLLMENT		
					YEAR	COUNTY	PAGE
1 McNally, John R.	NAMED	24	M	3/8	1897	Chick residing in Choctaw N. 1st Dist.	67
2 " Lula	Wife	23	F	I.W.	1897	" " " "	82
3 " Lena	Dau	5	"	3/16	1897	" " " "	67
4 " William Otie	Son	2	M	3/16			

TRIBAL ENROLLMENT OF PARENTS

NAME OF FATHER	YEAR	COUNTY	NAME OF MOTHER	YEAR	COUNTY
1 V.N. McNally	Dead	Creek Citz.	Sukey McNally	Dead	Chick residing in Choctaw N. 1st Dist.
2 John Duncan	"	Non citizen	Fanny Durham	"	Non citizen
3 No. 1			No. 2		
4 No. 1			No. 2		

(NOTES)

No. 1 also on Creek roll card #3160.
No. 2 on Chickasaw roll as Lou McNally   *(No. 2 Dawes' Roll No. 488)*
No. 3 " " " " Luca "
      Enroll all as Chickasaws; not included on final *(remainder illegible)*

Mar. 23/99.
No. 4 April 9/99.

RESIDENCE: Choctaw Nation   COUNTY   CARD NO.

POST OFFICE: Hartshorne, Ind. Ter.   FIELD NO.

NAME	RELATION-SHIP TO PERSON	AGE	SEX	BLOOD	TRIBAL ENROLLMENT		
					YEAR	COUNTY	PAG
1 King, Cornelia	FIRST NAMED	32	F	Full	1897	Chick residing in Choctaw N. 1st Dist.	70
2 " Billy	Son	6	M	3/4			
3 " Allie	Dau	1	F	3/4			
4 " Arthur	Son	1	m	3/4			

	TRIBAL ENROLLMENT OF PARENTS						
NAME OF FATHER	YEAR	COUNTY	NAME OF MOTHER	YEAR	COUNTY		
1 Pete Benton		Chick residing in Choctaw N. 1st Dist.	(Name Illegible)	Dead	Chick residing ir Choctaw N. 1st Dis		
2 Philip King		Choctaw Freedman	No. 1				
3 " "		" "	No. 1				
4 " "		" "	No. 1				

(NOTES)

No. 1 on Chickasaw Roll as Cornelia Prolla.   *(No. 2 Dawes' Roll No. 4773)*

Nos. 2 and 3 Affidavits as to birth to be supplied. Received Mar. 27/99,   *(No. 4 Dawes' Roll No. 4982)*

No. 2 not found on any roll. Entered on this card under instructions of A.S. McKennon, Commissioner.

(Entry illegible)

Nos. 2 & 3 are children of Philip King on Chickasaw Freedman Card No. 1366.

No. 4 placed on this card in accordance with provisions of Act of Congress approved March 3, 1902.

Application for enrollment received March 11, 1902. Proof of birth filed August 4, 1902.

No. 4 transferred from Chickasaw N.B. Card #209, August 4, 1902.

                                                          Mar. 21/99.

RESIDENCE: Choctaw Nation   COUNTY   CARD NO.

POST OFFICE: Red Oak, Ind. Ter.   FIELD NO.

NAME	RELATION-SHIP TO PERSON	AGE	SEX	BLOOD	TRIBAL ENROLLMENT		
					YEAR	COUNTY	PAG
1 Green, Ida	FIRST NAMED	23	F	Full	1897	Chick residing in Choctaw N. 1st Dist.	71
2 " Robert	Son	1	M	1/2			
3 Alberson, Edmon	Bro	15	M	Full	1897	Chick residing in Choctaw N. 1st Dist.	71

190

Chickasaw Enrollment Cards 1898-1914
Chickasaw by Blood   Volume II

TRIBAL ENROLLMENT OF PARENTS

	NAME OF FATHER	YEAR	COUNTY	NAME OF MOTHER	YEAR	COUNTY
1	Ben Alberson		Chick residing in Choctaw N. 1st Dist.	Tennessee Alberson	Dead	Chickasaw roll
2	Morris Green	1896	Sugar Loaf Co. Choctaw Roll	No. 1		
3	Ben Alberson		Chick residing in Choctaw N. 1st Dist,	Tennessee Alberson	Dead	Chickasaw roll

(NOTES)

No. 1 on Chickasaw roll as Ida Alberson
No. 1 on 1896 Choctaw census roll as Ida Colbert, page 52 #2164.
No. 1 is wife of Morris Green on Choctaw card #2889.
No. 2 Affidavit of mother and of midwife to be supplied. Rec'd, June 19/99.
No. 2 is Son of Morris Green on Choctaw card #2889,
Nos. 1 & 2 transferred to Choctaw Card No. 5679
Aug 6/03. See decision of July 21, 1902.

Mar. 21/99.

RESIDENCE: Choctaw Nation	~~COUNTY~~				CARD NO.		
POST OFFICE: Wilburton, Ind. Ter.					FIELD NO.		

	NAME	RELATION-SHIP TO PERSON FIRST NAMED	AGE	SEX	BLOOD	TRIBAL ENROLLMENT		
						YEAR	COUNTY	PAGE
1	Ward, John Harris		26	M	1/2			

TRIBAL ENROLLMENT OF PARENTS

	NAME OF FATHER	YEAR	COUNTY	NAME OF MOTHER	YEAR	COUNTY
1	Williston Ward	Dead	Choctaw Roll	Betsey Ward	Dead	Chick residing in Choctaw N. 1st Dist.

(NOTES)

On Choctaw Roll, Gaines Co., No. 12937, transferred to Chickasaw roll by Dawes Com.

Mar. 21/99.

CANCELLED *Stamped across card.*

RESIDENCE: Choctaw Nation	~~COUNTY~~				CARD NO.		
POST OFFICE: Goodland, Ind. Ter.					FIELD NO.		

	NAME	RELATION-SHIP TO PERSON FIRST NAMED	AGE	SEX	BLOOD	TRIBAL ENROLLMENT		
						YEAR	COUNTY	PAGE
1	Locke, Wilson		22	M	1/4			
2	" Marion	Bro	20	"	1/4			
3	" Mary Jane	Sister	18	F	1/4			

Chickasaw Enrollment Cards 1898-1914
Chickasaw by Blood   Volume II

	NAME OF FATHER	YEAR	COUNTY	NAME OF MOTHER	YEAR	COUNTY
1	Benj. F. Locke		White man	Hattie Locke	Dead	Chick residing in Choctaw N. 3rd Dist.
2	" " "		" "	" "	"	" " " "
3	" " "		" "	" "	"	" " " "

(NOTES)

No. 1 on Choctaw Roll Kiamitia Co., No. 8086, transferred to Chickasaw roll by Dawes Com.

No. 2 "   "   "   "   "   " 8087   "   "   "   "   "   "   "

No. 3 "   "   "   "   "   " 8088   "   "   "   "   "   "   "

No. 3 on Choctaw Roll as Kittie Locke.

Mar. 21/99.

CANCELLED *Stamped across card.*

RESIDENCE:	COUNTY					CARD NO.			
POST OFFICE:	Lebanon, Ind. Ter.					FIELD NO.			

	NAME	RELATIONSHIP TO PERSON FIRST NAMED	AGE	SEX	BLOOD	TRIBAL ENROLLMENT		
						YEAR	COUNTY	PAGE
1	Cochran, Arnaca	NAMED	51	F	Full	1897	Pickens	93
2	" Martin	Son	25	M	1/2	1893	"	54
3	McDaniel, Jennie	Dau	22	F	1/2	1897	"	93
4	Cochran, Turner	Son	21	M	1/2	1897	"	93
5	" Nellie	Dau	16	F	1/2	1897	"	93
6	" Ruth	"	14	F	1/2	1897	"	93
7	" Lettie	"	10	F	1/2	1897	"	93
8	McDaniel, Annid L.	Gr.Dau	16mo	F	1/4			

TRIBAL ENROLLMENT OF PARENTS

	NAME OF FATHER	YEAR	COUNTY	NAME OF MOTHER	YEAR	COUNTY
1	Joseph Wolf	Dead	Chickasaw roll	Jennie Wolfe	Dead	Chickasaw roll
2	Olie Cochran	"	Cherokee "	No. 1		
3	" "	"	" "	No. 1		
4	" "	"	" "	No. 1		
5	" "	"	" "	No. 1		
6	" "	"	" "	No. 1		
7	" "	"	" "	No. 1		
8	Alex L. McDaniel		Cherokee	No. 3		

(NOTES)

(No. 1 Dawes' Roll No. 696) (No. 2 Dawes' Roll No. 697) (No. 3 Dawes' Roll No. 698) (No. 4 Dawes' Roll No. 699)
(No. 5 Dawes' Roll No. 700) (No. 6 Dawes' Roll No. 701) (No. 7 Dawes' Roll No. 702) (No. 8 Dawes' Roll No. 703)

No. 1 on 1880 Cherokee Roll, page 87, #703 Coo. Dist. as Annie Cochran

No. 2 " 1880   "   "   " 87 #706 "   "

No. 3 " 1880   "   "   " 87 #707 "   " as Jane Cochran
No. 4 " 1880   "   "   " 87 #708 "   "
All but No. 2 are also on Cherokee Roll of 1896, page 127, Coo Dist.
All but No. 2 "   "   "   "   "   " 1894 " 157 "   "
No. 2 on 1893 Pay Roll as Clem Cochrane
No. 7 " 1897   Roll   " Lettie Cochran
No. 8 Born June 4, 1901. Enrolled Oct. 22, 1902.
Nos. 1, 2, 5, 6 and 7 Enrolled Feb. 20, 1901 on Cherokee roll card #7337.
No. 3 Enrolled Oct. 27, 1900 on Cherokee roll card #4995.
No. 3 is now the Wife of Alex L. McDaniel a Cherokee, Oct. 22, 1902.
No. 4 Enrolled Feby 20, 1901, on Cherokee roll card #7338.
See additional testimony of No. 1 taken Oct. 17, 1902.
"   "   "   " " 3 "   "   "   "

P.O. Address is now Claremore, I.T.   Mar. 21/99,

RESIDENCE: Choctaw Nation ~~COUNTY~~   **CARD NO.**
POST OFFICE: Caddo, Ind. Ter.   **FIELD NO.**

	NAME	RELATION-SHIP TO PERSON FIRST NAMED	AGE	SEX	BLOOD	TRIBAL ENROLLMENT		
						YEAR	COUNTY	PAGE
1	Nail, David Oscar	NAMED	26	M	1/8			
2	" Pearl E.	Wife	20	F	I.W.			
3	" Claud B.	Son	6mo	M	1/16			
4	" Haskell E.	Son	6wks	M	1/16			

TRIBAL ENROLLMENT OF PARENTS

	NAME OF FATHER	YEAR	COUNTY	NAME OF MOTHER	YEAR	COUNTY
1	Joe H. Nail		Chick residing in Choctaw N. 1st Dist.	Nettie Nail	Dead	Non Citizen
2	Ben Brewer		Non Citizen	Tennie Brewer		" "
3	No. 1			No. 2		
4	No. 1			No. 2		

(NOTES)
No. 1 On Choctaw roll, Blue Co, No. 9793 as Oscar H. Nail, transferred to Chickasaw Roll by Dawes Commission.
No. 3 Enrolled Mar. 27/99.
No. 4 Enrolled Mar. 9/01.

                                Mar. 21/99.
CANCELLED *Stamped across card.*

Chickasaw Enrollment Cards 1898-1914
Chickasaw by Blood   Volume II

RESIDENCE: Choctaw Nation ~~COUNTY~~   CARD NO.
POST OFFICE: Caddo, Ind. Ter.   FIELD NO.

NAME	RELATION-SHIP TO PERSON FIRST NAMED	AGE	SEX	BLOOD	TRIBAL ENROLLMENT		
					YEAR	COUNTY	PAGE
1 Nail, Joel H.	NAMED	49	M	1/4			
2 " Lou	Wife	24	F	I.W.			
3 " Vivia	Dau	23	F	1/8			
4 " Ethel	"	21	"	1/8			
5 " Ishtoyapi	Son	18	M	1/8			
6 Fulsom, Catherine	Mother	65	F	1/2			
7 Robertson, Wesley L.	Gr.Son	5mo	M	1/16			

TRIBAL ENROLLMENT OF PARENTS

NAME OF FATHER	YEAR	COUNTY	NAME OF MOTHER	YEAR	COUNTY
1 Jonathan Nail	Dead	Choctaw roll	Catherine Nail now Fulsom		Chick residing in Choctaw N. 1st Dist.
2 (Illegible) Daily	"	Non citizen	A.M. Daily		Non citizen
3 No. 1			Nettie Nail	Dead	" "
4 No. 1			" "	"	" "
5 No. 1			" "	"	" "
6 Jim Perry	Dead	Choctaw Roll	(Name Illegible)	"	Chickasaw Roll
7 Albert M. Robertson		White man	No. 3		

(NOTES)
No. 1 on Choctaw roll, Blue Co., No. 9791, transferred to Chickasaw roll by Dawes Com.
No. 3 "   "   "   "   "   9794 "   "   "   "   "   "   "
No. 4 "   "   "   "   "   9795 "   "   "   "   "   "   "
No. 5 "   "   "   "   "   9796 "   "   "   "   "   "   "
No. 6 "   "   "   "   "   4406 "   "   "   "   "   "   "
No. 3 is now Wife of Albert M. Robertson on Chickasaw Card #0348, Aug. 29, 1901.
No. 7 Born Nov. 6, 1901; enrolled May 13, 1902.
No. 4 is now the Wife of Armal H. Perkins on Chickasaw D.364. Evidence of marriage filed Sept. 4, 1902.

Mar. 21/99.

RESIDENCE: Choctaw Nation ~~COUNTY~~   CARD NO.
POST OFFICE: Coalgate, Ind. Ter.   FIELD NO.

NAME	RELATION-SHIP TO PERSON FIRST NAMED	AGE	SEX	BLOOD	TRIBAL ENROLLMENT		
					YEAR	COUNTY	PAGE
1 Chuffatubby	NAMED	50	M	Fuill	1897	Chick residing in Choctaw N. 3rd Dist.	74

TRIBAL ENROLLMENT OF PARENTS

	NAME OF FATHER	YEAR	COUNTY	NAME OF MOTHER	YEAR	COUNTY
1	*(Name Illegible)*	Dead	Chickasaw Roll	Po-wak-ke	Dead	Chickasaw Roll

(NOTES)

Mar. 20/99.

RESIDENCE: Choctaw Nation ~~COUNTY~~   CARD NO.

POST OFFICE: Kosome, Ind. Ter.   FIELD NO.

	NAME	RELATION-SHIP TO PERSON FIRST NAMED	AGE	SEX	BLOOD	TRIBAL ENROLLMENT		
						YEAR	COUNTY	PAGE
1	Impson, Melvina	NAMED	36	F	1/2			
2	" Harriet	Dau	13	"	1/4			
3	" Ammizon B.	Son	10	M	1/4			

TRIBAL ENROLLMENT OF PARENTS

	NAME OF FATHER	YEAR	COUNTY	NAME OF MOTHER	YEAR	COUNTY
1	Allendon Anderson	Dead	Choctaw roll	Louisa Impson		Chick resding in Choctaw N. 3rd Dist.
2	Isaac J. Impson		Jacks Fork Co. Choctaw roll	No. 1		
3	" " "		" "	No. 1		

(NOTES)

No. 1 Wife of Isaac J. Impson, Choctaw card No. 463

No. 1 on Choctaw Roll, Jacks Fork Co., No. 6334. transferred to Chickasaw roll by Dawes Com.

No. 2 "   "   "   "   "   "   " 6335   "   "   "   "   "   "   "

No. 3 "   "   "   "   "   "   " 6336   "   "   "   "   "   "   "

Mar. 29/99.

RESIDENCE: Choctaw Nation ~~COUNTY~~   CARD NO.

POST OFFICE: Alderson, Ind. Ter.   FIELD NO.

	NAME	RELATION-SHIP TO PERSON FIRST NAMED	AGE	SEX	BLOOD	TRIBAL ENROLLMENT		
						YEAR	COUNTY	PAGE
1	Nail, Alfred	NAMED	40	M	1/2	1897	Chick residing in Choctaw N. 1st Dist.	69

TRIBAL ENROLLMENT OF PARENTS

	NAME OF FATHER	YEAR	COUNTY	NAME OF MOTHER	YEAR	COUNTY
1	Ben Nail	Dead	Choctaw roll	Sutsie	Dead	Chickasaw roll

(NOTES)

Children and step children on Choctaw card No. 461.

Mar. 20/99.

Chickasaw Enrollment Cards 1898-1914
Chickasaw by Blood   Volume II

RESIDENCE:	Choctaw Nation ~~COUNTY~~				CARD NO.			
POST OFFICE:	Savannah, Ind. Ter.				FIELD NO.			

NAME	RELATION-SHIP TO PERSON FIRST NAMED	AGE	SEX	BLOOD	TRIBAL ENROLLMENT		
					YEAR	COUNTY	PAGE
1 Carney, Norris		32	M	Full			

	TRIBAL ENROLLMENT OF PARENTS						
NAME OF FATHER	YEAR	COUNTY	NAME OF MOTHER	YEAR	COUNTY	
1 Tombey Carney	Dead	Chickasar roll	Kitsey Alberson		Chick residing in Choctaw N. 1st Dist.

(NOTES)
On Choctaw Census Record, Atoka Co, No. 2944, transferred to Chickasaw roll by Dawes Com.
Wife and children on Choctaw card No. 460.

Mar. 20/99,

CANCELLED *Stamped across card.*

RESIDENCE:	Choctaw Nation ~~COUNTY~~				CARD NO.			
POST OFFICE:	Tuskahoma, Ind. Ter.				FIELD NO.			

NAME	RELATION-SHIP TO PERSON FIRST NAMED	AGE	SEX	BLOOD	TRIBAL ENROLLMENT		
					YEAR	COUNTY	PAGE
1 Colbert, William		32	M	Full	1897	Chick residing in Choctaw N. 1st Dist.	71

	TRIBAL ENROLLMENT OF PARENTS						
NAME OF FATHER	YEAR	COUNTY	NAME OF MOTHER	YEAR	COUNTY	
1 Jim Colbert	Dead	Chickasaw roll	Martha Ann Colbert	Dead	Chickasaw roll

(NOTES)
No. 1 on Chickasaw card #0.367 claims to be the Wife of No. 1 on this card.
See her testimony of Sept. 19, 1902.

Mar. 20/99.

RESIDENCE:	Choctaw Nation ~~COUNTY~~				CARD NO.			
POST OFFICE:	Wilburton, Ind. Ter.				FIELD NO.			

NAME	RELATION-SHIP TO PERSON FIRST NAMED	AGE	SEX	BLOOD	TRIBAL ENROLLMENT		
					YEAR	COUNTY	PAGE
1 Ward, Henry		32	M	1/2			

	TRIBAL ENROLLMENT OF PARENTS						
NAME OF FATHER	YEAR	COUNTY	NAME OF MOTHER	YEAR	COUNTY	
1 Williston Ward	Dead	Choctaw roll	Patsy Ward	Dead	Chickasaw roll

(NOTES)

On ChoctawCensus Record, Gaines Co., No. 12979, transferred to Chickasaw roll by Dawes Commission.
Has a child, Plenna Ward, on Choctaw card No. 459.

Mar. 20/99.

RESIDENCE: Choctaw Nation	~~COUNTY~~				CARD No.			
POST OFFICE: Lehigh, Ind. Ter.					FIELD No.			
NAME	RELATION-SHIP TO PERSON FIRST	AGE	SEX	BLOOD	TRIBAL ENROLLMENT			
					YEAR	COUNTY		PAGE
1 Battiest, Cain	NAMED	18	M	1/2				
2 " Allen	Bro	8	"	1/2				

TRIBAL ENROLLMENT OF PARENTS

	NAME OF FATHER	YEAR	COUNTY	NAME OF MOTHER	YEAR	COUNTY
1	Allen Battiest	Dead	Choctaw roll	Wisey Battiest	Dead	Chick residing in Choctaw N. 1st Dist.
2	" "	"	" "	" "	"	" " " "

(NOTES)

No. 1 on Choctaw Roll, Atoka Co., No. 1796, transferred to Chickasaw roll by Dawes Commission.
No. 2 "   "   "   "   " No. 1804   "   "   "   "   "   "   "

Mar. 20/99.

CANCELLED *Stamped across card.*

RESIDENCE: Choctaw Nation	~~COUNTY~~				CARD No.			
POST OFFICE: Legal, Ind. Ter.					FIELD No.			
NAME	RELATION-SHIP TO PERSON FIRST	AGE	SEX	BLOOD	TRIBAL ENROLLMENT			
					YEAR	COUNTY		PAGE
1 King, Hayes	NAMED	18	M	1/2				
2 Keener, Maulsey	Sister	17	F	1/2	1897	Chick residing in Choctaw N. 1st Dist.		69
3 Keener, Thomas Butler	Newborn	5mo	M	1/4				

TRIBAL ENROLLMENT OF PARENTS

	NAME OF FATHER	YEAR	COUNTY	NAME OF MOTHER	YEAR	COUNTY
1	Anderson King		Atoka County Choctaw Roll	Susan King	Dead	Chick residing in Choctaw N. 1st Dist.
2	" "		" "	" "	"	" " " "
3	Thomas Butler		Non citizen	No. 2		

(NOTES)

No. 1 on Choctaw Census Record, Atoka County, No. 7644; transferred to Chickasaw Roll by Dawes Commission
No. 1 transferred to Choctaw Card No. 5488 October 20, 1902.

Chickasaw Enrollment Cards 1898-1914
Chickasaw by Blood   Volume II

No. 2 on Chickasaw Roll as Maulsey Kinney.
No. 3 Enrolled Sept. 4, 1901. See letter of T.N. Foster relative to enrollment of No. 2, filed Sept. 4, 1901.

Mar. 20/99.

	NAME	RELATIONSHIP TO PERSON FIRST NAMED	AGE	SEX	BLOOD	TRIBAL ENROLLMENT		
						YEAR	COUNTY	PAGE
1	Nichols, Louis	NAMED	21	M	I.W.			
2	" Hannah	Wife	18	F	3/4	1897	Pontotoc	61
3	" Earnest Lee	Son	7mo	M	1/2			
4	" Bessie May	Dau	1/2	F	1/2			

RESIDENCE: COUNTY — CARD NO.
POST OFFICE: McGee, Ind. Ter. — FIELD NO.

TRIBAL ENROLLMENT OF PARENTS

	NAME OF FATHER	YEAR	COUNTY	NAME OF MOTHER	YEAR	COUNTY
1	Daniel Nichols		Non Citizen	Mary Nichols	Dead	Non citizen
2	Charles Strickland	Dead	Chickasaw Roll	Elizabeth Strickland	Dead	Chickasaw Roll
3	No. 1			No. 2		
4	No. 1			No. 2		

(NOTES)
No. 2 transferred from Chickasaw card #383.   *(No. 1 Dawes' Roll No. 175)*
No. 3 Enrolled June 12, 1900,
No. 4 Born May 27, 1901; enrolled Nov. 13, 1901

P.O. Roff, I.T.   No. 1 enrolled   Mar. 20/99.

RESIDENCE: COUNTY — CARD NO.
POST OFFICE: Wynnewood, Ind. Ter. — FIELD NO.

	NAME	RELATIONSHIP TO PERSON FIRST NAMED	AGE	SEX	BLOOD	TRIBAL ENROLLMENT		
						YEAR	COUNTY	PAGE
1	Hoffman, Jesse	NAMED	18	M	I.W.			
2	" Fannie	Wife	16	F	1/2	1897	Pickens	19
3	" Georgie L.	Son	6mo	M	1/4			
4	" Willie Thomas	Son	2mo	M	1/4			

TRIBAL ENROLLMENT OF PARENTS

	NAME OF FATHER	YEAR	COUNTY	NAME OF MOTHER	YEAR	COUNTY
1	Larkin Hoffman		Non Citizen	Mollie Hoffman	Dead	Non citizen
2	Wm Talley		White man	Agnes Talley	Dead	Pickens
3	No. 1			No. 2		

198

Chickasaw Enrollment Cards 1898-1914
Chickasaw by Blood   Volume II

4	No. 1			No. 2		

(NOTES)

No. 2 is daughter of William Talley on Chickasaw card #052.   *(No. 1 Dawes'Roll No. 174)*
No. 2 transferred from Chickasaw card #478.
No. 3 Enrolled Aug. 6, 1900.
No. 4 Born Feby 1, 1902; enrolled April 5, 1902.

No. 1 enrolled Mar. 20/99.
No. 2 first " Sept. 16/98.
as Fannie Talley.

RESIDENCE:	COUNTY					CARD NO.		
POST OFFICE: Davis, Ind. Ter.						FIELD NO.		

	NAME	RELATION- SHIP TO PERSON FIRST NAMED	AGE	SEX	BLOOD	TRIBAL ENROLLMENT		
						YEAR	COUNTY	PAGE
1	Myers, Winfield Scott	NAMED	21	M	I.W.			
2	" Alice M	Wife	16	F	1/16	1897	Pickens	19
3	" Gretchen Ethel	Dau	4mo	F	1/32			
4	" Mary Elizabeth	Dau	3mo	F	1/32			

TRIBAL ENROLLMENT OF PARENTS

	NAME OF FATHER	YEAR	COUNTY	NAME OF MOTHER	YEAR	COUNTY
1	W.H.H. Myers		Non Citizen	Mary J. Myers		Non Citizen
2	D.A. Brittenburg I.W.	1897	Pickens	Maria Brittenburg	1897	Pickens
3	No. 1			No. 2		
4	No. 1			No. 2		

(NOTES)

No. 2 transferred from Chickasaw card #468.   *(No. 1 Dawes'Roll No. 173)*
No. 3 Enrolled May 24, 1900.
No. 4 Born Nov. 7, 1901. Enrolled Jan. 29, 1902.
No. 4 Died June 23, 1902. proof of death filed Sept. 3, 1902.

No. 1 enrolled Mar. 20/99.
No. 2 " Sept. 16/98.
as Alice M. Brittenburg.

RESIDENCE: Choctaw Nation	COUNTY					CARD NO.		
POST OFFICE: Stringtown, Ind. Ter.						FIELD NO.		

	NAME	RELATION- SHIP TO PERSON FIRST NAMED	AGE	SEX	BLOOD	TRIBAL ENROLLMENT		
						YEAR	COUNTY	PAGE
1	Folota, Martin	NAMED	45	M	1/2			

Chickasaw Enrollment Cards 1898-1914
Chickasaw by Blood   Volume II

TRIBAL ENROLLMENT OF PARENTS						
NAME OF FATHER	YEAR	COUNTY	NAME OF MOTHER	YEAR	COUNTY	
1 Folota	Dead	Choctaw Roll	Siney Folota	Dead	Chickasaw Roll	

(NOTES)

On Choctaw Roll, Jacks Fork Co., No. 4548A, transferred to Chickasaw Roll by Dawes Commission.

Mar. 22/99.

CANCELLED *Stamped across card.*

RESIDENCE: Choctaw Nation   *COUNTY*   *CARD NO.*

POST OFFICE: Stuart, Ind. Ter.   *FIELD NO.*

NAME	RELATION-SHIP TO PERSON FIRST NAMED	AGE	SEX	BLOOD	TRIBAL ENROLLMENT		
					YEAR	COUNTY	PAGE
1 Seely, Isham		49	M	Full	1893	Choc. Dist.	

TRIBAL ENROLLMENT OF PARENTS						
NAME OF FATHER	YEAR	COUNTY	NAME OF MOTHER	YEAR	COUNTY	
1 Abel Seely	Dead	Chickasaw roll	Tema Seely	Dead	Chickasaw roll	

(NOTES)

No. 1 on Ieshatubby 1893 Pay Roll. [sic]

Mar. 20/99.

RESIDENCE: Choctaw Nation   ~~COUNTY~~   *CARD NO.*

POST OFFICE: South McAlester   *FIELD NO.*

NAME	RELATION-SHIP TO PERSON FIRST NAMED	AGE	SEX	BLOOD	TRIBAL ENROLLMENT		
					YEAR	COUNTY	PAGE
1 Harris, Louisa		60	F	3/4	1897	Chick residing in Choctaw N. 1st Dist.	70

TRIBAL ENROLLMENT OF PARENTS						
NAME OF FATHER	YEAR	COUNTY	NAME OF MOTHER	YEAR	COUNTY	
1 Tunubby (or Davis)	Dead	Chickasaw roll	Mary		Dead	Chickasaw roll

(NOTES)

Widow of Dr. E. Poe Harris
On Chickasaw Roll as Lula Harris.

March 20/99.

235

www.ingramcontent.com/pod-product-compliance
Lightning Source LLC
Chambersburg PA
CBHW030241030426
42336CB00009B/197